Ladies Laughing

Studies in Humor and Gender

A series edited by Regina Barreca, *University of Connecticut, Storrs*, and Nancy Walker, *Vanderbilt University, Nashville, Tennessee*

This book is part of a series. The publisher will accept continuation orders which may be cancelled at any time and which provide for automatic billing and shipping of each title in the series upon publication. Please write for details.

Ladies Laughing

Wit as Control in Contemporary American Women Writers

Barbara Levy

Gordon and Breach Publishers

Australia Canada China France Germany India Japan
Luxembourg Malaysia The Netherlands Russia Singapore
Switzerland Thailand United Kingdom

Copyright © 1997 OPA (Overseas Publishers Association) Amsterdam
B.V. Published in The Netherlands under license by Gordon and Breach
Science Publishers.

Amsteldijk 166
1st Floor
1079 LH Amsterdam
The Netherlands

British Library Cataloguing in Publication Data

Levy, Barbara
    Ladies laughing : wit as control in contemporary American
    women writers.—(Studies in humor and gender ; v. 3)
    1. American literature—Women authors—History and
    criticism   2. Humor in literature
    I. Title
    818.5'4'09

ISBN 90-5699-543-X

To the memory of my mother
Jeanne Kaufman Levy

and

To all my students
at the University of Puerto Rico

CONTENTS

CONTENTS

INTRODUCTION TO THE SERIES

Humor as a human activity crosses—and double-crosses—many lines and boundaries, including those of gender. *Studies in Humor and Gender* will explore these boundaries and the territories encompassed by them. The monographs and collections published in this series will provide useful and original perspectives on the interaction of gender and humor in many of their possible combinations. An interdisciplinary field by its very nature, the study of humor, comedy, joking, and play draws together the interests and expertise of those working in literature, anthropology, sociology, linguistics, communication, film studies, folklore, medicine, and, increasingly, gender studies. The works published under the aegis of *Studies in Humor and Gender* will offer scholars, writers, and general readers alike a forum for examining and discussing insights into a vital field of study.

By making available the best discoveries and theories about humor and comedy in books framed by issues of gender, we believe that this series will inevitably also shed light on the larger questions of culture, power, sexuality, and the imagination. Its texts will feature sound scholarship, integrative approaches to the study of humor and gender, and clear, lively prose. We have no doubt that the volumes published in *Studies in Humor and Gender* will generate interest, debate, dissent, recognition, and attention. Destined for personal bookshelves as well as libraries, these volumes will be widely read, consulted, quoted, and discussed both inside and outside classroom walls.

ACKNOWLEDGMENTS

I first wish to thank the University of Puerto Rico for granting me the sabbatical that allowed me to begin this project. Then I wish to acknowledge the Center for Research on Women at Wellesley College, where I presented early versions of several chapters as a visiting research scholar. I particularly thank Jan Putnam of the Center for her enthusiasm and encouragement.

I am grateful to those who offered me teaching positions in the Boston area, enabling me to relocate and continue writing: Patsy Yaeger, head tutor of History & Literature at Harvard; Anne Dow, director of English as a Second Language at Harvard; Wini Wood, director of The Writing Program at Wellesley College; Lilith Haynes, director of the Institute for English Language Programs at Harvard; and Fritz Fleischmann, chairman of Arts and Humanities at Babson College.

Many thanks to Steve McCauley for introducing me to the works of Dawn Powell, and to Dimi Berkner for help in finding a publisher. I gratefully acknowledge the proofreading assistance of my friends and colleagues: Liz, Hank, Sarah and Naomi Lieberman; Carol Anastasi, Sybil Schlesinger and Sarah Gates.

On the personal side, for providing encouragement and necessary diversions, I am grateful to Carolyn Graham, George and Sylvia Kaufman, June Hime, Alan Del Castillo, Carolyn Boren and Thomas Noel. I especially thank my daughter Nadine Beck and my son-in-law Alan Pearson, both of whom proofread as well, and the last and littlest—but far from least—diversion, my grandson Matthew Pearson Beck, born as this book was nearing completion.

Finally, my sincere gratitude to Carol Hollander, Regina Barreca and Karen Wolny for their shrewd editing skills.

1

Introduction

WHAT WIT CONTROLS:

Women are not accustomed to calling the shots. Nor have they ever been encouraged to be funny. On the contrary, women have consistently been told they have no sense of humor whatsoever.[1] And yet more and more women are learning to enjoy the power of wit, learning to disregard the connections of wit to witch and bitch and write on. This book will focus on the wit of recent women writers, explore the relationship between wit and control, and consider how lives as well as texts have benefited from the alliance.

Wit may seem to offer a false control, a sort of last-ditch effort to salvage *something* from a situation slipping beyond one's grasp. When all else fails, make a joke. While this may be true of wit at its most desperate, with writers we are always dealing with wit at its least desperate, with wit at its most strategic and manipulative. Shirley Jackson once claimed that "The only way to turn something that really happened into something that happens on paper is to attack it in the beginning the way a puppy attacks an old shoe. Shake it, snarl at it, sneak up on it from various angles." Nora Ephron admits to an incredible number of draft copies, although her final versions always create the illusion of effortlessness. She estimates that one six-page double-spaced typewritten essay, written in pre-word processor days, could use up to 300 or 400 pieces of typing paper. Lisa Alther allows that it takes

1

her six drafts and about five years to complete a novel. Rita Mae Brown, who may sound like the sassiest and most spontaneous in this collection of voices, claims that she never thought of being anything but a writer, and that her Dad gave her a typewriter when she was only eight. Alison Lurie remembers that she received parental encouragement to see herself as a writer when she was only six or seven. Grace Paley recalls that her attentive older brother and sister encouraged her to play with words even before she was old enough write. She made up songs or poems and they wrote them down. The young Shirley Jackson, on the other hand, received little or no encouragement, but that didn't stop her from shutting herself in her room every day after school to write.[2] Clearly, none of these writers ever considered wit to be a last-ditch effort to salvage a desperate situation. Quite the contrary, their wit has always been a carefully executed writing strategy used to shape and control their fiction.

All of these writers recognized the controlling possibilities of fiction, some at a remarkably early age. Several have used writing to enhance what they perceived as an uneventful childhood. As a young girl, Anne Tyler felt that what happened in books was more "reasonable and interesting and *real*, in some ways, than what happened in life." When she ran out of books she made up her own. And when she couldn't sleep, "she made up stories in the dark."[3] As an adolescent, Alison Lurie discovered she could even control non-fiction in her letters home from boarding school. Whatever version of her teacher she chose to present would be the truth— "if I said so, the whole truth."[4] As an adult, Lisa Alther used fiction to revise certain adolescent disappointments. She made the heroine of *Kinflicks* a flag-swinger for her high school, something Alther had failed to become despite years of practicing in the back yard. "At last," Alther notes wryly, "I get to be a flag-swinger."[5] As adults, both Jackson and Ephron acknowledge using fiction to improve their lives. It is easier, Jackson claims, to write a story about raising children than to cope with their daily problems: "It helps a good deal—particularly with children around—if you can see them through a flattering veil of fiction."[6] Ephron, in an essay called "Revision and Life," argues that fiction gives you the "chance to rework the events of your life so that you can give the illusion of being the intelligence at the center of it, simultaneously managing to slip in all the lines that occurred to you later."[7] In each of these observations, the writer suggests that she uses her wit to control her own version of her life by reshaping it into a more interesting and promising one.

The more people she can convince of the validity of her version, the more in control she becomes. A witty writer gains some degree of control over the events in her life, then, by retelling her story her own way, by putting herself, as Ephron said, as the intelligence at the center of it.

Shirley Jackson's son Barry made this telling observation about his mother's writing:

> She realized that the only tools the magician needs are in the head. You make the world, you decide what your name is, your role, decide what people are going to think of you by your own force of will. And that's real magic in the real world.[8]

A witty writer learns to control her material with one main goal—to convince her reading audience that her viewpoint is a valid one. Of course, all effective writers cast a spell over their readers, who willingly push aside their own consciousness to fall sway to the author's. One great attraction of reading, in fact, is that it *does* give our own overworked consciousness a break by allowing us to escape into someone else's. But there is an added aggressive quality to the control of witty writers. This is partly due to the stance of feigned vulnerability they adopt. Nora Ephron likes to recreate herself in adolescence as gawky, flat-chested, and unpopular, Shirley Jackson projects herself on paper as an incompetent and overwhelmed mother, while Faith, the narrator of so many of Grace Paley's short stories, seems haplessly manipulated by the men in her life. For a while, we seem to manage everything better than these fictional heroines: our love lives, our finances, our moral positions. But ultimately they are going to emerge in the position of superiority. In point of fact, they have been there all along.

MALE FEAR OF WITTY WOMEN:

The potential power of a witty woman has not been not lost on men. Male writers as far back as Chaucer have portrayed women with quick wits as dangerous ones to wed. While *The Canterbury Tales* offers many examples of such shrews, The Wife of Bath coming immediately to mind, Chaucer's clearest portrayal of the dangers to men of witty women can be found in "The Merchant's Tale." The Merchant's diatribe can be read simply as a bitterly humorous warning to other old men about what to expect if they foolishly lust after young brides. The characters' names alone—January and May—anticipate the problem. We are set up to expect that fresh young May will betray withered old January and we are not disappointed. But it is not the fact of May's betrayal so much as her astonishingly clever excuse when January catches her in the very act of sex that concerns us here. Nor is it merely the cleverness of her words, nor the fact that they were granted her magically by the fairy queen, but rather that this queen has promised to grant all women equally clever answers to extricate themselves from equally compromising situations that becomes distinctly worrisome. For she vows to grant a witty tongue not only to May, but to "alle women after:"

> For lak of answere none of hem shal dyen.
> Al hadde men seyn a thyng with bothe his yen, (2271–2)

> [None of them shall die for lack of an answer,
> Even if the men have seen the thing with his two eyes][9]

The misogynistic assumption that all women after May will *need* such magical aid is troublesome enough, but it is in the assurance that all women will *get* it—that we will all have clever and effective answers for gross misconduct—that we best see the projection of male fear of women's wit.

January, who has inexplicably grown blind, is trying to enjoy his young wife in the private garden he created for them alone. But he has become so jealous that, once blinded, he always keeps a hand on her. Nevertheless, May has managed to get her young lover, Damyan, inside the garden and to signal for him to climb a pear tree. All that remains is for her to free herself from January's hand. So she feigns so sharp a longing for a pear (thereby flattering the old man by suggesting he has impregnated her) that he allows her to climb the tree, using his own back as a step up. No sooner is she in the tree than Damyan is in her:

> And sodeynly anon this Damyan
> Gan pullen up the smok, and in he throng (2352–3)

At precisely this moment, of course, January's sight returns. He roars his protest. 'What ails you?' May soothes, not missing a beat, 'I was taught there was no better thing to make you see than to struggle with a man in a tree.' At first January doesn't believe her: " 'Struggle!' quod he, 'ye algate (nevertheless) in it wente!' "(2376). 'Then,' retorts May, 'the medicine was false': "Ye had som glymsing, and no parfit sighte" (2383). When January protests that his sight is perfect, May grows indignant: "This thank have I for I have made you see" (2388). Here January gives up. Either he believes her or he pretends to believe her, choosing to be blind to the truth rather than lose his young wife. However one chooses to interpret January's acquiescence, what is clear is that the woman's cunning gave her the last word and that word, quite obviously, was false.

WOMEN, WIT, AND WITCHCRAFT:
THE BURDEN OF STEREOTYPES

Before any witty woman could write, then, she had to learn to ignore such negative associations in literature and legend, reaffirmed more recently on television, in newspapers, and the movies, between a woman and her wit. Until very recently, the picture of the clever woman has nearly always been the picture of the witch, the shrew, or the bitch. Margaret Atwood deplored the literary and legendary models for women in a clever essay she called "The Curse of Eve—Or, What I Learned in School." Her list explodes with

> . . . Old Crones, Delphic Oracles, the Three Fates, Evil Witches, White Witches, White Goddesses, Bitch Goddesses, Medusas with snaky heads who turn men to stone, Mermaids with no souls, . . . evil step-mothers, comic mothers-in-law, . . . Medea who slew her own children, Lady Macbeth and her spot, Eve the mother of us all, . . .[10]

Atwood is clearly enjoying herself but she is not exaggerating. In the past, when women showed signs of cleverness they were often suspected of being witches. And if enough "proof" could be gathered they were killed. In both the Middle Ages and the Renaissance, according to Gilbert and Gubar, "even the most talented literary women were constrained by cultural strictures which implied that any intellectual ambition might mean they were evil."[11] Virginia Woolf expressed the connection from the opposite direction:

> When, however, one reads of a witch being ducked, of a woman possessed by devils, of a wise woman selling herbs, or even of a very remarkable man who had a mother, then I think we are on the track of a lost novelist, a suppressed poet, of some mute and inglorious Jane Austen, some Emily Brontë who dashed her brains out on the moor or moped and mowed about the highways crazed with the torture that her gift had put her to.[12]

The relationship of the witch to the community, simultaneously powerful but feared and ostracized, must have appeared to many a woman writer as a relationship ominously analogous to her own, or to her *fears* of her own, situation. For women have always occupied a marginal position in society. Judy Little's opening chapter of *Comedy and the Women Writer* is a thoughtful and thorough presentation of how the norms and values of society have pushed women into this marginal position:

> . . . the monomythic norm—the varied quest myth described by Northrop Frye and Joseph Campbell—has allotted to women a peripheral role. . . . The women is catalyst, landscape,. . . but not herself the adventurer.[13]

Little's book explores the comedy of Virginia Woolf and Muriel Spark in depth, and adds a final chapter which includes Jean Rhys, Margaret Drabble, Penelope Mortimer, and Beryl Brainbridge. All these British novelists., Little notes, "perceive themselves to some extent as outsiders" (6). The peripheral position of women in society is one more reason the image of the witch, the eternal outsider, has kept surfacing in their writing.

Alison Lurie admits to an interest in witchcraft but claims she reinterprets the supernatural as the psychological:

> Witchcraft is an old interest of mine. It's something that I've always been rather keen on, and it keeps coming up. I'm interested in it, not so much as a believer. It works, but it doesn't work in the strict magical way. Magic does work. But it works psychologically rather than supernaturally. It's certainly a very significant part of life, more than we mostly think.[14]

Shirley Jackson did not make it so easy for her public to accept her interest in witchcraft. Although her husband, the critic Stanley Edgar Hyman, wrote the jacket description of her first novel, *The Road through the Wall*, and described her as "perhaps the only contemporary writer who is a practicing amateur witch," Jackson herself was never this straightforward. She had the trappings of witchcraft in her home (the books, the cats, the charms) and she *seemed* to practice it. She simply would never admit whether or not she was in earnest. Jackson's relationship to witchcraft will be discussed in chapter four and Lurie's in chapter five. For now it is enough to acknowledge the haunted houses and supernatural events in Jackson's fiction, and explain them with Isaac Bashevis Singer's insight, similar to Lurie's, that "The supernatural expresses the subconscious better than any other event a writer can write about."[15]

Other contemporary women have brazenly celebrated the powers associated with witchcraft and scorned the negative associations. This is the tone of the french feminist Helen Cixous' important essay published in 1975, "The Laugh of the Medusa."[16] Cixous observes that the blackness of witchcraft has cast its shadows over all women for too long: women have become "the dark continent," made to feel secretive and ashamed of their bodies and their strengths:

> Who, surprised and horrified by the fantastic tumult of her drives (for she was made to believe that a well-adjusted normal woman has a . . . divine composure), hasn't accused herself of being a monster? Who, feeling a funny desire stirring inside her (to sing, to write, to dare to speak, in short, to bring out something new), hasn't thought she was sick? (246)

The phallic-obsessed male world has made woman see herself as lacking— lacking not only a phallus, but a voice, a presence, indeed, a clearly-delineated self. According to Cixous, "Men say that there are two unrepresentable things: death and the feminine sex" (255). But women are only unrepresentable because men refuse to look at them: "You only have to look at the Medusa straight on to see her. And she's not deadly. She's beautiful and she's laughing" (255). Cixous' essay urges women to recognize the ways they have been shamed, silenced, and erased. Only when a woman learns to celebrate her body and her desires can she write with all her creative ("dark," "secret," "shameful") juices flowing.

Mary Daly, in *Gyn/Ecology* gleefully celebrates the power of witches.[17] She writes that "Hag-ography" is the tradition behind her book, the basis for her *Metaethics of Radical Feminism*, the book's subtitle. Hagiography, Daly observes, is a term used for the biography of saints. "Hag-ography," Daly's wry neologism, is the study of hags, witches, and crones:

> . . . a Crone is one who should be an example of strength, courage and wisdom.
> For women who are on the journey of radical be-ing, the lives of the witches, of the Great Hags of our hidden history are deeply intertwined with our own process. As we write/live our own story, we are uncovering their history, creating Hag-ography and Hagology. . . . Women traveling into feminist time/space are creating Hag-ocracy, the place we govern. To govern is to steer, to pilot. . . . The vehicles of our voyages may be any creative enterprises that further women's process. The point is that they should be governed by the Witch within—the Hag within.(15)

But not all recent scholars have seen the witch figure in so unambiguously positive a light. Judith Wilt's provocative article "The Laughter of Maidens, The Cackle of Matriarchs" argues that the optimistic sassy laughter of young maidens in literature evolves into the compromising "cackle of matriarchs" when they marry.[18] Wilt argues that matriarcal humor is merely survival humor, since the older woman stays in her unhappy position and can only pile "sandbags of wit against the flood of anger and pain" (193). That is, the matriarch laughs at male foibles as well as the injustices done her, but does not imagine that she can change her position in society. Some examples Wilt offers of comic matriarchs are the "acceptable female comics" (Phyliss Diller, Joan Rivers, Jean Kerr) as well as the women in Erma Bombeck's fiction and the married women in Marilyn French's novel *The Women's Room*. Although the matriarch is ultimately a figure of compromise and reconciliation, her laughter is still seen as a threat, and she is drawn as a witch: "when we have to do with women comics, matriarchal comics, we have to do with witches" (179).

WOMEN'S EXCLUSION FROM
TRADITIONAL DEFINITIONS OF WIT:

Another stumbling block to aspiring witty women writers stems from
their exclusion from the traditional definitions of wit, grounded in eighteenth-century thought. Pope's well-known couplet, claiming that

> True wit is Nature to advantage dressed,
> What oft was thought, but ne'er so well expressed ("An Essay on
> Criticism," II.297–8)

left "true wit" a matter of judgment, and the prevailing eighteenth-century
judgment was that wit involved both proper subject matter and proper language. This is what Dryden meant by describing wit as a "a propriety of
thoughts and words."[19] Anything written by women would have been dismissed out of hand, of course, since not only would their subject matter be
ridiculed, but so would the very fact of their writing at all. For writing was
not considered an appropriate occupation for the fairer sex. The prevailing
eighteenth-century attitude toward witty women writers foreshadowed
Johnson's famous dismissal, later in the century, of a woman preacher. She
reminded him, he said, of a dog dancing on his hind legs—one marvels not
at how well it was done, but that it was done at all.

But, women are now learning to ask, whose standards determine whose
language is the wittiest? Wit, according to an editor of *The Norton
Anthology*, "implies quickness of mind, inventiveness, a readiness to perceive resemblances between things apparently unlike and so to enliven literary discourse with appropriate images, similes, and metaphors.[20] While
he was describing the traditional eighteenth-century approach to wit, no
modern writer better illustrates this technique than Virginia Woolf.
Commenting on a procession of educated, powerful men parading across
the Thames, Woolf speculates on women's future potential:

> Who can say whether, as time goes on, we may not dress in military
> uniform, with gold lace on our breasts, swords at our sides, and some-
> thing like the old family coal-skuttle on our heads, save that that ven-
> erable object was never decorated with plumes of white horsehair.[21]

While this wry observation brilliantly illustrates the traditional definition of
wit, neither Pope or Dryden would have found the subject matter at all
proper. They would have considered it an impertinence for a woman to be
writing at all, much less sharpening her wit against male traditions.

The male bias that led to the exclusion of women's interests and values from the traditionally proper subject matter of wit is only now being

exposed. Although Virginia Woolf suggested the bias in 1929, when she observed that ". . . football and sport are 'important'; the worship of fashion, the buying of clothes 'trivial,' " scholars have only recently considered the many ramifications of her observation.[22] In 1988, Regina Barreca observed that "It is the inability of the critical tradition to deal with comedy by women rather than the inability of women to produce comedy that accounts for the absence of critical material on the subject."[23] Her clever book on women's humor, *They Used to Call Me Snow White . . . But I Drifted: Women's Strategic Use of Humor*, is part of her ongoing effort to supply some of that missing critical material. One of the premises behind Nancy Walker's *A Very Serious Thing: Women's Humor and the American Culture*, which traces women's humor from the beginnings of American literature, is that this tradition has been excluded from the canon because women's subjects have always been considered trivial.[24]

This study of witty women begins by considering the cautious reception given to three witty women writing early in the twentieth century: Dorothy Parker, Dawn Powell, and Betty MacDonald. Each of the seven following chapters concentrates on a single contemporary witty writer in order to examine how her wit controls her texts, her readers, and, to an extent, her life. Some, like Ephron, openly acknowledge the appeal of control. Others, like Jackson, discuss control only in terms of the craft of writing. Since I intend to argue that wit has led to control in both the writings and the lives of these women, I have mixed biographical information with critical commentary. But I have also included personal information because I feel that in the same way that subjects of interest to women have been undervalued and trivialized, so have their lives. The obstacles to writing when raising a family, for women writers who choose to have children, should not be ignored. Nor should the effect of their formative years. When Margaret Drabble was asked whether she saw literature as text and context, or text alone, she responded:

> No. I see it as social context. Also I see it a lot in terms of a writer's personal biography. I was taught not to pay attention to it, but I find it increasingly interesting. It's so obvious that writers are influenced by the way their parents behaved. It seems to me ridiculous to isolate a text, in fact, almost meaningless.[25]

In the discussions that follow, I have always included what I consider to be relevant information on the writers' lives, but been careful to distinguish fact from speculation. And one very clear fact is that these seven women are all effective story tellers whose wit has secured them a respected niche in the contemporary literary world.

NOTES

1. See Regina Barreca, introduction to *Last Laughs*, and Nancy Walker, *A Very Serious Thing:* esp. 73–80, for documentary evidence of this bias.
2. Shirley Jackson, "Experience and Fiction" *Come Along With Me; Part of a novel, sixteen stories, and three lectures,* ed. Stanley Edgar Hyman (NY: Viking, 1968) 199; Nora Ephron, "Revision and Life," *Nora Ephron Collected* (Ny: Avon, 1991) 214–215; Carol Edwards, "Interview with Lisa Alther," *Turnstile* 4.1 (1993): 48; Rita Mae Brown, *Starting From Scratch* (NY: Bantam, 1988) 3 & 9; Dorothy Mermin, "Aliuson Lurie," *Women Writers Talking,* ed. Janet Todd (NY: Holmes & Meier, 1983) 93; Kathleen Hulley, "Interview with Grace Paley," *Delta* 14 (May, 1982): 21; Judy Oppenheimer, *Private Demons:* The Life of Shirley Jackson (NY: Putnam, 1988) 23.
3. Anne Tyler, "Still Just Writing," *The Writer on Her Work,* ed. Janet Sternburg (New York: Norton, 1980) 13.
4. Alison Lurie, "No One Asked Me To Write a Novel," *New York Times Book Review* 6 June, 1982: 13.
5. Edwards 38.
6. Shirley Jackson 203.
7. Nora Ephron 215–16.
8. Judy Oppenheimer 190.
9. All translations from Chaucer are my own. The text used is *The Works of Geoffrey Chaucer*, ed. F.N. Robinson, 2nd ed. (Boston: Houghton Mifflin, 1957). In the following discussion, lines in single quotations not followed by a line reference indicate I am paraphrasing the original.
10. Margaret Atwood, *Second Words* (Boston: Beacon, 1982) 219.
11. Sandra Gilbert and Susan Gubar, *The Norton Anthology of Literature by Women* (New York: Norton, 1985) 4.
12. Virginia Woolf, *A Room of One's Own* 50–51.
13. Judy Little, *Comedy and the Woman Writer* (Lincoln: Univ. of Nebraska Press, 1983) 16–17.
14. Dorothy Mermin, "Alison Lurie," *Women Writers Talking* 85–6.
15. Oppenheimer *Private Demons*, 228.
16. Elaine Marks & Isabelle de Courtivron, eds, *New French Feminisms* (NY: Schocken, 1981) 255–264.
17. Mary Daly, *Gyn/Ecology: The Metaethics of Radical Feminism* (Boston: Beacon, 1978).
18. Judith Wilt, "The Laughter of Maidens, The Cackle of Matriarchs," *Gender and Literary Voice,* ed. Janet Todd (NY & London: Holmes & Meier, 1980) 173–195.
19. John Dryden, "The Author's Apology for Heroic Poetry and Heroic License, " *The Norton Anthology of English Literature,* ed. M, H. Abrams, 4th ed., vol.I (New York: Norton, 1979) 1805.

20. Samuel Holt Monk and Lawrence Lipking, "The Restoration and the Eighteenth Century," *The Norton Anthology,* 1729.

21. Virginia Woolf, *Three Guineas* (1938; New York: Harcourt Brace Jovanovich, 1966) 61–2.

22. Woolf, *A Room of One's Own,* (1929; NY: Harcourt Brace Jovanovich, 1957) 77.

23. Regina Barreca, introduction to *Last Laughs: Perspectives on Women and Comedy,* ed. Regina Barreca (NY: Gordon and Breach, 1988) 20.

24. Walker 72.

25. Gilian Parker and Janet Todd, "Margaret Drabble," *Women Writers Talking,* 171.

2

Forerunners: Dorothy Parker, Dawn Powell, Betty MacDonald

Despite efforts to suppress, ignore, or trivialize their writing, certain women writing early in the twentieth century learned to trust the potential power of their wit. Dorothy Parker, Dawn Powell, and Betty MacDonald, three witty writers born the generation before those featured in this book, all made their livings by their pens—creating new lives for themselves as they wrote.[1] It is far from coincidental that, early in their lives, all three underwent crises which forced them out of the conventional woman's plot. It was after the crisis that each began to write herself a new life script.

In *Writing a Woman's Life*, Carolyn Heilbrun credits Nina Auerbach with identifying this curious phenomenon in the life of many an accomplished woman who died before the middle of this century—an early crisis or event that ejected her from the male-scripted marriage plot: "For women who wish to live a quest plot, as men's stories allow, indeed encourage them to do," Heilbrun observes, "some event must transform their lives, all unconsciously, apparently 'accidentally,' from a conventional to an eccentric story."[2] Auerbach was discussing George Eliot, while Heilbrun sees a similar pattern in the life of Dorothy Sayers, the successful English writer of the Peter Whimsy detective novels. Heilbrun objects to the negative

13

framework in which Sayer's biographer, James Brabazon, places his subject's successful writing career. Brabazon presents Dorothy Sayers as a
physically unattractive woman who only fell back on her intellect because
of her failure to attract a husband. But, argues Heilbrun, Brabazon cannot
see that this "failure" to live within the conventional marriage script was
precisely what enabled her to have a successful writing career in the first
place. What is at issue is the biographer's emphasis. Heilbrun argues that
Sayer's life is "an excellent example of a woman's unconscious 'fall' into a
condition where vocation is possible and out of the marriage plot that
demands not only that a woman marry but that the marriage and its progeny
be her life's absolute and only center" (51). Heilbrun advises the potential
biographer of any accomplished woman who died before the middle of the
twentieth century to examine her life carefully in order to uncover the event
which put her outside of, thereby freeing her from, the marriage plot.

Although Dorothy Parker's mother died when she was five, and Dawn
Powell's when she was six, neither those early tragic losses nor the unconventional childhoods which followed were the precise crises which trans-
formed their lives. Parker led a privileged childhood in New York City until
the age of twenty, when her father died and, if Parker's account can be
trusted, left her penniless. Although she could have lived with an older
brother or sister, she chose to live alone, supporting herself by playing the
piano until her writing was recognized. In less than a year, she received her
first acceptance check from *Vanity Fair*, which marked the beginning of her
literary career.[3] Dawn Powell's crisis began when she was only twelve,
when her father remarried and moved Dawn and her two sisters to his second wife's farm. Although all three girls were unhappy, only Dawn ran
away. She did so not because of any general misery, but specifically because
her new stepmother had burned all her early writing efforts. Powell then
moved in with a sympathetic aunt until, at twenty-one, she finished college
and headed for New York City, determined to make her living with her pen.[4]
Betty MacDonald's crisis came through an early bad marriage she entered at
age eighteen. After four years, she could no longer endure her isolated life
as the wife of a chicken farmer in the wilds of the State of Washington.
Although divorce carried a stigma in 1931 unimaginable today, she preferred to move with her two infant daughters back to her mother's home in
Seattle, willing to work at anything rather than stay in the horrifying script
that had been written for her.[5] All three women then began new lives which,
while not excluding marriage, centered on their writing careers.

Despite their literary successes, the reputations of these three writers
were diminished by the bias against women who wrote with wit. Parker's
wit backfired in so far as it provided her readers with an excuse to dismiss
her politics and serious social commentary. Dawn Powell's caustic wit

caused her to be dismissed as a bitter cynic. Her novels and stories were largely overlooked until the 1990's, when reprints with highly complimentary introductions by Gore Vidal began to reintroduce her to the reading public. Betty MacDonald's merry wit, on the other hand, made her memoirs extremely popular when they first appeared from the mid-forties to the mid-fifties, but only because she was interpreted as endearingly frivolous and scatterbrained. Her merry memoirs have always been trivialized as the work of a conciliating, pacifying domestic humorist, although it is hard to see how any of her comments on marriage can be read as pacifying.[6] But the reception of witty women writers has been even more guarded than the reception granted other women writers. The reputations of Parker, Powell, and MacDonald illustrate three distinct ways wit could diminish a women writer's reputation, however large an audience she reached.

1. DOROTHY PARKER (1893–1967)

Both Dorothy Parker's biographers, John Keats and Marion Meade, present Parker as a confused, sad, and self-destructive woman. Nora Ephron wryly observes that "Dorothy Parker had not been very good at being Dorothy Parker either."[7] There is an implicit threat in such negative assessments—women can be funny and successful, this threat goes, but only at a high personal price. I feel that the degree to which Parker's politics and life are dismissed as frivolous or destructive is directly related to her great reputation as a wit: the more the one is praised, the more the other is criticized. And Parker's reputation as a wit is great. She had a tremendous impact on the New York literary scene in the first half of this century. Nor has this reputation faded. If a person in the 1990s can attach only one name to the legendary Algonquin Round Table it is, invariably, hers.

Dorothy Parker was twenty-one when she first had a verse accepted for publication. The magazine was *Vanity Fair*, the year 1914. The young Parker immediately marched into the editor's office seeking a job. Her boldness was to be emulated by Ephron fifty years later at the offices at *Esquire*. Unlike Ephron's, however, Parker's boldness was not cushioned by screenwriting parents. In fact, at twenty-one her life was not cushioned by any parents at all. Her father had died the year before, her mother when she was five, and her stepmother when she was ten.

Parker led an extremely unconventional childhood. Her father was a successful businessman, first in the growing garment industry and later in the cigar business. Jacob Henry Rothschild was from a German Jewish family with the same name as, but not the family connection to, the banking Rothschilds of Europe. He twice married Christian women and always

enjoyed a lavish life style. His first wife bore him four children, the
youngest being Dorothy. His second wife outlived his first by only five
years. When she died, the children had maids to run the house and dogs on
whom to lavish affection.

From the time of his second marriage in 1900, his two daughters attended
a private Catholic school in New York City, Blessed Sacred Academy,
which not only boasted a strong academic reputation, but was conveniently
located around the corner from their luxurious West Side brownstone.
Dorothy hated it and caused as much trouble as she could from the start. She
treated formal schooling as something to rebel against, as would Grace Paley
thirty years later. In 1907, at age fourteen, Dorothy left home for Miss
Dana's, a boarding school in New Jersey which she attended for less than a
year. In light of her future literary success, it may surprise many that this
marked the end of her formal education. It probably would not surprise
Carolyn Heilbrun, however, who would undoubtedly see the young Parker's
rebellion against formal education as an early attempt to step outside the
conventional script still being written for middle-class young ladies.

Parker spent most of the next six years as companion for her twice-
widowed father. He died in 1913 when she was twenty. Although there
seemed to be no lack of money throughout her childhood, when *Vanity Fair*
first published a poem of Parker's in 1914, she had been eking out a living
by playing the piano for a dance studio while living in a boarding house.
Interviewed in 1956 for the *The Paris Review*, Parker explained that when
her father died, there simply wasn't any money.[8]

It may now appear remarkable that in 1918, a twenty-four-year-old
woman with no literary connections nor even a high school diploma could
be chosen to replace *Vanity Fair's* renowned drama critic, P.G. Wodehouse.
But that is exactly what happened. Frank Crowninshield, the editor, had
continued to be impressed with Parker since he had first hired her for *Vogue*
and soon had her transferred to *Vanity Fair*. It was into his office she had so
boldly marched two years earlier. When Wodehouse asked for a leave,
Crowninshield decided to take a chance and replace him with the young
Dorothy Parker. His hunch paid off. In April of 1918, Parker wrote her first
drama review, launching her career as one of New York's leading wits. She
wrote under the name Parker, not Rothschild, as she had been married to
Edwin Pond Parker II in 1917, when both were in their early twenties,
shortly before Edwin joined the military. Although the marriage ended a
few years after he returned from Europe, and her second (and third) husband was Allen Campbell. she always kept the name Parker she so quickly
made synonymous with wit.[9]

Her drama criticism was brilliant and arresting from the start. Even
when she praised a play, which she did only rarely, she could find some-

thing to be sarcastic about. Her reviews are fresh, original and cleverly written. She makes her points even as she appears to be straying from them. The following review of a production she admired appeared in December of 1918, when Parker was twenty-five and had been reviewing for eight months:

> There are still a few rays of light, however, even in the gathering gloom of the season. There is Tolstoi's *Redemption*, for instance— although "ray of light" isn't exactly a happy term for it. It isn't what you might call sunny. I went into the Plymouth Theatre a comparatively young woman, and I staggered out of it, three hours later, twenty years older, haggard and broken with suffering. It won't fill you all full of glad thoughts, and it isn't just the sort of thing to take the kiddies to, but won't you please see it, even if you have to mortgage the Dodge, sublet the apartment, and sell everything but your Liberty Bonds, to get tickets? Go and see it, so that you may come out and proclaim to the world that at last you have beheld a perfectly done play.
>   A more extraordinary production I have never seen. It is difficult to speak of "atmosphere" and "feeling" without sounding as if one wore sandals and lived below Fourteenth Street, but you just can't mention Robert Jones scenery without using the words.

She ended the review with a reservation most English speakers share, though few could shape so adroitly:

> There's only one thing I could wish about the whole play—I do wish they would do something about those Russian names. Owing to the local Russian custom of calling each person sometimes by all of his names, sometimes by only his first three or four, and sometimes by a nickname which has nothing to do with any of the other names, it is difficult for one with my congenital lowness of brow to gather exactly whom they are talking about. I do wish that as long as they are translating the thing, they would go right ahead, while they're at it, and translate Fedor Vasilyevich Protosov and Sergei Dmitrievich Abreskov and Ivan Petrovich Alexandrov into Joe and Henry and Fred.[10]

Her book reviews were equally polished and original. Dorothy Parker was more than merely witty: she was well-read, intelligent, and had the courage of her perceptions. From 1927–1933 she wrote the "Constant Reader" column for *The New Yorker*, combining insight with wit. Probably her most quoted observation is the final line of her review of A.A. Milne's *The House at Pooh Corner*, whose cuteness put her off. Her review ends in a deadly mixture of direct quoting and observation:

> "Well, you'll see, Piglet, when you listen. Because this is how it begins. *The more it snows, tiddely-pom—*"

> "Tiddely what" said Piglet, (He took, as you might say, the very
> words out of your correspondent's mouth.)
> "Pom," said Pooh. "I put that it to make it more hummy."
> And it is that word "hummy," my darlings, that marks the first place
> in *The House at Pooh Corner* at which Tonstant Weader Fwowed up.[11]

But Parker's reputation has done her the injustice of stressing her quips
at the expense of her insights. Her assessment of Hemingway is a good
example of the latter. She was reviewing *Men Without Women*, a collection of his stories published after the highly-acclaimed *The Sun Also Rises*.
Both works had been published after his overlooked short story collection
In Our Time:

> Now *The Sun Also Rises* was as "starkly" written as Mr.
> Hemingway's short stories; it dealt with subjects as "unpleasant." Why
> it should have been taken to the slightly damp bosom of the public
> while the (as it seems to me) superb *In Our Time* should have been dis-
> regarded will always be a puzzle to me. As I see it—I knew this con-
> versation would get back to me sooner or later, preferably
> sooner—Mr. Hemingway's style, this prose stripped to its firm young
> bones, is far more effective, far more moving, in the short story than in
> the novel. He is, to me, the greatest living writer of short stories; he is,
> also to me, not the greatest living novelist[12]

From 1957 to 1962 Parker reviewed books for *Esquire*. Her willingness
to take an unpopular position never dimmed with age. The ban on
Nabokov's *Lolita* had hardly been lifted when she wrote her review:

> I do not think that *Lolita* is a filthy book. I cannot regard it as
> pornography, either sheer, unrestrained, or any other kind. It is the
> engrossing anguished story of a man, a man of taste and culture, who
> can love only little girls. . . .
> An anguished book, but sometimes wildly funny, as in the saga of
> his travel across and around the United States with her, in search of
> some place that might possibly please her; and in the account of that
> trek are descriptions of the American hinterlands that Sinclair Lewis
> could never touch. . . . [A brief plot summary follows]
> No. It is no good, I see at this late moment, to try to melt down the
> story. It is in its writing that Mr. Nabokov has made it the work of art
> that it is. Mr. Nabokov—the same man, you know, that wrote the del-
> icate stories in *Pnin*—started writing in English long after his first
> youth. His command of the language is absolute, and his *Lolita* is a
> fine book, a distinguished book—all right, then—a great book.[13]

From our vantage point in the 1990s, it is hard to imagine the consternation
this review must have caused, the puritanical eyebrows this must have
raised, in 1958. But neither Parker's writing nor her life was ever styled to
gain public approval.

In June of 1919, the twenty-six-year-old Parker was sufficiently established in the New York literary scene to receive an invitation for a luncheon party at the Algonquin Hotel celebrating the return from the war of *The New York Times* drama critic, Alexander Woollcott. The luncheon was such a success that someone suggested they meet daily. Hindsight established this party as the first meeting of the Algonquin Round Table, although the hotel manager had yet to establish them at the large round table he hoped would accommodate the growing group, and Edmund Duffy, a cartoonist for *The Brooklyn Eagle*, had yet to publish his caricature of the luncheon guests that he labeled The Algonquin Round Table, thereby making the name official. And thus was established the legend of a group of witty flamboyant writers enjoying stylish alcoholic lunches when not writing down their witticisms for posterity. Meade's account suggests that the writers functioned as a close-knit support group. But since the luncheon meetings spilled over into afternoon cocktails, evenings out, and weekend poker games, the Round Table did little to encourage sober working habits. Although it lasted barely ten years, the Algonquin Round Table has been granted a permanent place in the literary history of America. Dorothy Parker, along with Alexander Woollcott, Robert Benchley, George Kaufman, and Harold Ross, were among its charter members.

In 1928, Parker moved to Hollywood with her second husband, Alan Campbell, where they teamed up to write countless screenplays, including "A Star is Born" and "Five Little Peppers and How they Grew." By then her literary reputation was so well established that she was offered a salary four times as great as her husband's. During the pre-McCarthy years in Hollywood, their income remained high, and Parker enjoyed the lavish lifestyle their joint incomes allowed. She and Campbell restored an old farm in Bucks County, Pennsylvania, in the late thirties. But even in her new home Parker remained true to a lifelong aversion to domesticity. Meade quotes a friend describing their life style: "Dottie and Alan went to bed half-drunk at four in the morning and then slept until the next afternoon. They expected their help to stay up till dawn cleaning up and then to be awake whenever they got up" (268). Parker steadfastly refused to learn how to cook, and for the rest of her life, during the years she was not with Campbell, preferred to live in hotels.

Although Parker had a vivid reputation, and was extremely sought after (in the 1930s, she and Fanny Brice "divided New York between them"[14]), the sadder aspects of her private life have been as carefully documented as her accomplishments. In both Keats and Meade's biographies, Parker's depressions, problems with alcohol, and suicide attempts are painstakingly recounted, as is her aversion to domestic skills. It is as if we expect a woman who is so in control of her words to display an equal control of her private life, and blame her for disappointing us. While not unduly alarmed at the lack of empathy in John Keats' biography, *You Might As Well Live*, I found the accumulating criticism of the female commentators dismaying, which only exposes an expectation of my own.[15]

Consider Marion Meade's assessment of an affair Parker had in the mid-1920's, which ended in an unwanted pregnancy. Legally, she was still married to Edwin Parker, who had suffered both alcohol and morphine addictions. Meade accuses Parker of avoiding two crucial questions: "What caused her attraction to an addict in the first place, and what was it about her that drew unstable men?" (111). Yet these would have been singularly foolish questions for Parker to ask herself in view of the fact that all of her friends, male and female, drank heavily. Indeed, her entire circle of friends would be considered unstable by any middle-class standard.

When Nora Ephron criticized Parker's life, she at least acknowledged that she had grown up besotted with the legend of Dorothy Parker, with the romanticized and idealized version of reality.[16] And Lillian Hellman, in her reminiscence of Parker, does admit that she "enjoyed her more than I enjoyed any other woman," describing a comment by Parker as startling and sudden "as if a curtain had opened and you had a brief and brilliant glance into what you would never have found for yourself."[17] But, on balance, Hellman's portrait of Parker, as Ephron points out, is "of a sad lady who misspent her life and talent."[18]

I feel it would be more accurate to say that the critics *misrepresent* Dorothy Parker's life and talent. Her lavish life style is served up as if that were the source of her unhappiness. Parker's politics and serious social commentary were ignored even in her lifetime, and only her merry quips remembered: "A 'smartcracker' they call me," Parker commented in the 1956 *Paris Review* interview, "and that makes me sick and unhappy. . . . Wit has truth in it; wisecracking is simply calisthenics with words."[19]

Even her friends dismissed her political activities, calling them theatrics. Yet her political beliefs were remarkably consistent: she always tried to help the victims of political injustice. She went to jail for Sacco and Venzetti,[20] raised money to help the refugees of the Spanish Civil War, and again to fight the Nazis. During the McCarthy purge, she was blacklisted in Hollywood. When she died in 1967, she left her money to Martin Luther King, a man she had never met, and, in the event of his death, to the NAACP. In view of his subsequent assassination, the contingency in her will proved her to be rather politically astute.

Parker knew that her reputation as a wit was undermining her political efforts. In 1937 she went to Spain, but her protests against Franco were largely ignored. According to Keats:

> She beat her head against the walls of her reputation. She told all who would listen that she wished she had never written a humorous line. She wanted everyone to forget her wit and listen to the alarm she was trying to sound. But Harold Ross wanted her to be funny, and Alan Campbell wanted her to shut-up, and Metro-Goldwin-Mayer wanted her to write film fantasies . . .[21]

Parker wrote at least one report for *The New Masses*, a cultural and political magazine of the American radical literary left, whose contributors included Dreiser, Hemingway, Richard Wright, and Langston Hughes. Parker grew so frustrated at the way her opinions were dismissed (and so fed up with people accusing her of being a card-carrying communist in order to discount her opinions) that she included this disclaimer in the report:

> I am not a member of any political party. The only group I have ever been affiliated with is that not particularly brave little band that hid its nakedness of heart and mind under the out-of-date garment of a sense of humor. I heard someone say, and so I said it too, that ridicule is the most effective weapon. I don't suppose I ever really believed it, but it was easy and comforting, and so I said it. Well, now I know. I know that there are things than never have been funny, and never will be. And I know that ridicule may be a shield, but it is not a weapon.[22]

Parker grew so frustrated over the public's refusal to take her seriously that she would have traded in her reputation as a wit if it meant that her social commentary would be heard.

What Parker's critics have ignored is that she held firm to certain key values throughout her lifetime, none of them traditional middle-class ones. She never aspired to bourgeois goals, be they educational, political, domestic, monetary, or literary. She left school at fourteen, refused to ever cook or keep house, never kept track of her money, and certainly never saved for a rainy day. She did believe in having a good time. During her final years, when she lived alone as a semi-invalid in a hotel room in New York City, she had one consistent greeting for Lillian Hellman, who admits she should have visited more often and would have understood had Parker greeted her with a reproach. But her greeting was always the same: "Oh Lilly, come in quick. I want to laugh again."[23]

Parker always believed in speaking out and acting on her beliefs. She risked traveling to war-torn Spain in order to send back first-hand reports of Franco's atrocities, and consistently spoke up for victims of oppression.

That her beliefs did not prove effective at keeping personal depression at
bay seems entirely irrelevant to the quality of her writing or, for that matter,
to the romantic and reckless quality of her life. But the public rarely admires
a woman who adopts a Bryronesque persona. Byron, after all, was a man. It
is telling that Hemingway's flamboyant life style, politics, and suicide
served only to enhance his reputation, while Parker's life style, politics, and
unsuccessful suicide attempts served only to undermine hers.

2. DAWN POWELL (1897–1965)

Dawn Powell lived "under the burden of being known as the second
Dorothy Parker."[24] But today even that burden has been lifted—most contemporary readers do not know of her at all. Yet Powell was a devastatingly
witty and prolific writer who spent all of her adult life in Greenwich
Village, where she wrote thirteen novels, several plays, short stories which
appeared in such major periodicals as *The New Yorker* and *The Saturday
Evening Post*, and turned out radio, TV, and film scripts. Although she was
friends with Edmund Wilson, Hemingway, Malcolm Cowley, and Robert
Benchley ("adored by" claimed Jacqueline Rice, the executor of her
estate),[25] her books never created the stir they deserved and often went out
of print even as she was working on the next.

The target of her satire was always the middle class, which, according to
her obituary, "did not add to her popularity."[26] This is a peculiar rationale,
since the middle class had also been the satiric target of such successful
writers as Sinclair Lewis and Theodore Dreiser. Gore Vidal feels that
Powell *should* have been as widely read as Hemingway, Fitzgerald O'Hara
or Katherine Anne Porter. He suggests that not only her caustic wit but also
her subject matter worked against her:

> . . . Powell was that unthinkable monster, a witty woman who felt no
> obligation to make a single, much less a final, down payment on Love
> or the Family; she saw life with a bright Petronian neutrality, and every
> host at life's feast was a potential Trimalchio to be sent up.[27]

Vidal is undoubtedly right. The more careful reader, of course, could make
a similar observation about Dorothy Parker's subject matter. But since all of
Parker's better known stories ("Big Blond" and "Telephone" for example)
feature women who appear incomplete without their men, they can also be
read as if Parker were suggesting the importance of love by exploring the
sufferings of those who yearned for it. This interpretation is a more comfortable one, since it is in keeping with a woman's traditional role. But to
read Parker so, one has to slur over the fact that she was satirizing, not

endorsing, the behavior of these women. In fact, all of Parker's female characters are in nearly the same position as Powell's: both writers depict gay and sophisticated New York ladies who are trying to combat their disappointments in love by hiding behind glittering sassy personae.

"For decades," wrote Vidal, "Dawn Powell was always just on the verge of ceasing to be a cult and becoming a major religion."[28] Thanks to Vidal's efforts as well as a more tolerant climate towards women writers and women's roles, Dawn Powell is in the process of being rediscovered today. In 1995, Tim Page edited Powell's diaries and wrote a new introduction for *My Home Is Far Away* (both published by Steerforth Press, South Royalton, Vermont). Several of her novels have been reprinted since 1989: *The Golden Spur* (Viking, 1962, Random House 1990), *The Wicked Pavilion* (Riverside Press 1954, Vintage 1990), *Angels on Toast* (Scribner 1940, Vintage 1990) *The Locusts Have No King* (Scribner 1948, Yarrow Press 1990) and *A Time to be Born* (Scribner 1942, Yarrow 1991). Most of the rest are available in libraries. Her early novels are set in the Midwest and her later ones in New York—where there is always at least one transplanted Midwesterner who is making (or, more often, *not* making) a name in the arts.

Dawn Powell, like Dorothy Parker, had a highly irregular childhood. She was born in Mount Gilead, Ohio in 1897. Her mother died when she was six, and her father, who traveled, boarded out his three small daughters with various relatives. The children were often moved yearly, from "village life in small-town boarding houses, to rougher life in the middle of little factory-towns." When Powell was twelve, her father remarried and moved his three daughters to his new wife's farm near Cleveland. There Dawn Powell's troubles began in earnest. All three sisters were unhappy with the new arrangement, but it was only when her stepmother burned all her writing that young Dawn decided she had had enough. She ran away with just thirty cents in her pocket earned from berry-picking. Moving in with a sympathetic aunt in Shelby, Ohio, she attended high school and, in 1918, graduated from Lake Erie College. Then the twenty-one-year-old woman headed straight for New York City. For a few months she was a "yeomanette" with the Naval Reserve, but soon learned to make her living with her pen.[29]

Powell began her writing career humbly, doing publicity work. She met her future husband, Joseph Roebuck Gousha, who was in advertising, while doing publicity for the Inter-Church World movement. They were married in 1920 and remained married until he died in 1962. Joseph Roebuck Jr, a son, was their only child. According to Gore Vidal, Dawn Powell "did every sort of writing" throughout her married life because her only child was brain damaged, and the special education and nurses required were

costly.[30] Curiously, *The New York Times* obituary reports that Powell educated their only child at home because she believed schools repressed children's creativity. The contradiction is explained in Guare's introduction to
The Locusts Have No King. He quotes Jacqueline Rice, friend and executor
of Powell's estate, who explained that Powell covered the truth by telling
everyone her son was so exceptional that she had to keep him at home with
tutors in Italian and piano to meet his superior talents.[31] Apparently the life
she was creating for herself in New York had no room for pity.

Although her photographs show a plump, almost motherly sort of person, her life style and writings belie her appearance. Vidal recalls a party at
her place on 35 East Ninth Street, around 1950, also attended by E.E.
Cummings and his wife Marion: "Conversation flows. Gin flows. Marion
Cummings is beautiful." Finally, Vidal wakes up to the fact that Coby,
Powell's "eternal escort," was her lover, while Joe, looking down from a
balcony high up in the second story of her living room, was her husband: "I
realize, at last, that this is a ménage à trois in Greenwich Village. My mar-
tini runs over."[32]

Powell's novels evoke the same atmosphere as Vidal's memory of that
afternoon party in her Village home. The novels are filled with sophisticated people living New York lives. The narrator is merciless at exposing
the self-centered panic beneath the suave facades, and fortune's wheel
seems to spin quite arbitrarily over them all. Such a medieval image as fortune's wheel is apt, since all Powell's novels tend to read like updated
Canterbury Tales, intent on exposing human weaknesses in all walks of
life. And, like Chaucer's pilgrimage, the different life stories are loosely
bound. Her novels do not contain plots so much as isolated vignettes, held
together by the fact that the characters know each other, however superficially, in their New York society. At times she includes too many characters, so that the brilliance of her satire can become dulled by the reader's
confusion in trying to remember who is who.

One of her most successful novels is *The Happy Island*, written in
1938. A good example of how Powell operates is her description of smug
Anna, who unwittingly outwits her philandering husband Neal as well as
his mistresses:

> Eventually Anna's unwavering faith in her own happiness broke
> through other women's claims to Neal like a soulless mighty tank. It is
> impossible for other women to rejoice in a lover whose wife is so con-
> spicuously complacent, so suspiciously content, who gently smiles at
> his open flirtations as if this was all charming child's play well-under-
> stood and often discussed between the happy couple, so customary that
> the wife could well afford a benign indifference, touched, perhaps,
> with pity for the new, alas only temporary, slave.

But Powell has saved the final irony for the next paragraph:

> So Neal's women—and for that matter even Neal—were mystified, and believed Anna was cruelly, diabolically clever, while Neal, fairly shallow himself, respected Anna for her deep devotion to himself, always an impressive and moving thing to a man. Anna was neither clever nor deep but so thoroughly narcissistic she honestly did not see how any man could fail to see how superior she was to all other women in looks, brains, and general nobility.[33]

As this passage illustrates, Powell's wit comes in her subtle insights rather than in the clever turn of phrase we associate with Parker.

If *The Happy Island* can be said to have a main plot (really a recurring vignette), it is the story of Prudence and her Midwestern lover Jeff. Jeff is a budding playwright who comes to New York just long enough to produce his first play. They have a brief romantic encounter back home in Silver City, Ohio, before Prudence escapes to New York and recreates herself as a provocative entertainer in a small nightspot. Jeff is the foil to Prudence's self-created New York persona. He wants her to return to Silver City as his wife, even though he objects to almost everything about her other than their mutual sexual attraction. After he leaves New York, they correspond. Here is his reply to one of her typical letters:

> For God's sake, Prudence, what do you believe in if you can't believe in your own friends? What fun do you get out of being so damnably wise? Please remember that your remarks on paper, without benefit of your personal attractions, are frightening and make me suspect I fell in love with a witch. (256)

But ultimately his downhome values do not prevail. Although Prudence ultimately agrees to go live with him, the narrator captures her desperation as her train pulls into her hometown station:

> . . . here was the land against which your own will was helpless, the land that dictated what you would be and what you would do, here was the land of little homes, wilted lettuce, apple pie, sugar on cucumbers, noodles, pot roast, bean soup, fried potatoes, rice pudding, pop, icebox cake, new mown grass, bonfires, chicken suppers. (*The Happy Island*, 281)

Here, as in all of her novels, Powell does not seem able to visualize a positive option for her characters. Her women can choose small towns and male dominance or the big city and survival masks. The latter is presented as the lesser of two evils rather than as a positive good. For a time, Prudence is caught between the two:

> She was lost between her worlds; and if Jeff went away, there would
> be nothing left, not that real self he was so proud of rescuing, small
> unhappy reality that it was, nor that cruel swaggering false self that at
> least had perfected a technique of living, a way of using a mask as a
> shield behind which she might go about her secret destiny. (*The Happy
> Island*, 295)

It is impossible to ignore an autobiographical strain in Prudence's story.
Prudence returns to New York and her city lover, who grew "a little phonier
every year but at least he was gay, he did know how to play" (299). Powell
also chose to live in New York, and maintain a gay facade. For if it is true
that she led a sophisticated "mènage à trois" and enjoyed partying with literary luminaries like E.E. Cummings, it is also true that she diligently wrote
anything and everything to provide special care for her retarded son, while
pretending he was gifted and needed exceptional training. In 1965, at age
67, she died of cancer. True to her merry facade to the end, she refused to
let her friend Jacqueline Rice bring over her baby for daily visits when the
cancer grew worse. Rice told John Guare that:

> She hid her fear and despair. She showed her best face to the world.
> And what a glorious face. I wake up some mornings so happy because
> I've dreamt that that whole world is still alive.[34]

3. BETTY MACDONALD (1908–1958)

Unlike the poor reception given Powell's works, Betty MacDonald's
four autobiographical memoirs, published between 1945 and 1955, sold so
well that in 1959, the year after her death, a fifth volume was published
which was no more than a collection of selected chapters from the earlier
four.[35] But today's reader can only retrieve them from libraries. Portions of
MacDonald's first memoir, *The Egg and I*, originally appeared in install-
ments in *The Atlantic Monthly*, was published as a book by Lippincott in
1945, and stayed at the top of the best seller list for months. It then earned
her an additional $100,000 plus a percentage of the film profits when
International Pictures bought the rights and turned it into a mawkish comedy starring Claudette Colbert and Fred MacMurray. The movie opened in
Radio City Music Hall in April, 1947.[36]

The Egg and I describes MacDonald's life with her first husband,
Robert Eugene Heskett, an insurance salesman who no sooner married her
than left the insurance business to become a chicken farmer. The year was
1927. She was eighteen and he thirty-one. They bought an abandoned farm
in a remote area of the state of Washington near Chimacum, where their

nearest neighbors were four miles distant. In her memoir she calls her neighbors, with their large brood of slovenly children, The Kettles. Thus were Ma and Pa Kettle born. Unfortunately, MacDonald's memoir, published in 1945, was so popular that those characters (or the movie's version, with Marjorie Main and Percy Kilbridge playing Ma and Pa Kettle) apparently reached even the remote areas around Chimacum. For in 1950, five years after her book appeared and nearly twenty years after the event, nine members of a single family filed an unsuccessful $900,000 suit against MacDonald and Lippincott, claiming they were humiliated by being identified as the original Kettle family.[37]

MacDonald stuck out this isolated marriage for four years before leaving and returning with her two infant daughters to her mother's home in Seattle. In the Hollywood version, as one might expect, she and her husband patch up their differences and live happily ever after. But MacDonald's life followed a different script. She left her husband in 1931. During those post-depression years, encouraged by her elder sister Mary, she was game to try her hand at almost anything: she was secretary to a mining engineer and manager of a chain letter office, she sold advertising, worked for a number of government agencies, and became the only woman labor adjuster in the National Recovery Administration. She was employed by the Treasury Department, and from 1939–42 served as director of publicity for the National Youth Administration.[38]

Anybody Can Do Anything (1950) merrily chronicles these years, except for the time spent in a Seattle sanitorium for tuberculosis from 1938 to mid-1939. That experience had already been written as *The Plague and I* (1948), the title playing off of her earlier success, *The Egg and I*. This second memoir did a clever and witty balancing act between exposing the undue harshness of certain health care workers while remaining grateful for the care received in a public institution.

MacDonald was always adept at extracting the pith from difficult times. She puts me in mind of a minor character in one of Anne Tyler's novels, a fortune teller who shrewdly reassured a worried client that she could not only change her future but also her past. That is, the client could not change what had happened, but she *could* change the hold it had over her.[39] Betty MacDonald clearly shared this philosophy, for not only did she turn a disastrous marriage into one best seller, and her struggles to support her family into another, but even managed to turn her bout with a potentially fatal disease into a third. Her wit controlled both her outlook and her income.

James Hart, in *The Popular Book: A History of America's Literary Taste*, ascribed the popularity of MacDonald's initial success with *The Egg and I* to the general appeal of Americana during the forties, a period when

many people were warily learning to live in cities.[40] He felt that her rural
hardships reassured the new city dwellers that "a return to nature could be
even more irksome than an escape from it" (268). While confirmation of
city life may well have contributed, MacDonald's success is due mainly to
her wit and her tact. She seems to sense just when to mock and when to keep
silent. She never ridicules her first husband's ability to run a chicken farm,
for example, but acknowledges that he is an informed and successful
farmer. However his shortcomings as a husband are never glossed over. Nor
does she ever try to turn sad moments into funny ones—her description of
the end of the marriage is brief. It does not even appear until her third memoir, and then only by way of contrast between her life at age eighteen and
her sister Mary's life at twenty:

> While Mary changed jobs and met people, I raised chickens, had two
> children and didn't meet anybody. Finally in March, 1931, after four
> years of this, I wrote to my family and told them that I hated chickens,
> I was lonely and I seemed to have married the wrong man. (*Anybody
> Can Do Anything*, 35)

Her sister Mary also wrote a novel about life married to the "right man"
and dedicated it "to my sister Betty who egged me on." But it seems that
anybody could not quite do anything. For though *The Doctor Wears Three
Faces* by Mary Bard (Lippincott, 1949) is an interesting confirmation of
Betty MacDonald's picture of their common childhood, it is too filled with
self-deprecating humor and uncontrolled exaggeration of her doctor/hus-
band's virtues to stand on its own merits. By contrast, even marriage to the
right man didn't blind sister Betty to faults. In 1942 she married her second
husband, Donald Chauncy MacDonald, pure Scot on both sides, and "not
exactly an optimist:"

> In fact, if I were to be absolutely truthful, and I wouldn't dare because
> we are so happily married, I would say that Don is a charter member,
> perhaps the founder, of that old Scottish brotherhood sworn always to
> bring bad news home even if it means mounting a rabid camel and rid-
> ing naked over the Himalayas in winter. (*Onions in the Stew*, 33)

Because of her surface lightheartedness, MacDonald has been mistak-
enly classified as a breezy writer of domestic humor, the often cloying literature of the determinedly happy housewife whose clever but tiresome
tone is summed up in Erma Bombeck's title *If Life is A Bowl of Cherries,
What Am I Doing in the Pits*? Relentless cheer and merry self-deprecation
makes much of this literature readable only in very short doses. MacDonald
consciously set out to refute such good sports. She recalls her attitude
before meeting a publisher's representative for the first time:

> ... I was going to write a sort of rebuttal to all the recent successful I-love-life books by female good sports whose husbands had forced them to live in the country without lights and running water. I would give the other side of it. I would give a bad sport's account of life in the wilderness without lights, water or friends and with chickens, Indians and moonshine. (*Anybody Can Do Anything*, 252)

What distinguishes MacDonald's memoirs from those of the domestic humorist is her refusal to blame herself for her unhappiness or misrepresent her miseries. Unlike the comic matriarch discussed by Judith Wilt, MacDonald's character is extremely able to imagine herself in a different and better role. Twenty years before Betty Freidan, Betty MacDonald had this to say about "Monday—Washday!":

> I entered all of the soap contests in the vain hope that I would win $5000 and never have to use theirs or any other washing powder ever again as long as I lived. I failed to understand why farmers' wives were always talking about the sense of accomplishment they derived from doing a large washing. I would have had a lot more feeling of accomplishment lying in bed while someone else did the washing. (*The Egg and I*, 70)

Her hope to win a contest may have been in vain, but her desire to remove herself from the daily chores was not. In an interview for *The New York Times Book Review* in 1948, she describes her life on Vashton Island, where she and her second husband were raising peaches and cherries and, believe it or not, just starting in on chickens: "Don here and a man who helps run the place will nurse them along," MacDonald quickly adds, "not I. I'm going to write another book."[41] And this is just what she did.

MacDonald's last memoir, *Onions in the Stew*, chronicles her life on Vashton Island with her second husband and her two daughters from the first marriage. It is another merry memoir with flashes of fine writing. MacDonald describes a friend's voice as "husky to that fascinating point just short of asthma" (116). And even her comic exaggerations seem justified:

> If you live on salt water, I am informed by the old-timers, you can expect everything you own, even a great big stone fireplace, to break down eventually. This, they say, has something to do with the corrosive effect of salt air. My private opinion, solidified by experience, is that it has more to do with the corrosive effect of the eight million houseguests attracted by the salt air. (*Onions in the Stew*, 137)

MacDonald and her husband lived in Vashton Island until 1956, when they moved to a cattle ranch they purchased in Carmel Valley, California. Sadly, she was forced to return to Seattle for medical treatment just two years later,

and died of cancer in February of 1958, one month short of her fiftieth birthday. Although her life was cut short, she had had the time to reshape it by
leaving her early misguided marriage and enriching her second happier
union through her clever and successful writing.

DOMESTIC SUBJECTS VERSUS DOMESTIC HUMOR

The domestic humorists, those who write what Wilt has labeled
"Matriarchal Humor," have been omitted from this study—writers like
Erma Bombeck and Jean Kerr. Bombeck is extremely popular as well as
prolific: *I Lost Everything in the Post-Natal Depression, Motherhood: The
Second Oldest Profession, and The Grass Is Always Greener Over The
Septic Tank* are the snappy titles to three of her eight books. Jean Kerr is
probably best known for *Please Don't Eat the Daisies*. It is not that these
writers lack wit—they can be, in fact, very witty. But their wit is always
self-deprecating. Rita Mae Brown once said that Erma Bombeck was on
safe "feminine" territory. Brown is partly right—it is not the territory,
exactly, but rather the writer's *approach* to it that makes her material safe.
The main characters of domestic humor are always good-natured wives and
mothers, who, in spite of witty grumblings over car pools, pets, and dirty
laundry, never seriously question their traditional role as the family's care-
taker. Although it is becoming fashionable to see domestic humor in a more
positive, feminist light, and argue that the wit of housewives actually
debunks the myth of Supermom, I am not convinced. I still feel such writing ultimately reinforces the status quo.[42] The Moms who appear in these
fictions may be realistically overweight, overwrought and overburdened,
but they are also at the center of loving, if hectic and demanding, homes.
The implied message is to hold the line: you only have to recognize the
humor of your position for you to enjoy it. Your *attitude* towards your
demanding role has to change, rather than the role itself. Wit is used to control frustrations, to quiet doubts. It is a safe and reassuring message—particularly for husbands and editors. This safe route, admittedly, may have
been the only one towards publication at one time. Nancy Walker is
undoubtedly right that domestic humor usually had a subtext,[43] and one
ought to recognize that these domestic humorists have helped pave the way
for the more outspoken witty writers of today.

The older traditional women comedians, Lucille Ball and Gracie Allen,
as well as the character of Edith Bunker from *All in the Family*, fall into a
similar category. A clever article on both Gracie and Lucy has appeared
suggesting that both were, in fact, subversive in the way their "dumb" personae exploded the logic of rational thought processes (ie, George Burns

directs his wife to "Say goodnight, Gracie" and she responds "Goodnight Gracie.")[44] While the insight has merit, it doesn't erase the fact that the route used to subvert the command was stupidity. The surface source of Gracie Allen's wit was a labored literal-mindedness, and if there was a hidden subversive agenda, the general public was not invited to reckon with it. We laughed at the results of the surface slow-wittedness, not at any subtly-informed rebelliousness. What her audience fondly remembers are the antics of a foolish but loveable wife.

But lest the baby gets thrown out with the bathwater, it is important to distinguish between domestic humor and domestic issues. Domestic issues are subjected to many a contemporary woman writer's wit. Although "domestic humor" is the label describing the self-deprecating and exaggerated humor written by women about their lives, one should not then conclude that all witty women who write wittily about women's lives use self-deprecating tactics. If we do not make this distinction we are in danger of buying into the old notion that women's concerns are automatically less important than men's, and thereby worthy only of self-deprecating jokes. Virginia Woolf gamely observed as early as 1929 that while women's values often differ from men's, it is the masculine values that always prevail:

> This is an important book, the critic assumes, because it deals with war. This is an insignificant book because it deals with the feelings of women in a drawing-room.[45]

All of the contemporary women included in this study deal with, among other topics, those that were once the exclusive province of women's magazines—children, marriage, body image, relationships. But the manner in which they do so distinguishes their work from that of traditional domestic humorists. Granted, Grace Paley admitted that for a long time she fell into a self deprecating frame of mind and thought her "life as a woman was shit." Although she was interested in her life, she didn't have enough social ego to put her thoughts in writing. But when she finally decided she "didn't give a damn" and was going to write about it anyway, she never made a single deprecating jest against a woman's life.[46] Quite the contrary, her wit always questions the injustices of a woman's traditional position: "What is man, that woman lies down to adore him" she jokes.[47] Lisa Alther's main character in *Kinflicks*, Ginny Babcock, may first appear as one more insecure indecisive female by virtue of the exaggerated way she adapts to her current partner's life style, but the fact that she continually sheds these roles and struggles to understand what is happening to her makes her into something else entirely. Ginny becomes a courageous individual who may not know exactly where she is headed but realizes she cannot get there by hiding inside of someone else's set of beliefs. Nora Ephron's writing deals almost exclusively with "women's issues," but with such an informed, intelligent, and witty voice at the center no one would call her wit self-deprecating. Even in her oft-anthologized essay "A Few Words on Breasts," a topic which seems to lay itself open to self-deprecation, she acknowledges that the root of her hang-up was the terrible fifties in American society, with its emphasis on large breasts, rather than her flat-chested self. Alison Lurie plays with belittling attitudes towards older women when she creates Vinnie Miner, her fifty-four-year-old plain heroine of *Foreign Affairs*. Vinnie is determined to take care of herself, so that it is not so much self-deprecation as self-pity that she has to battle, an understandable problem in a society that honors youth and beauty. Vinnie is aware of her problem and objectifies it—she imagines her self-pity as a dirty white dog named Fido who follows her about and even crawls into her lap when things get very bad. With this clever strategy, Lurie both playfully acknowledges the problem and detaches it from Vinnie's essential character.

Stated simply, the wit of the domestic humorist turns inward against herself. She merrily puts what she sees as her own inadequacies on display: if her children drive her crazy, she is lacking patience; if her schedule is too full, she lacks organization. She lets her wit cloud her judgment. But the witty writers I am studying turn their wit outward. They judge society, reject traditional roles, and ask questions. None accepts the idea that the frustrations and pain she encounters in life are either incurable or her own fault. Their wit is empowering, used to strengthen their convictions rather than to curb their (unwomanly) desires.

The wit of Parker, Powell, and MacDonald is directly connected to the witty women writers of today.[48] The sharp satirical portraits of the characters in Alison Lurie's fiction is in the same tradition as those in the earlier novels of Dawn Powell. The same anger beneath the merriment of Shirley Jackson's two family memoirs can be found in the memoirs of Betty MacDonald, as can the disillusionment suffered by Lisa Alther's heroine in *Kinflicks* whenever she accepts any socially sanctioned role. Finally, the position of a powerful woman wit in the New York scene, currently occupied by Nora Ephron, belonged to Dorothy Parker in the twenties and thirties.

NOTES

1.   The seven women in this study actually span two generations, which makes the eldest closer to the generation of these forerunners. Alther and Brown were born in 1944 and Ephron and Tyler in 1941, but Lurie, Paley, and Jackson were born in 1926, 1922, and 1916, respectively. Although Parker and Powell

were born at the end of the nineteenth century, in 1893 and 1897, MacDonald was born in 1908, only eight years before Shirley Jackson.

2. Carolyn Heilbrun, *Writing A Woman's Life* (NY: Ballantine, 1988), 48.

3. The facts of Parker's life, unless otherwise indicated, are from Marion Meade, *Dorothy Parker: What Fresh Hell is This?* (NY: Penquin, 1989).

4. "Dawn Powell, Novelist, is Dead; Author of Witty, Satirical Books," Obituary, *The New York Times* 16 Nov 1965: 47.

5. William McCann, *Dictionary of American Biography*, Supplement Six: 1956–1960 (NY, Scribner, 1980) 409.

6. Nancy Walker also stresses MacDonald's non-pacifying tone in *A Very Serious Thing* (Minneapolis, Univ. of Minn. Press, 1988) 51–52.

7. Nora Ephron, *Crazy Salad* (NY: Bantam, 1976) 140.

8. Marion Capron, "Dorothy Parker," *Women Writers at Work: The Paris Review Interviews*, ed. George Plympton (NY: Viking, 1989) 110.

9. Campbell's and Parker's first marriage dissolved in the early 1940's, but they remarried in 1950 and stayed married until his death in 1963.

10. Dorothy Parker, rev. of *Redemption* by Leo Tolstoi, *Vanity Fair* Dec. 1918; rpt. in *The Portable Dorothy Parker*, rev.ed. (NY: Penguin, 1976) 419–20.

11. Parker, "Constant Reader," *The New Yorker* 20 Oct.1928; rpt. in *The Portable Dorothy Parker*, 518.

12. Parker, "A Book of Great Short Stories," *The New Yorker* 29 Oct. 1927; rpt. in *The Portable Dorothy Parker*, 460.

13. Parker, rev. of *Lolita* by Vladimir Nabokov, *Esquire*, Oct. 1958; rpt. in *The Portable Dorothy Parker*, 565–66.

14. Meade 225.

15. My expectation that an enlightened woman critic would be more generous in assessing another woman's life is shared by Heilbrun in *Writing a Woman's Life* 15–19.

16. Ephron, *Crazy Salad* 140.

17. Lillian Hellman, *An Unfinished Woman* (NY: Bantam, 1970) 187–88.

18. Ephron 140.

19. Capron, *Women Writers at Work* 115.

20. Nicola Sacco and Bartolomeo Vanzetti were Italian-American anarchists, a fish peddler and a shoemaker, who had been found guilty of murdering a paymaster and a guard in Massachusetts in 1920. Because their case gained so much attention, and because prominent figures like Dorothy Parker were willing to be arrested to protest the verdict, their executions were put off for seven years (Meade 180–81).

21. John Keats, *You Might As Well Live* (NY: Simon and Schuster, 1970) 221.

22. Joseph Norton, ed., *New Masses: An Anthology of the Rebel Thirties* (NY: International Publishers, 1969) 190.

23. Hellman, *An Unfinished Woman* 195.

24. John Guare, introduction to *The Locusts Have No King* (NY: Yarrow, 1990) vii. Guare is quoting an unnamed friend, a member of the Dramatists Guild.

25. Guare, intro to *Locusts* x.

26. Obituary, *New York Times* 47.

27. Gore Vidal, introduction to *Angels on Toast* (1938; NY:Vintage, 1990) ix.
28. Vidal, introduction to *Angels* viii.
29. Obituary, *NY Times* 47.
30. Vidal, intro. to *Angels* xiii.
31. Guare, intro. to *Locusts* x.
32. Vidal, intro. to *Angels* xii.
33. Dawn Powell, *The Happy Island* (NY: Farrar & Rinehart 1938) 191.
34. Guare, intro. to *Locusts* x.
35. Betty MacDonald's memoirs, all published by Lippincott, are: *The Egg and I* (1945), *The Plague and I* (1948), *Anybody Can Do Anything* (1950), and *Onions in the Stew* (1955). After she died, her second husband, Donald Chauncy MacDonald, edited *Who Me* (1959), made up of excerpts from all four.
36. "Betty M'Donald, Writer, is Dead," Obituary, *New York Times* 8 Feb. 1958: 19.
37. McCann, *Dict. of American Biography* 409.
38. McCann, *Dict. of Amer. Bio.* 409.
39. Anne Tyler, *Searching For Caleb* (NY: Berkeley, 1983) 135.
40. James Hart, *The Popular Book* (NY:Oxford, 1950) 267–68.
41. Ralph Thompson, "In and Out of Books," *New York Times Book Review* 5 Dec. 1948: 8.
42. For sympathetic interpretations of domestic humor see Zita Dresner, "Domestic Comic Writers," *Women's Comic Visions*, ed. June Sochen (Detroit: Wayne State Univ,. Press, 1991) 93–114 and Nancy Walker, "The Female Humorist in America," *A Very Serious Thing*, 15–37.
43. See Walker, *A Very Serious Thing* 21, where she illustrates how a passage from Francis Whitcher is "a text on two levels."
44. Patricia Mellencamp, "Situation Comedy, Feminism, and Freud: Discourses of Gracie and Lucy," *Studies in Entertainment*, ed. Tanya Modleski (Bloomington: Indiana Univ. Press, 1986) 80–95.
45. Woolf, *A Room of One's Own* (1929; NY: Harcourt Brace Jovanovich, 1957) 77.
46. Kathleen Hully, "Interview with Grace Paley," *Delta* 14 (1982): 26.
47. Grace Paley, "A Subject of Childhood" in *The Little Disturbances of Man* (1956; NY: Viking, 1985) 143.
48. For a discussion of earlier witty women writers in America, particularly in the nineteenth century, see Nancy Walker, *A Very Serious Thing*, and also her article "Nineteenth Century Women's Humor" in *Women's Comic Visions*, ed. June Sochen, 85–92.

3

Nora Ephron: All You Ever Wanted to Know About Control. . . . . (But feared you'd appear too manipulative if you asked)

CONTROLLING FOOD

If people remember just one thing about *When Harry Met Sally* beyond her faked orgasm over lunch, it is the fastidious way that Sally orders her food.[1] What few people realize is that Sally's restaurant quirks are Nora Ephron's, that it is actually Ephron's relationship to food we are witnessing in Sally. Rob Reiner had approached Ephron with an idea for a script, but it wasn't until he came up with a theme that allowed her to incorporate large pieces of their own opinions and character traits that he awakened her interest. According to Ephron, when they met for lunch a second time, they

> threw around some more ideas, none of which I remember. But finally, Rob said he had an idea—he wanted to make a movie about a man and a woman who become friends, as opposed to lovers; they make a deliberate decision not to have sex because sex ruins everything; and then they have sex and it ruins everything. And I said, let's do it.
> (Introduction: *When Harry Met Sally*, viii)

35

Ephron based Harry on Rob, on bleak, depressed, clever Rob Reiner. Sally
she based on herself, whom she considers "cheerful and chirpy and relentlessly, pointlessly, unrealistically, idiotically optimistic" (Intro. x). Ephron
was aware of the connection between Sally's love of control and the way
she ordered food when eating out:

> Sally loves control—and I'm sorry to say that I do too. And inevitably,
> Sally's need to control her environment is connected to food. I say
> inevitably because food has always been something I write about—in
> part because it's the only thing I'm an expert on. (Intro. x)

In spite of Ephron's insight, the idea to use her ordering quirks in the movie
came from Rob Reiner and Andy Scheinman, Reiner's producing partner.
They were watching her order lunch, an avocado and bacon sandwich, for
the fifth day in a row. She wanted the mayonnaise on the side, the bread
toasted and slightly burnt, the bacon crisp. They pointed out the pattern. "I
just like it the way I like it," she retorted and that line went in the script as
well as her detailed way of ordering her food preparation (Intro. xi).

In this anecdotal introduction to the published screenplay, Ephron uses
an elaborate pizza metaphor to explain her feelings about screenwriting. It
is a pizza parable, really, wherein she manages to illustrate the interconnec-
tions between screenwriting, control, herself, and food. Writing a script,
Ephron explains, is

> like delivering a great big beautiful plain pizza, the one with only
> cheese and tomatoes. And then you give it to the director, and the
> director says, "I love this pizza. I am willing to commit to this pizza.
> But I really think this pizza should have mushrooms on it." And you
> say, "Mushrooms! Of course! I meant to put mushrooms on the pizza.
> Why didn't I think of that? Let's put some on immediately." And then
> someone else comes along and says "I love this pizza too, but it really
> needs green peppers." "Great," you say. "Green peppers. Just the
> thing." And then someone else says, "Anchovies." There's always a
> fight over the anchovies. And when you get done, what you have is a
> pizza with everything. Sometimes, it's wonderful. And sometimes you
> look at it and you think, I knew we shouldn't have put the green pep-
> pers onto it. Why didn't I say so at the time? Why didn't I lie down in
> traffic to prevent anyone's putting green peppers onto the pizza?
> (Intro. xiii–xiv)

The fact that Ephron manages to make a joke about the interfering input
from others is a good sign that it bothers her. And what better way to point
out the pitfalls of the inevitable collaboration of screenwriting than by creating a witty food parable? When the subject is food she is the expert—in
the kitchen she never needs a collaborator. She is presenting the problem in

a way certain to garner admiration for her own clever writing style. Ephron *should* be left in absolute control of the script, the witty presentation implies, look how well she manages when she is.

Food has always been something Ephron writes about, and she seems fond of titles with food references. *Crazy Salad* is the title of her collected articles on women's issues, originally written as a column for *Esquire* from 1972–74.[2] The title comes from a poem by William Butler Yeats called "A Prayer for My Daughter," written in 1919 shortly after his daughter was born. He prayed she be not too beautiful, like Helen of Troy, or too great, like Venus, since very fine women usually have character flaws causing them to choose poor mates. Paris is a fool and Vulcan bandy-legged, which shows that

> It's certain that fine women eat
> A crazy salad with their meat
> Whereby the Horn of Plenty is undone. (11.30–32)

Crazy Salad devotes only one article entirely to food—the Pillsbury Bake Off. Granted, Ephron takes a mocking tone towards the contest, but she also took a mocking tone toward her Wellesley Reunion, where she admitted that she can mock but still care (36). Her constant interest in food works its way into many of the other articles as well. In "A Few Words About Breasts," for example, she digresses with relish into the way the mother of her childhood best friend, Diane, filled her kitchen with junk food, unlike the wholesomely-stocked kitchen in Ephron's home:

> My house was full of apples and peaches and milk and homemade chocolate-chip cookies—which were nice and good for you but-not-right-before-dinner-or-you'll-spoil-your-appetite. Diane's house had nothing in it that was good for you, and what's more, you could stuff it right up until dinner and nobody cared. Bar-B-Q potato chips . . ., giant bottles of ginger ale, fresh popcorn with melted butter, hot fudge sauce on Baskin-Robbins jamoca ice cream, powdered-sugar doughnuts from Van de Kamp's. (*Crazy Salad*, 4–5)

A distinct complicity springs up between Ephron and her readers in digressions like these. She can presume that most of her readers come from homes with sensible kitchens like hers, and will enjoy poking fun at the memory of having been raised with so bourgeois and timid an approach to indulgence. Moreover, her comic style, her engaging strung-together adjective phrase (but-not-right-before-dinner-or-you'll-spoil-your-appetite) charms the reader into an agreeable frame of mind. Such complicity and charm help to put her in control of our sympathy, which is precisely what she is after in her digressions.

The title of her one autobiographical novel, *Heartburn*, is, obviously, a pun on overindulging. The story shows how Rachel has overindulged and overinvested in both food and love. Interestingly enough, however, she pays only for her indulgences in love. Nevertheless, food plays an excessive role in the book. Excessive but not unplanned. Excessive but purposeful. What does it accomplish? It keeps Rachel in control of *something*. She cannot control her husband's sexual appetite but she can control and enhance her own and her reader's appetite for wonderful taste sensations. In addition to the obvious but clever embedding of recipes in the text, in addition to Rachel's career as the Julia Child of Educational TV, there is the constant absorption with food: the trips in search of "the world's creamiest cheesecake and the world's largest pistachio nut and the world's sweetest corn on the cob" (132). Rachel may be able to believe Mark could leave *her*, but not her perfect vinaigrette. There is a strategy behind her recipes, her quests for the perfect food, and the jokes. How miserable can this woman be, their existence in the text implies, if she can joke and give recipes? She is hurt but not defeated, wounded but still fighting. Her sense of humor is still in place, as are her taste buds.

Susan Leonardi offers a witty discussion of the Key lime pie-throwing incident at the end of the novel.[3] In "Recipes for Reading," she sees recipes embedded in texts as narrative strategies that would only fall flat (no pun intended) in a cinematic version:

> In the end, the narrative itself becomes a kind of recipe—how to survive a disastrous marriage, And the recipe is this: turn it into a story. . . . The key lime pie is both dessert and dessert of the story—dessert for Betty's dinner, Mark's dessert as an unfaithful husband. And it is a dessert to which we as readers have the recipe or key. No wonder, then, that the scene does not work in the film, where the pie is just a pie like any other pie and not a dessert to which the viewer has access, not a point of trust and inside knowledge between narrator and reader, not, that is, a pie that can be either eaten, read, or thrown into someone's face. (346–7)

As Leonardi's article explains, and Ephron's text illustrates, recipes embedded in a text can do a great deal more than tell you how to make a certain dish. In *Heartburn*, they save Rachel from feeling totally victimized by keeping her in control of something even at the worst of times. She has special foods she likes to eat when she is blue: shrimp fried rice and bacon hash, the former from a chinese restaurant, the latter from a recipe she is not so depressed that she cannot include. The recipes are also a witty gift, a gay offering to the reader. The recipe index at the end captures her cocky spirit—if you do not like my story, the index implies, at least you have bought some useful recipes. The constant intrusion of so many recipes, all irrelevant to the story line, also functions as a reminder of Rachel's inde-fatigable resourcefulness as a woman. Her nurturing instincts lead to the creation and care of two children and many wonderful dishes, the recipes suggest, while her husband's sexual instincts lead only to the destruction of two families. The recipes help create the persona she is after—a witty, resourceful, somewhat-sexually-naive-but-aren't-we-all sort of wife who chose to use the kitchen (where her control was complete) rather than the bedroom (where it was, at best, partial) as the arena of her love.

CONTROLLING PITY

In October of 1973 Ephron chose Dorothy Parker as the subject of her monthly Esquire column. Since Parker's writing often features helpless women with little control over anything, Ephron's disillusionment with Parker is probably heightened by Ephron's alleged love of control, and her subsequent exasperation with characters like Parker's who refuse to take it.

Ephron explains that she grew up infatuated with Dorothy Parker. Although Parker had attended a few parties given by Ephron's parents, suc-cessful Hollywood screenwriters, there were many young women who aspired to be Dorothy Parker who had never met her at all, as Ephron found out when she moved to New York. She (and they) were apparently in love with the legend, not the actual woman:

> All I wanted in this world was to come to New York and be Dorothy Parker. The funny lady. The only lady at the table. The woman who made her living by her wit. Who wrote for *The New Yorker*. Who always got off the perfect line at the perfect moment, . . . (*Crazy Salad*, 139)

The adult Ephron's objection to Parker's writing at its worst is what she calls Parker's

> unbearable girlish sentimentality. The masochist. The victim. The sen-timental woman whose moods are totally ruled by the whims of men. . . . Many of the women poets writing today about love and men write with as much wit as Parker, but with a great deal of healthy anger besides. (*Crazy Salad*, 141)

Ephron's criticism is understandable, since even in her best works, Parker coyly veils her anger. In "Big Blonde," which Ephron acknowledges as one of Parker's first-rate stories, the ageing, flagging female is aroused when she sees an old horse being beaten for stumbling to his knees. She senses the similarity of their plights, hers and the old horse's, but the only

action that follows her insight is a failed suicide attempt.[4] Parker undoubtedly intended to awaken a social conscience in her readers by awakening
their pity. But awakening pity, for whatever purpose, is precisely what
Ephron wants to avoid.

In *Heartburn*, written ten years after the Parker article, Ephron spells
out her intent to head off any pity, her own or her reader's. *Heartburn*
does not only embed recipes in a clever text, but also presents one version
of the break-up of Ephron's marriage to Carl Bernstein, of Watergate
Fame. It is a sad story made into a funny story—heartbreak into heartburn: "The most unfair thing about this whole business," Rachel tells us
on page one, "is that I can't even date." Rachel knows exactly what her
wit is controlling. Towards the end of the novel, her therapist asks her
why she feels she has to turn the painful events of her life into stories.
Rachel responds:

> Because if I tell the story, I control the version.
> Because if I tell the story, I can make you laugh, and I would rather
> have you laugh at me than feel sorry for me
> Because if I tell the story, it doesn't hurt as much.
> Because if I tell the story, I can get on with it. (*Heartburn*, 221)

It is hard to imagine a clearer statement of the use of wit to control both one-
self and one's audience. Rachel is using wit to distance herself from pain
("If I tell the story it doesn't hurt as much") and to manipulate her friends so
that they will not pity her ("I would rather have you laugh at me than feel
sorry for me"). Since Rachel's story is, in fact, Nora Ephron's story, the
"you" being manipulated is "us," the reading audience. Ephron has turned
the breakup of her marriage into a funny story so that she can control her
version of it and head off any misplaced pity we, her reading audience,
might feel.

One amusing but revealing difference between Ephron and Parker is in
their attitudes toward food and cooking. When identifying her own characteristics that made up the character Sally (*When Harry Met Sally*), Ephron
claimed that she writes about food because it is the only thing she is an
expert on. But Parker, her one-time role model, was utterly phobic about
anything to do with cooking or homemaking. Moreover, it would have gone
against Parker's persona to claim expertise about anything, even in jest: "I
was just a little Jewish girl trying to be cute" she said late in life.[5] According
to Meade's biography, Parker would starve rather than boil herself an egg.[6]
This doesn't seem to be empty hyperbole, since Meade adds that Parker ate
bacon raw all her life claiming "she had no idea how to cook it" (46). Rather
than learn, she chose to rely on servants.

CONTROLLING THE MOOD

Lois Gould, the novelist (author of *Not Responsible for Personal Articles*), interviewed Nora Ephron for the *NY Times Book Review* of April 16, 1978. This was before *Heartburn* (1983), but just after *Scribble Scribble* (1978). One of Ephron's most arresting observations comes as a follow-up to Gould's comments on why it seems new and daring for women to be writing with wit. Gould is describing the inherent aggression of wit, or humor:

> Speaking and writing are also aggressive acts, but expressing humor is somehow a more powerful weapon of action, than simply saying "I think this" in a soft, serious way. So if you make a joke of something other people have done, you have deflated it, you have taken action against it, you have changed the mood. It's considerably more active, isn't it? (34)

And Ephron responds, briefly:

> And you've stepped aside from it, which is actually a betrayal of the mood. (34)

Ephron's reply is an interesting twist on the notion that wit allows distance, on the notion that we laugh so we don't cry. Betraying the mood provided the therapeutic motivation behind *Heartburn*, even though Ephron verbalized the therapeutic strategy well before the fact. In 1978 she had only been married to Bernstein for two years.

Ephron's mother realized that betraying the mood can be comforting as well as controlling, and had been trying to get that idea across to her daughter from her hospital bed as early as 1971. "You're a reporter, Nora," she said about a week before she died, "Take notes." Henry Ephron writes that he burst into tears when his daughter repeated the conversation to him and even Nora thought it made her mother sound tougher than she was.[7] But Phoebe Ephron was undoubtedly offering her daughter a way to handle her grief, a way her daughter shows she perfected by the time she wrote *Heartburn*. The very words made their way into that text. Rachel, Ephron's alter-ego, is wishing her mother were alive to offer her advice on what she should do now that she has discovered that her husband is in love with someone else while she is seven months pregnant with their second child. Then she admits that

> Even in the old days, my mother was a washout at hardcore mothering; what she was good at were clever remarks that made you feel immensely sophisticated and adult and, if you thought about it at all, foolish for having wanted anything so mundane as some actual nurturing. Had I been able to talk to her at this moment of crisis, she would probably have said something fabulously brittle like "Take notes." (*Heartburn*, 39–40)

Nora's use of her real mother's deathbed comment in a fictional situation
proves she is faithfully following another of her mother's writing maxims:
"Everything is copy."[8]

Reactions to Ephron's following her mother's advice are mixed. The
critical response to *Heartburn*, to so audacious and self-serving a use of a
private tragedy, ranged from annoyance to endorsement. Garrett Epps was
clearly put off:

> An intelligent writer like Nora Ephron cannot really have put
> together an entire (although admittedly tiny) "novel" simply to bring
> her friends up to date on what's been happening to her. Is there anyone
> in America who has so many friends that a circular letter to them—not
> intended for the rest of us—could sell in hardback?[9]

This, obviously, was before the movie version appeared.

Grace Glueck was more amused than Epps but still not convinced of
Heartburn's literary merit. She had great fun reading it, she admitted, but
seemed uncomfortable with its revenge theme:

> How awfully lucky for those who treat them badly, I thought as I
> read Nora Ephron's *Heartburn*, that when journalists get mad they
> reach for a typewriter instead of a gun.[10]

Recently, Regina Barreca endorsed Ephron's witty treatment of a potentially tragic subject. Granted, she was writing a book on women's strategic
use of humor rather than reviewing *Heartburn*. Barreca's discussion of how
women can get away with aggressive humor ("you have to do it with
finesse") led straight to *Heartburn*:

> Look how well Nora Ephron did with *Heartburn*. Using anger, hurt, or
> the desire for revenge to propel yourself into an activity is not the
> worst that can happen. As the writer Naomi Bliven has pointed out,
> "Behind almost every woman you ever heard of stands a man who let
> her down."[11]

CONTROLLING YOUR LIFE IN FICTION

In 1986 Ephron wrote an article called "Revision and Life" which was
originally intended for a college writing handbook. The article now appears
at the end of her 1991 collection called, straightforwardly enough, *Nora
Ephron Collected*.[12] In her thirties, she tells us, just as she was learning to

revise her articles for *Esquire*, so she was learning to wish she could revise her behavior in life:

> What should I have done instead? What could I have done? What if I hadn't done it the way I did? What if I had a chance to do it over? What if I had a chance to do it over as a different person? These were the sorts of questions that kept me awake and led me into fiction, which at the very least (the level at which I practice it) is a chance to rework the events of your life so that you give the illusion of being the intelligence at the center of it, simultaneously managing to slip in all the lines that occurred to you later. Fiction, I suppose, is the ultimate shot at revision. (*Ephron Collected*, 215–16)

If fiction is the ultimate shot at revision, than perhaps letters home is the penultimate. Ephron's own letters home from Wellesley College became the basis of her parents' successful Broadway play "Take Her She's Mine." She had a wonderfully supportive mother, who once told her that the best way to learn how to write was to write a letter to your mother and tear off the salutation. Ephron wrote to her faithfully:

> because you didn't get a letter back from her if you didn't write one yourself. And I know that in writing my mother with whom I felt completely confident, I began to become a writer.[13]

She was as gifted a letter writer as her mother, according to her father. The following excerpt from one of her letters, reproduced verbatim in the play, bears him out:

> We just heard Norman Thomas speak on disarmament, which, naturally, he regards as absolutely necessary, and isn't the world situation abysmal? Sometimes I think it won't last another week, and here am I, still a virgin. (*We Thought We Could Do Anything*, 197)

Her parents wrote the play in only six weeks. It was a hit on Broadway and Twentieth-Century Fox bought the movie rights.

Ephron could revise the events of her college life in letters home with the confidence that her parents would believe in her flattering rendition since they already saw her as the intelligence at the center of her life. She was considered the brain and wit of the family, as both the play and her father's memoirs make clear. So Ephron's most optimistic self-image colluded with the image her parents already held of her, not to mention the one society came to reward in later years. Since she felt confident in her parents' high opinion of her, writing home gave her the opportunity to sharpen her wit without worrying whether her flattering rendition would be believed.

But not all aspiring women writers enjoyed so positive a relationship with their mothers. Consider Shirley Jackson and Sylvia Plath, to take two extreme examples. Jackson was the proverbial ugly duckling, the pudgy intellectual child born to an ambitious California socialite. She married Stanley Edgar Hyman, a New York Jewish intellectual, moved to Bennington, Vermont, had four children, and lived and wrote within a creative chaotic world of books, talk, witchcraft, and all night poker games (Stanley's). Stanley and Shirley both overindulged in eating, drinking and gift-giving. But, according to Judy Oppenheimer, rather than turn her back on her disapproving mother, Jackson wrote "long cozy letters" to her parents throughout her relatively short, troubled life:

> letters of a mature, well-orga.1ized, serene housewife and mother and hostess who handled every contingency with a minimum of fuss and just happened, on the side, to have a flourishing career.[14]

According to Barry Hyman, Jackson's fourth child:

> Her letters were her revenge.... They were sort of: "I'm going through the vicissitudes of raising children without becoming a sterile negative old bitch and I'm still alive and have a sense of humor." (Oppenheimer 135)

These letters may have been her revenge, but the need to write them at all showed she was still trying to win her mother's affection and acceptance, as Barry wisely acknowledged (Opp. 135). The persona in the letters is a blend of her mother's version of success and Shirley's, not unlike the persona of the mother in Jackson's autobiographical writings.

If Aurelia Plath hoped that publishing her daughter's letters home would counterbalance the image of the pushy insensitive mother of *The Bell Jar*, she was mistaken. Sylvia's chirpy overearnest tone in her letters home makes painful reading and only aggravates the strained mother-daughter picture that emerged in the novel. According to Stevenson:

> The letters Sylvia wrote to her mother from Smith (and indeed throughout her life)—the hundreds of letters that opened with "Dear Mum" or "Dearest Progenitor" or "Dearest darling beautiful saintly mother!" and ended with "Your happy Sivvy" or occasionally "Your hollow girl, Sivvy"—were cries for self-confirmation from an anxious daughter....[15]

There *was* collusion between Sylvia and her mother, to be sure. But they colluded in creating an idealized version of Sylvia that neither Sylvia nor any other mortal could possibly uphold. After graduating from Smith, Sylvia

Plath crossed the ocean to do graduate work in Cambridge, England. "So long as Mrs. Plath stayed in America," Stevenson comments wryly, "letters home could tell the 'truth' both the mother and daughter wanted to hear" (78).

There are unanswerable questions hovering just beneath these examples. Why did Plath kill herself? Why was Jackson's life so troubled? As writers, both are as impressive and successful as Ephron. Both, moreover, enjoyed success within their life span. When, then, is a flattering self-image nurturing and when is it harmful? When does parental support build confidence and when does it create undue pressure? When does wit put you in control of your own life and when does wit only allow you the temporary illusion of control? When is the illusion strengthening and when is it debilitating? Is there a point when the illusion of control passes over into actual control, perhaps when you have convinced enough people?

Undoubtedly, the degree to which the writer believes in the image she has created of herself on paper is crucial, as is the degree to which those closest to her share this belief. Despite a successful writing career and four beautiful, healthy, and lively children, Shirley Jackson could never convince her mother that she was the intelligence at the center of her own life. Sylvia Plath seemed unable to convince herself. Nora Ephron, on the other hand, has been able to convince pretty much everybody.

EPHRON'S FAMILY INFLUENCE

Even though Nora Ephron was considered the brain and wit in her family, five of the six members of her immediate family have appeared in print, repeatedly and successfully. She is the eldest of four daughters. Two of her sisters became writers. Delia, the second oldest, is another comic writer whose works include *Funny Sauce* (1986) and *How to Eat Like a Child* (1978). Amy, the youngest, published *Bruised Fruit* in 1987 and a second novel in 1991, *Biodegradable Soap*. Amy's first novel was a promising serious one. At that point, she was not a comic writer, rewriting her life in a funnier dimension, as are her two older sisters. All three, Nora, Delia, and Amy, have written screenplays, but only Nora has also become a movie director.

Ephron's parents produced three successful Broadway plays as well as over thirty Hollywood screenplays, including *Deskset, Daddy Long Legs*, and *Captain Newman, M.D.*, which was nominated for an Oscar. Her mother, Phoebe Wolkind Ephron, also wrote one Broadway Play, *Howie*, on her own. In 1977, after Phoebe Ephron's untimely death at age fifty-seven, Henry wrote the story of their lives and called it (aptly enough) *We Thought We Could Do Anything*. It is filled with the image of the two of them, Henry and Phoebe Ephron, successfully maneuvering against the odds in Hollywood and New York. Despite his nostalgic idealizations, Henry sounds genuine in his respect for his wife's writing talent and in his adoration of his daughters. He includes a family legend of Nora's witty repartee while still in nursery school. A little boy had taunted her with "I can speak Spanish. I'll bet you can't." Nora didn't hesitate a second: "I certainly can—The Niña, the Pinta, the Santa Maria." Henry wonders if this wasn't the beginning of Nora's reputation as a wit (63).

In 1958, Nora chose to travel east to attend Wellesley College. She graduated in 1962, and headed for New York to emulate Dorothy Parker and make her living by her wits. Her family was then living in Beverly Hills, where she had been raised. In 1963, Ephron became a journalist at the *New York Post*. About eight years later, in the early seventies, she gamely approached *Esquire* and told the editors they needed a witty column on women—and that she was the one to write it. They agreed.

In the early sixties, most middle-class young women succumbed to society's expectations and married as soon after college graduation as possible. Ephron, however, had the confidence to put off marriage and head directly to New York to seek her fortune with her pen. By 1972, ten years after graduation, Ephron had her own column in *Esquire*. *Crazy Salad* is the collected result of that column. Her reputation was growing, and deservedly so. She was developing a wonderful voice—cocky but aware of her own shortcomings, opinionated, and, above all, witty—very very witty. Ephron has always had a good sense of rhythm and a clever way of stringing together pithy adjectives. What's more, she never says things for the sake of a laugh, alone. Her opinions always sound genuine and her view of the world around her is an engagingly optimistic and convincing one.

PHOEBE WOLKIND EPHRON AS ROLE MODEL

Nora Ephron did have a role model, but it was not Dorothy Parker. It was her mother, Phoebe Wolkind Ephron. Phoebe had her own role model—an aunt who was a dentist at Lord & Taylor's. According to Henry Ephron, this aunt had probably been the most important influence on Nora's mother's life. Phoebe's aunt worked while her husband ran the house, cooked, and cared for the kids.[16] What the model of her aunt's life showed Phoebe was that she need not feel guilty about letting someone else clean the house and mind the children.

Nor would Phoebe compromise her life style, even rhetorically, to placate society's expectations. As early as 1958, she refused to present herself as a mother and housewife first, who wrote plays only in her spare time. In an interview for the *New York Times*, occasioned by the opening of her Broadway Play *Howie*, she claimed:

> I don't go into the kitchen very often except for ice cubes for a drink. . . . We have a cook for the cooking and a nurse for the children. I've been a full-time screenwriter since 1943, and I put in a full day at the office.[17]

Hindsight suggests that she gave her four daughters something more nourishing than their afternoon milk and cookies. Still, what bravado and courage for a woman in 1958 to admit in print that she put her work first.

Phoebe was a more encompassing role model for Nora than was her aunt for her, since both private and professional spheres were involved. Not only were both Ephron and her mother writers, but they were both comic writers. Ephron began as a journalist, however, a field her mother left untouched. And Nora has yet to write a Broadway play. But both mother and daughter have written successful screenplays. Nor did the mother's influence stop with Nora. She clearly encouraged all her daughters, who are busily writing faster than I can acknowledge their work. It is unusual enough for a woman born in 1914 to achieve what Phoebe Wolkind Ephron did, but to be comfortable enough with what she was doing to bequeath her confidence to her four daughters may be the most astounding part of it.

Nor did Phoebe's influence on and encouragement of young women stop with her family. In the eulogy Nora delivered at her mother's funeral service on October 13, 1971, she read from a letter she received from her former college roommate written when her mother went into the hospital:

> I have been trying to think all through this letter how to say what I want to say to you about your mother. I have found myself thinking about her a great deal since we talked. The point is that she is not just the mother of my dear friend, but that she really had a tremendous effect on all of us. You know how dazzled we were by the career, by the working with her husband, by the four children, by the approach to life. I once told you, midst all my babies, that I was practicing the Phoebe Ephron family plan, and don't think for a minute that I had not conned myself into truly believing that. What she has gotten across to me was a let's-do-everything-in-life attitude. . . . You know that she is wildly talented and successful and the original liberated woman and all that. What you might not have realized was the extent to which we all admired her, considered her somehow our own, looked forward to her letters to you, managed to drop her name in conversation.[18]

Nora Ephron's achievements have been impressive. She writes brief but formidable pieces, excelling in the essay, screenplay, and novella. She also seems to enjoy collaborating, in spite of what she has said about the loss of control involved in collaborations. She collaborated on the screenplay for *Silkwood*, which was nominated for an Academy Award, as was *When Harry Met Sally*. One is tempted to conclude that, despite the mother's very real achievements, the daughter has probably surpassed her. Yet I hesitate to make this judgment. For one thing, several of Nora's parents' screenplays were nominated for Oscars, and they did write three quite successful Broadway plays. But a more crucial reason for hesitating is that competition doesn't seem to have been an issue between the parents and children in the Ephron family. Encouragement, nourishing of talents, building of confidence—yes. Competition? No. I am quite certain that no one would be happier to hear of the achievements of her eldest daughter, indeed, of all her daughters, than Phoebe Ephron. Nora's eulogy supports this suspicion:

> What I think she gave us, most of all, was the sense that we could do anything, anything at all, that anything was possible. Being women had nothing to do with it, just as it had had nothing to do with it for her. That is a remarkable thing to pass on to daughters. She was not doctrinaire or dogmatic about it; although she named me after the heroine of *The Doll's House*, she could not bear being called a feminist. She merely was, and simply by her example, we all grew up with blind faith in our own abilities and destinies. (210–11)

And that says it all.

A POSTSCRIPT ON CONTROL

Or almost all. Shortly after this chapter was completed, Ephron made her debut as a movie director. Thus far, she has directed two movies: *This Is My Life* and *Sleepless in Seattle*. Her sister Delia collaborated with her on the screenplay for *This Is My Life*. The movie is based on the witty novel by Meg Wolitzer called *This is Your Life*, although the title had to be altered after Ralph Edwards protested the recycling of the name of his old television show, still rerun on cable television.[19]

The screenplay is a clever adaptation of the book with many Ephron family reminiscences worked in. In the novel, Dottie Engels has two major problems: one is her massive weight and the other her impossible double life as mother and performer. The movie dropped the weight issue and concentrated on how Dottie (played by Julie Kavner) learns to cope with her two daughters' feelings of neglect while she pursues her career as a stand-up comic. This brought the Ephron sisters into familiar territory. The four Ephron daughters had grown up in Hollywood with a mother who put her career as screenwriter first. And Nora Ephron is currently performing her own juggling act as both mother and writer. Ephron, speaking of Dottie's children but undoubtedly thinking of her own two sons, said she was "foolish enough to believe that they are better off because their mom got her dreams," but she immediately added:

> ... but who are we kidding? If you give your kids a choice, your mother in the next room on the verge of suicide versus your mother in Hawaii in ecstasy, they'd choose suicide in the next room.[20]

What most of the articles on Ephron's directing debuts stress is her urge to control. A feature story in the *Boston Globe* opened this way: "Words like 'bossy' and 'scary' seem to foam up in Nora Ephron's wake, wherever she travels.[21] Ephron takes such remarks in stride. She quipped to the *Vogue* interviewer that:

> If I were basically roasting myself, I would say that I have an incredible compulsion to tell everyone what to serve for dinner. . . . But the truth is, I am a fairly controlling person who has only in recent years gotten a grip on my need to control people. (145)

"Well maybe" the interviewer adds. In the same article Sally Quinn, friend and author, reports that Nora "said that all of her friends are just gonna love it because she's gonna leave us all alone now. She can boss everybody [on the set] around instead" (147). The day may come when a woman director will not have to sound apologetic over enjoying the control that comes with the job. But, until then, Ephron knows how to diffuse the negative reactions her controlling skills evoke: she will simply incorporate such criticism into her witty repartees.

NOTES

1. Nora Ephron, *When Harry Met Sally* (NY: Knopf, 1990).
2. Nora Ephron, *Crazy Salad* (NY: Bantam, 1976).
3. Susan J. Leonardi, "Recipes for Reading: Summer Pasta, Lobster a la Riseholme, and Key Lime Pie," *PMLA* 104 (1989): 340–347.
4. For a slightly different reading of "Big Blond," see Nancy Walker, *A Very Serious Thing* (Minneapolis: Univ. of Minnesota Press, 1988) 30–31, where she argues that only Parker and the reader are aware of Hazel's dependent position.
5. Ephron, *Crazy Salad* 140.
6. Marion Meade, *Dorothy Parker: What Fresh Hell Is This* (NY: Penguin, 1987) 46.

7.   Henry Ephron, *We Thought We Could Do Anything* (NY: Norton, 1977) 210.
8.   Henry Ephron 210.
9.   Garrett Epps, "Of Recipes and Revenge," *The New Republic* 23 May 1983: 37.
10. Grace Glueck, "A Dishy Roman a Clef With Recipes," *The New York Times Book Review* 24 April 1983: 3.
11. Regina Barreca, *They Used To Call Me Snow White . . . But I Drifted* (NY: Viking, 1991) 98.
12. Nora Ephron, *Nora Ephron Collected* (NY: Avon, 1991).
13. Henry Ephron 210.
14. Judy Oppenheimer, *Private Demons: The Life of Shirley Jackson* (NY: Putnam, 1988) 135.
15. Anne Stevenson, *Bitter Fame: A Life of Sylvia Plath* (Boston: Houghton Mifflin, 1989) 22.
16. Henry Ephron 6.
17. Qtd. in Obituary: "Phoebe Ephron, Comedy Writer, Dies" *New York Times* 14 Oct. 1971: 48.
18. Henry Ephron 211.
19. Matthew Gilbert, "This Is Her Life," *The Boston Sunday Globe* 1 March 1992: B34.
20. Lesley Jane Nonkin, "take one," *Vogue* Jan 1992: 146.
21. Gilbert B31.

4

Shirley Jackson: "In the country of the story, the writer is King."

In 1962, Shirley Jackson opened *Notes for a Young Writer*, written originally for her younger daughter Sally, with this royal proclamation.[1] She was forty-six years old and the mother of four. Sally was fourteen and had an older sister and brother, Joanne seventeen, Laurence twenty, and one younger brother, eleven-year-old Barry. Sally was the one Jackson felt had a mind most like her own and the one who, supposedly, wanted to be a writer. But Sally seemed to have had so much encouragement at so early an age it could not have been clear to her whether she genuinely wanted to write or whether she was simply being groomed, even pushed into it by a mother who recognized her daughter's talents from the outset. Jackson's story "The Intoxicated" describes a teenager who thinks and speaks exactly like Sally, although it was written before her daughter born. The story prompted family and friends to claim that Shirley Jackson conceived of her daughter's original mind even *before* she was born.[2]

Actually, both Sally's parents showed an interest in her writing. Shirley Jackson, her successful fiction-writer mother, insisted she write ten pages a night, although she did not have to show anyone what she wrote. Meanwhile her father, Stanley Edgar Hyman, corrected her writing like the professor and literary critic he was—looking for grammar and logic errors. "Between them," Sally said to Jackson's biographer, "I didn't stand a chance" (264). When Sally was only sixteen, she had a story published in *Gentleman's Quarterly*, sold to the magazine by Shirley's agent, Carol Brandt. But when Sally was only seventeen, her mother died, unexpectedly, during a nap on a "hot stuffy Sunday afternoon in August" (268). And Sally has not written since (264).

WRITING TECHNIQUES TO
CONTROL YOUR AUDIENCE

The fact that these notes were written for a promising young talent who turned away from a writing career in no way invalidates them. Shirley Jackson recognized their value outside of her home circle and used them at writing conferences during her last three years of life. They are not only clear and clever but absolutely above-board on the issue of control. Jackson knew that every effective writer has techniques to manipulate her audience, and decided to let her fourteen-year-old daughter privy to some of hers. She would have to keep her readers interested and play fair, Jackson explained, by not asking more of their imaginations than they could reasonably grant. The readers will be able to suspend reason and agree that there really is a Land of Oz, for example, but not that it can be seen from their windows. But then,

> for as long as the story does go on you are the boss. You have the right to assume that the reader will accept the story on your own terms. You have the right to assume that the reader, however lazy, will exert some small intelligence while he is reading. (*Notes*, 234)

That last sentence does not sound quite so patronizing in context, since Jackson goes on to say that her daughter need not describe everything, that she "need only describe one gardener to imply that the castle is well stocked with servants" (235).

Jackson is well aware of the control she has over her readers, over how she can sneak up on them, affect the speed at which they read, and help them digest complicated passages. Easy sections, simple clear paragraphs, provide "benches for the reader to sit down upon," a phrase she attributes to another writer, whose name she has forgotten. On these benches, "the poor reader who had struggled through the complex maze of ideas for several pages could rest gratefully" (241). But sometimes the rest is a set-up:

> If you would like him to rest for a minute so you can sneak up behind him and sandbag him, let him have a little peaceful description, or perhaps a little something funny to smile over, or a little moment of superiority. (*Notes*, 241)

The idea that the writer might have the ability and the desire to affect the speed at which her text can be read is, at first, surprising, and, on reflection, obvious:

> And if you want your reader to go faster and faster make your writing go faster and faster: "The room was dark. The windows were shaded, the furniture invisible. The door was shut and yet from somewhere, some small hidden precious casket of light buried deep in the darkness of the room, a spark came, moving in mad colored circles up and down, around and in and out and over and under and lighting everything it saw." (Those adjectives are unspeakable in every sense of the word, and wholly unnecessary; this is an example, not a model.) If you want your reader to go slower and slower make your writing go slower and slower: "After a wild rush of water and noise the fountain was at last turned off and the water was gone. Only one drop hung poised and then fell, and fell with a small musical touch. Now it rang. Now."
> (*Notes*, 241)

Another technical strategy Jackson revealed to her daughter that seems so obvious in hindsight involves what she calls conversation, and reviewers usually call dialogue. When a writer is praised for realistic and convincing dialogue, the critic, duped along with the general reader, often claims the writer has a good ear for how people really talk. But, according to Jackson, convincing written dialogue has little to do with the way people really talk. Jackson explains that you mustn't let your characters speak the way real people talk because "the way people usually talk is extremely dull" (236). Of course she is right. Listen to the way people repeat, stumble, hesitate. The writer's trick is to convince the reader that the characters *sound* like real people talking, even though they speak with far more economy of speech, with far more thought given to the choice and effect of their words. Characters usually use short sentences, but if they have to tell a long story, do so "only in the most carefully stylized and rhythmic language" (237). If you are not convinced that Jackson is correct about the high degree of stylization in written conversation, just

> ... look at some written conversation that seems perfectly smooth and plausible and natural on the page, and then try reading it aloud; what looks right on the page frequently sounds very literary indeed when read aloud; remember that you are writing to be read silently.
> (*Notes*, 237)

The following, from Jackson's last fragment of a novel, *Come Along With Me*, where Angela Motorman (age and size both forty-four) is explaining a

little about herself to the woman in whose home she plans to rent a room, is
a good example of the economy of written conversation:

> "I've just buried my husband," I said.
> "I've just buried mine," she said.
> "Isn't it a relief?" I said.
> "What?" she said.
> "It was a very sad occasion," I said.
> "You're right," she said, "It's a relief." (*Come Along With Me*, 10–11)

The fact that Jackson is writing these notes to nurture her daughter's
writing efforts must have awakened memories of the very different reception her own childhood writing received. Her mother was interested in the
social graces and did not know how to handle her intelligent, strong-
willed, overweight bookworm of a daughter, except to criticize her
appearance constantly (Opp. 24). The most intense part of young Shirley's
day was spent privately in her bedroom, writing. In an unpublished piece
written at Syracuse University between 1937 and 1940, which
Oppenheimer, her biographer, found in the Library of Congress Jackson
collection (after her death, Jackson's husband donated forty-two boxes of
her scrapbooks, diaries, letters, and journals to the Library of Congress),
Jackson tried to write about a painful part of her childhood, putting herself
in the third person:

> Every day all the way home from school she would think about going
> into her room and closing the door. She would think about her desk
> and the sunlight coming into the room and being alone with her desk
> and writing . . . She would touch her pocket to make sure that the key
> to her desk was safe. (Opp. 23)

But one day she came home and found her grandmother reading the papers
she had locked in the desk:

> She opened the door of her room quietly; there was no need to let
> them know she was home. When she opened her door she saw her
> grandmother at the desk; the desk was open and her grandmother was
> reading the papers from the desk. . . . She stood in the doorway watch-
> ing and finally she said "You mean it doesn't lock any more? My desk
> doesn't lock?" (Opp. 23, Ellipsis Jackson's)

This brazen invasion of privacy, practiced by her mother as well as her
grandmother, so enraged Jackson that before leaving home permanently she
openly burned every page of her childhood writing (24). If she couldn't
control the invasion, she could at least destroy what had been invaded. Nor

did she forget this experience. As an adult, she never once went through any of her children's papers (24).

CONTROLLING ONE'S ENVIRONMENT WITH WITTY FICTION

As an adult, Jackson tried to control unpleasant events with a lighter touch. In 1958, at forty-two, she wrote a lecture in an enchantingly good-humored vein which she called "Experience and Fiction."[3] The lecture opens with a whimsical anecdote from her life, an anecdote which appeared in a different form in her autobiography, *Raising Demons*.[4] The anecdote involves her old refrigerator, whose door always stuck in damp weather. Her daughter Sally, after watching her mother struggling one rainy morning, suggests she use magic to unstick it. Here the lecture parts company with the version in her autobiography. In the autobiographical version, Jackson allows Sally to use magic until the whole door comes off in her husband's hands. (" 'Jeekers,' Sally said, eyes wide. 'I went and unstuck the wrong side' " 649.) In the lecture version, she points out that Sally's suggestion need not be taken so literally. Jackson goes to her type-writer and writes the version that appeared in *Raising Demons*. She then sells the story to a magazine and buys a new refrigerator with the money received. The point? According to Jackson, looking for a lead-in for her lecture, this anecdote illustrates "the practical application of magic" and also answers the question she is posing for herself in the talk: "where do stories come from?" (195).

In all probability, neither version of the refrigerator story is precisely what happened, since both versions were edited when fictionalized. All fiction comes from life, according to Jackson, but has to be reworked:

> . . . the genesis of any fictional work has to be human experience. This translation of experience into fiction is not a mystic one. It is, I think, part recognition and part analysis. A bald description of an incident is hardly fiction, but the same incident, carefully taken apart, examined as to emotional and balanced structure, and then carefully reassembled in the most effective form, slanted and polished and weighed, may very well be a short story. (*Exp. & Fict.* 196)

Fiction, then, improves on the experience by reshaping it, giving it a form, a point, granting it what Ephron referred to as the illusion of having an intel-ligence at the center—the writer herself. Jackson's lecture quarrels "with the statement that this event cannot be improved upon because that is the way it really happened" (199). According to Jackson, there is nothing sacred about reality. Fiction is always preferable:

> It is much easier, I find, to write a story than to cope competently with the millions of daily trials and irritations that turn up in an ordinary house and it helps a good deal—particularly with children around—if you can see them through a flattering veil of fiction. It has always been a comfort to me to make stories out of things that happen, things like moving, and kittens, and Christmas concerts at the grade school, and broken bicycles. It is easier, as Sally said, to magic the refrigerator than it is to wrench at the door. (*Exp. & Fict.* 203)

The lecture goes on to illustrate the psychological control and comfort fiction afforded Jackson the day the local IRS representative came to audit their tax return. While her husband was sealed up in the study with the tax man, Jackson sat down to defend herself the only way she knew how—at her typewriter. She began straightforwardly enough, intending to write a letter to the government protesting such harassment of law-abiding citizens. But "she could not resist a few words of description" and, before she knew it, the letter turned into a story. When the interview was over, she "was well along in a story about a quietly lunatic investigation" (204). In her lecture, she could not resist adding that the income-tax man stopped by her typewriter on his way out and, recalling she was a writer, asked her where writers got their ideas. This last ironic twist seals the event in such vintage Jackson style that it is hard to believe the conversation actually took place. But it could have, and if life were as polished and pointed as fiction, it would have. Nevertheless, a version of the tax man story does appear in *Raising Demons*, which proves to skeptics that she really did, at least, turn the tax man's visit into a story, and, simultaneously, turn a situation where she and her husband were the victims of the IRS into one where she could pull all the strings.

CONTROLLING FEAR: JACKSON'S "SERIOUS" WRITING

Jackson was aware of the therapeutic value of her writing. During her last years, 1962–65, she was consciously using her writing, along with therapy, to combat the fears that had developed into a full-blown breakdown. But she had been aware of the way writing controlled her fears before that. We know that she began lecturing at the Suffield Writer's Conference in the summer of 1956. So even though the lecture notes which Oppenheimer uncovered and included in her biography are undated, they were most likely written in the late fifties. A comment in one of these lectures reveals her personal awareness of the therapeutic value of her writing, although it is presented as a generalization useful for all writers:

> The very nicest thing about being a writer is that you can afford to indulge yourself endlessly with oddness, and nobody can really do anything about it, so long as you keep writing and kind of using it up, as it were. All you have to do—and watch this carefully, please—is keep writing. So long as you write it away regularly nothing can really hurt you. (Opp. 211)

What Jackson feared would hurt her most was loss of control. She was afraid of losing control of her own words, which implied losing control of herself, of her identity. In an unsent letter to the poet Howard Nemerov, who taught at Bennington College with her husband, Jackson tried to put this fear of words *into* words. The unsent letter began in anger and ended in fear. What prompted her outburst was a misinterpretation of an earlier novel, *Hangsaman*,[5] in an English publication called *Sex Variant Woman in Literature*. Jackson's novel was referred to as "an eerie novel about lesbians" (Opp. 232). But Jackson had not meant Natalie and Tony, the two female characters in *Hangsaman*, to be lesbians, any more than she intended a lesbian reading of the two female characters she was currently creating (Merricat and Constance in *We Have Always Lived in the Castle*). In *Hangsaman* she had been trying to represent two warring psyches within the same person. In the letter to Nemerov, Jackson said she was writing about the "ambivalence of the spirit, or the mind, not the sex" (233). She was writing of the fear of a word, but the word she feared was not "lesbianism." The word she feared was "fear," fear of losing control to a stronger conscience which would destroy what she thought of as herself:

> We are afraid of being someone else and doing the things someone else wants us to do and of being taken and used by someone else, some other guilt-ridden conscience that lives on and on in our minds, something we build ourselves and never recognize, but this is fear, not a named sin. Then it is fear itself I am writing about . . . fear and guilt and their destruction of identity. . . . Why am I so afraid?
> So here I am. I am frightened by a word. I am frightened by a word because it tells me I am frightened. But I have always loved to use fear, to take it and comprehend it and make it work and consolidate a situation where I was afraid and take it whole and work it from there . . . I delight in what I fear. (Opp. 233, Ellipses Jackson's)

Jackson's articulation of what she fears elucidates nearly all of her so-called "thrillers." In *Hangsaman*, Natalie nearly succumbs to the will of Tony, who is no more than a second guilt-ridden conscience living in

Natalie's own mind ("some other guilt-ridden conscience that lives on and on in our minds, something we build ourselves and never recognize"). Natalie is guilt-ridden by the fact that she has no friends, that her father thinks she is so wonderful, but she knows the truth: that she is isolated, friendless, unhappy, and ashamed. But the novel is actually a triumph of Natalie's healthier conscience, which escapes the efforts of the second guilt-ridden conscience to commit suicide. Natalie ends up escaping from Tony and a dark, damp, deserted wood and hitching a ride to the edge of her college campus, which she reenters alone but alive.

The Bird's Nest is another variation on the theme of absorption into another's conscience.[6] Unable to deal with the reality surrounding her mother's death, Elizabeth has become fragmented into four incomplete personalities. The novel follows her struggles back to one reintegrated whole. But Jackson teases us with the fear of absorption by making each fragmented personality feel complete, whenever each is able to gain control and surface. Towards the end of the treatment, each worries about the fact that she will be lost or dead when the whole person is cured. One of the personalities tries to explain her worries to her Aunt Morgen:

> "He said, the doctor, that when I was cured it would be that all of us, Betsy and Beth and all, were all back together. He said I was one of them. Not myself, just one more of them. He said he was going to put us all back together into one person."
>
> "So? . . . Why not wait and see what happens?" Morgan suggested, inspired.
>
> "Look," Elizabeth turned and looked at her. "I'm just one of them, one *part*. I think and I feel and I talk and I walk and I look at things and I hear things and I eat and I take baths—. . . But I do it all with *my* mind." Elizabeth spoke very slowly, feeling her way. "What he's going to have when he's through is a new Elizabeth Richmond with *her* mind. *She* will think and eat and hear and walk and take baths. Not me. I'll maybe be a part of her, but I won't know it—*she* will."
>
> "I don't get it," said Morgen.
>
> "Well," said Elizabeth, "when *she* does all the thinking and knowing, won't I be . . . dead?" (*Bird's Nest*, 333)

"Fear of being someone else and doing the things someone else wants us to do," Jackson's words in her unsent letter to Nemerov, aptly describes the frightening touches in this novel.

The Haunting of Hill House can and has been read as a struggle between Eleanor and a haunted house, but the plot is more understandable if we recognize that Eleanor's struggles are also against that other guilt-ridden conscience "living on and on" within her own mind.[7] Eleanor feels guilty over her mother's death. She is certain that her dying mother had knocked on the wall and called for her medicine, as usual, but that she had not awakened as usual. (If Eleanor had not awakened, a rational, non guilt-ridden person might ask, how can she be certain that her mother had called?) Eleanor is also guilty and ashamed because she is thirty-two, unmarried, alone, has wasted eleven years caring for her invalid mother, is more relieved over her mother's death than sorry, has taken the car she and her sister own jointly (against her sister's wishes), and is now having rather a good time at Hill House. She is there by invitation, which means she belongs somewhere for the first time in her life. Since we can all manage to feel guilty over joy as well as misery, we all live in constant danger of absorption by that other guilt-ridden conscience living in our own minds, as Jackson well knew. In this novel Jackson chose to have Eleanor succumb to that second conscience, which drives her into a tree to her death: "*Why* am I doing this? Why am I doing this? Why don't they stop me?" blurts Eleanor's primary conscience, aware to the end (246).

We Have Always Lived in the Castle presents the confrontation even more obscurely.[8] It describes the struggle between the joint conscience of two sisters, Merricat and Constance, where our sympathies are directed, and the threatening group conscience of the townsfolk. Because the girls keep their "castle" (really a large estate), albeit in a battered and mostly burnt condition, and because the townfolk guiltily slink up one by one to the house under cover of night with offerings of food to atone for their attack, this novel reads like a triumph.

Triumphant or not, it was writing this novel that helped destroy the balance in Jackson's mind, turning her from a clever functioning writer into a severely troubled woman who was afraid to leave her bedroom. For this tale of two sisters isolating themselves from hostile and evil townsfolk came very close to voicing Jackson's own fears of her position in Bennington, Vermont, as Oppenheimer observes (233–237). Jackson had many other stresses at the time: Stanley had fallen in love with another woman, Jackson's role as a mother had become less demanding with the two eldest children away at school, she was suffering from colitis, and she had been taking amphetamines and tranquilizers since a doctor began the cycle over ten years before to help her lose weight (Opp. 238–241).

Unable to quiet the fears writing this novel had awakened, Jackson grew unable to leave home: "I have written myself into the house" she wrote to a friend (Opp. 237). She admitted to others that she had, in fact, written into the novel what it was like for her in North Bennington, where she was taunted by the villagers on her daily walks to the grocery store (Opp. 234). By Thanksgiving of 1962, Jackson refused to leave her bedroom. After staying indoors for three months, she agreed to see a psychiatrist. But it was to be three years before she began another novel. Twenty-nine pages of text were completed when she died in 1965 at age forty-nine.

Probably her most masterful use of fear, the story that was banned in South Africa, the one for which she is best known, is "The Lottery." Rather than approach this as the cynical exposure of the evil in human nature (a perfectly valid if overused approach), it is more interesting to approach it from Jackson's love of using fear, from her constant need to control it, to "use it up," as she put it. All her life, Jackson played with fear, prodded it the way you would a sore tooth. The fears she played with were both private: the fear of being swallowed by that second guilt-ridden conscience; and social: the fear of rejection, isolation, and persecution. She learned to frame these fears within the safe confines of a plot. All she need do to stay sane was to redirect her feeling of annihilation, rejection, or persecution into a plot which justified such fears. By doing so, by putting her fears into the story, Jackson was able to contain her paranoid feelings against the townsfolk in Bennington, Vermont. She was able to control her suspicions that the grocer would just as soon stone her as sell her a pork chop. Within the confines of the plot, such hostility would feel impersonal. It was not anything Shirley Jackson deserved, nor was it anything Tess Hutchinson had done, to merit being blackballed. "The Lottery" was illustrating how that other side of human nature, that other "guilt-ridden conscience," could take over en masse and control the more civilized everyday conscience under which we usually operate. Even little Davy Hutchinson was given a few pebbles to throw at his mother.

CONTROLLING FEAR:
JACKSON'S WITTY AUTOBIOGRAPHIES

I am reluctant to write that Shirley Jackson was misunderstood. She was, but my saying so suggests that I, alone, understand her, which would set myself up on a pompous, precarious, and doomed critical podium. While I do not claim to understand *everything* about Shirley Jackson's writing, I can make one important observation: her witty autobiographies and her so-called supernatural horror tales are not so far apart as everyone has assumed. Hovering over all reviews of her work is always the question of how the same person who wrote "The Lottery" could come up with the warm family autobiographical stories of *Life Among the Savages* and *Raising Demons*. The book critic for *Time* magazine, reviewing *We Have Always Lived in the Castle*, one of Jackson's last publications, had a wonderful time presenting the division:

> Shirley Jackson is a kind of Virginia Werewoolf among the
> seance-fiction writers. By day, amiably disguised as an embattled

mother, she devotes her artful talents to the real-life confusions of the four small children (*Life Among the Savages, Raising Demons*) in her Vermont household. But when shadows fall and the little ones are safely tucked in, Author Jackson pulls down the deadly nightshade and is off. With exquisite subtlety she then explores a dark world (*The Lottery, Hangsaman, The Haunting of Hill House*) in which the usual brooding old houses, fetishes, poisons, poltergeists and psychotic females take on new dimensions of chill and dementia under her black-magical writing skill and infra-red feminine sensibility. (21 Sept. 1962: 93)

The split was presented in her obituary in *The New York Times* so straightforwardly that it seems pedestrian by contrast, despite its adjective-overload:

> Shirley Jackson wrote in two styles. She could describe the delights and turmoils of ordinary domestic life with detached hilarity; and she could with cryptic symbolism, write a tenebrous horror story in the Gothic mold in which abnormal behavior seemed perilously ordinary. (10 Aug. 1965: 29)

Her husband skirted the issue by showing a patronizing, critical grudge against the naïveté of people who raise the question in the first place:

> People often expressed surprise at the difference between Shirley Jackson's appearance and manner, and the violent and terrifying nature of her fiction. Thus, many of the obituaries played up the contrast between a "motherly looking" woman, gentle and humorous, and that "chillingly horrifying" short story "The Lottery" and other works. When Shirley Jackson, who was my wife, published two lighthearted volumes about the spirited doings of our children, . . . it seemed to surprise people that she should be a wife and mother at all, let alone a gay and apparently happy one. This seems to me to be the most elementary misunderstanding of what a writer is and how a writer works, on the order of expecting Herman Melville to be a white whale.[9]

Hyman is upholding the notion of Art for Art's sake, the study of the corpus divorced from the person, as if there were no connection between what a person writes about and what that person needs to write about, no connection between who you are and what issues you are struggling with. His wife knew better than that, as all her words on the act of writing show.

A few critics *were* able to admit they did not understand her "gothic" or "supernatural" tales. These novels have never seemed particularly gothic to me, for while they do contain castle-like estates, these estates are filled with quirky characters rather than the cardboard counts, villains, and maidens of gothic thrillers. Nor do they deal precisely with the supernatural. For Jackson, the supernatural is mainly a way to express the subconscious, an observation made by Isaac Bashevis Singer, an admirer of Jackson's work (Opp. 228). And her fiction is at least as psychological as it is supernatural. It is difficult to know how to refer to these novels. I am calling them "serious" only to separate them from the lighthearted wit of the autobiographies. But the serious fiction is filled with (indeed, saved by) witty observations. And while the autobiographies are obviously meant to be witty, it does not follow that they are therefore frivolous. It is simply that they allow the reader to feel comfortable because they allow him to think he knows what is going on. Since he can then feel superior, he tends to write them off as lightweight. Jackson's serious fiction, on the other hand, is never written off, even when it is not understood. Confusion, in fact, tends to inspire awe. The less the critic understands, the more highly does he praise. Edmund Fuller starts his review of *The Haunting of Hill House* with rare honesty:

> This review of Shirley Jackson's new novel properly begins with the confession that I am not sure of anything about it except its almost unflagging interest.[10]

Ihab Hassan felt the same way about *We Have Always Lived in the Castle*, but he veiled his perplexity beneath a literary-sounding generalization:

> I have always felt that some writers should be read and never reviewed. Their talent is haunting and utterly oblique: their mastery of their craft seems complete. Even before reading Shirley Jackson's latest novel, I would have thought her case to be clear; she is of that company. And now Miss Jackson has made it even more difficult for a reviewer to seem pertinent: all he can do is bestow praise.[11]

But such humility, as well as such praise, was saved for the serious fiction. No one feels her witty autobiographical pieces deserve equal respect. Even Lenemaja Friedman, author of one of the two books that exist on Jackson to date (the other is Oppenheimer's biography), who devotes her last brief chapter to the family chronicles, makes this clear in a telling aside:

> She must have had tremendous resources of energy, for it was during these years, the 1950s, when her children were growing up that her literary output was the greatest: at least forty-four short stories were published during this decade (many of these, however, are the family-based stories for the women's magazines);[12]

Even her husband felt defensive about the image his wife projected in the autobiographies. When she granted a rare interview to Harvey Breit, playing up her cozy mothering role as well as the restful, non-physical side of writing, declaring "It's the only way I can get to sit down," Stanley would not take it silently.[13] He wrote a sarcastic little note to her which Oppenheimer tells us she saved in her "Lottery" scrapbook:

> dear neat detached miss jackson . . . writin? taint nothin but fun!!! neatly tucking a wisp of grey hair in place . . . d'ruther be raisin my passel of kids but since they laid henry off at the mill . . . flouring her apron with careworn hands . . . n'poppin blueberry pies in the oven . . . neatly detaching her goddamn head . . . shucks . . . yessir yessiree yesirreeindeedee! (Opp. 141)

Despite her husband's mockery, there was probably a serious motivation for the persona she created in her witty family sagas. The serious fiction is coping, or trying to cope, with fear by rechanneling it into plots. But Jackson is also combating fear in her witty autobiographies. In these, she is combating fear by distancing it, rather than rechanneling it. Between herself and her fears she places four children, one large but cozy house, any number of cats, a large cowardly dog, little wheels off things, a husband in his den, homemade brownies, inept maids, and terribly funny insights about it all:

> Our house is old, and noisy, and full. When we moved into it we had two children and about five thousand books; I expect when we finally overflow and move out again we will have perhaps twenty children and easily half a million books; we also own assorted beds and tables and chairs and rocking horses and lamps and doll dresses and ship models and paint brushes and literally thousands of socks. This is the way of life my husband and I have fallen into, inadvertently, as though we had fallen into a well and decided that since there was no way out we might as well stay there and set up a chair and a light of some kind;[14]

In about 98% of her two witty autobiographies, *Life Among the Savages* and *Raising Demons*, Jackson keeps a safe distance between herself and her fears. She presents herself as the wise, warm mother threading her way through her children's devious but demanding egos, her house's cantankerous furnace, and the daily meals and laundry.[15] But occasionally that distance shortens, giving us a fleeting glimpse of what her wit is keeping at bay. Even the popular story of Laurie's initial experience in kindergarten (which is often anthologized separately as "Charles") is but a cute rendition of what is, in fact, a difficult child. He not only bit, swore, and kicked a teacher, he had the panache to create a cover story to cover his misdeeds. The whole class stayed after school to keep Charles company, Laurie told his mother. But in this chapter Jackson's "wise mother" mask is so firmly in place that we are not at all disturbed by the fact that her eldest is what is usually called a problem child. Indeed, the self-centeredness of all her children is always so cleverly portrayed, and her mother's mask is always so firmly in place that we are not even disturbed by the story of Sally refusing to give the policeman her penny to put in the parking meter so her mother won't get a ticket. She tells him he can have her shilling, not her penny, but only if he promises "not to ask little girls for money ever again."[16]

But Jackson's mask slips somewhat in *Raising Demons* when she describes Sally's excursions into magic. One day Sally and her baby brother Barry disappear for a few hours, and her two older children try to reassure her they are safe with "Pudge," the ruler of an underground magic kingdom. The next morning she finds a large tub of spring flowers on her back porch with a thank-you note from Pudge. Since this is supposed to be autobiography, Jackson may not be playing fair, may be asking more than her reader could possibly grant. Sally's dealings with magic are never given an explanation, but left hanging in that murky area of the inexplicable which is not far from fear.

The other occasion in her autobiography when fear draws a little closer is when Jackson presents herself as a faculty wife. Her brilliant acerbic wit is sustained throughout the anecdote:

> I was not bitter about being a faculty wife, very much, although it did occur to me once or twice that young men who were apt to go on and become college teachers someday ought to be required to show some clearly distinguishable characteristic, or perhaps even wear some large kind of identifying badge, for the protection of innocent young girls who might in that case go on to be the contented wives of furniture repairmen or disc jockeys or even car salesmen. The way it is now, almost any girl is apt to find herself hardening slowly into a faculty wife when all she actually thought she was doing was just getting married. (*Raising Demons*, 639)

But her wit, however bright, cannot eradicate the disturbing facts beneath the surface cleverness: many of the students *were* young, beautiful, and idolatrous, while Jackson *was* older, fatter, and no longer infatuated by her husband, and her husband *did* love the adulation, not to mention the young nubile bodies, of his students.

These sections afford glimpses into a world that is not the safe, warm, and loving one Jackson is operating in for most of her two memoirs. Her children's self-centeredness suggests the self-absorbed world in which the adolescent Natalie was enmeshed (*Hangsaman*), the faculty wife's fears are similar to the fear of being forever left out of love which is eating away at Eleanor (*The Haunting of Hill House*), while Sally's adventures link up with the inexplicable parts of life expressed by the supernatural in all Jackson's serious novels.

Conversely, there are many witty touches in the serious fiction, as well as countless evocations of the cozy domestic safety which dominates the autobiographies. Although I have never cared for gothic tales, or tales of the supernatural, science fiction, or mystery, the intelligent, wry, domestic tone in all of Jackson's fiction lifts it into a category of its own. A brief tribute to her in *Newsweek* made a similar observation:

> In her art, as in her life, Shirley Jackson, who died last week at 45 [sic], was an absolute original. She belonged to no literary movement and was a member of no "school." She listened to her own voice, kept her own counsel, isolated herself from all fashionable intellectual and literary currents. She was not an urban, or existential, or "new," or "anti-"novelist. She was unique. (23 Aug. 1956: 83B)

By mingling wit and domestic detail with the inexplicable and fearful, Jackson has shortened the gap between her witty and her serious writing. Her wit also makes the serious fiction more acceptable. Many of the characters have sardonic sides which serve to ease a skeptical reader into the story. Mrs. Halloran, in *The Sundial*, is one such character. Although she goes along with her sister-in-law's vision of the end of the world (if Aunt Fanny proves to be right, Mrs. Halloran plans to be the queen in their new utopia), she is aware of Aunt Fanny's shortcomings, as well as the humor of their situation. Aunt Fanny has started to replace the library books with survival supplies:

> but Mrs. Halloran, looking in some surprise on a carton of cans of peaches, asked Aunt Fanny, "Surely we are entering a land of milk and honey? Must we take our own lunch? (*The Sundial*, 95)

Familiar domestic tensions add a comfortable touch. The doctor who is running the experiment at Hill House turns out to be a henpecked husband, and, though Eleanor has psychic abilities, she also has a dominating married sister who treats her like a servant. When Eleanor sets out for Hill House in their jointly-owned car, which she took despite her sister's objections, she becomes somewhat freed from her usual timid personality. Passing a tiny cottage en route to Hill House, she dares to daydream, to imagine a possible alternate life for herself inside:

> No one would find me there, either, behind all those roses, and just to make sure I would plant oleanders by the road. I will light a fire in the cool evenings and toast apples at my own hearth. I will raise white cats and sew white curtains and sometimes come out of my door to go to the store to buy cinnamon and tea and thread. People will come to me to have their fortunes told, and I will brew love potions for sad maidens; I will have a robin . . . (*Hill House*, 22–23)

All the cozy domestic details, the cinnamon and tea and thread, make her sudden urge to hide ("No one would find me there, either"), and to establish herself as a kindly witch for young maidens, that much easier to accept. Moreover, the emotional motivation behind Eleanor's daydream has been carefully established. In her dream she hides from those who have been powerful enough to hurt her in the past and enjoys a skill which will draw harmless and powerless people to her in the future. Above all, she will be safe, with her cats, her curtains, her toasted apples—safe, useful, and maybe even loved. And Jackson has presented the daydream to us with her own unique, wry, domestically-informed wit.

WIT AS CONTROL IN JACKSON'S PRIVATE LIFE

Jackson's biographer spoke to an old friend of Stanley Edgar Hyman's about the marital relationship. Frank Orenstein, whose friendship with Stanley went back to their high school days, had this to say:

> He was the czar, but she was the real ruler. It was her house, her rule. Stanley was probably smarter than anybody, but he didn't have the quick wit—and I think that was part of what evened up the balance. (Opp. 179)

It was her quick wit that had impressed Stanley from the start. What first brought Shirley to Stanley's attention was a piece she had written for *The Threshold*, a magazine published by her creative writing class at Syracuse University in 1938 (Opp. 61). And wit remained important in their relationship. "They were big fans of each other," recalls their eldest son, Laurence, thinking of their wonderful family dinners (Opp. 198). "Both of them were total suckers for anything slapstick," remarked Barry, the younger son. Their elder daughter, Joanne, recalled one of her mother's most memorable dinner table performances, the night she did an impression of a drunken goldfish (Opp. 198).

The more ominous side to Jackson's wit was her interest in witchcraft. After her death, no one was willing to take a definite position as to whether Jackson was serious about being a witch. She did fill her home with books on witchcraft, with charms, and cats. A hedged reference to her witchcraft abilities crept into *The New York Times* Obituary:

> In that connection [to the subject of witchcraft], Brenden Gil, the critic, who was a friend of Miss Jackson, said yesterday that she had considered herself responsible for an accident to an enemy by having fashioned a wax figure of him that had a broken leg. (10 Aug. 1965: 29)

Even if the controlling aspect of witchcraft *did* appeal to Jackson, she undoubtedly knew that any show of interest, let alone declaration of belief, would provoke scorn. She usually packaged her public allusions in an acceptable form: "I have always been interested in witchcraft and superstition but never had much traffic with ghosts" she said in one of her writing lectures.[17] Her language makes the observation that much more palatable. The phrase "never had much traffic with ghosts" mocks the whole enterprise and suggests that her interest in witchcraft is purely intellectual. That is, in fact, what her brother believed: "She studied it like you'd study history," he told Oppenheimer, "I always thought it was a little tongue-in-cheek" (37).

But if we accept her brother's version, what do we make of her eldest son's comment that "my mother believed strongly and firmly in the supernatural. She believed it and was very tuned in to it, perhaps more than she cared to be" (Opp. 37). Or how do we react to Jackson's more candid words uncovered by Oppenheimer in the draft version for another writing lecture: "No one can get into a novel about a haunted house without hitting the subject of reality head-on; either I have to believe in ghosts, which I do, or I have to write another kind of novel altogether" (226).

Her tarot readings were reputed to be so accurate that several of her friends nervously refused to let her tell them their fortunes. After the family moved to Vermont in 1945, she never had fewer than six cats at a time. A friend of her elder daughter recalled a dinner when a grey cat jumped on Shirley Jackson's shoulder and seemed to whisper in her ear, at which point Jackson announced that the cat had told her a poem—which she then repeated. Joanne reported another light side to her witchcraft. She kept all the small kitchen tools crammed in one drawer. When she wanted one, she would slam the drawer shut, call out the desired utensil's name, and open the drawer. According to Joanne, it would always be on top (Opp. 189).

Still, these intriguing details are hardly conclusive proof that Jackson considered herself a witch. We probably have to settle for ambiguity. Harriet Fels, wife of the president of Bennington College and friend of Jackson, summed up the ambiguity nicely: "She would allude to witchcraft. She acted as if she believed in it on the one hand, but it was a game on the other hand. She wasn't above stricking pins in dolls, it was a real thing—but she treated it in conversation as a game" (Opp. 189).

According to Oppenheimer, everyone knew Jackson had the tools of magic in her home—her books, devices, and amulets were in plain sight. But she wouldn't even tell her children whether or not she practiced magic in earnest:

> "When she was asked, she would say nothing about whether she did or
> didn't," said Laurence. She could joke—or seem to joke—about being

a witch, she could allude to certain charms and spells in passing, but
the actual practice of magic was very private and real to her, something
she felt strongly should be hidden from the outside world. "I wouldn't
want to violate any secrets," Laurence said.

While Laurence's comments suggest he believed her to be in earnest,
Barry, her younger son, offered the explanation I quoted in my introduction,
which leads away from the question of belief and back to the relationship
between witchcraft, writing, and control:

> She realized that the only tools the magician needs are in the head. You
> make the world, you decide what your name is, your role, decide what
> people are going to think of you by your own force of will. And that's
> real magic in the real world. (Opp. 190)

This, as Oppenheimer observes, is "not unlike writing itself" (190).

While Jackson's wit could put her in complete control in her fiction ("for
as long as the story does go on you are the boss"), it could never function
quite so effectively in daily life. Stanley Edgar Hyman had his own agenda,
and an active participation in parenting or household duties was not on it. He
was the professor and literary critic. Their den was always called Stanley's
study, however many best sellers Shirley wrote in it (Opp. 170). What *was*
on his agenda, however, was sexual promiscuity. Also, Jackson's difficult
relationship with her parents could never be resolved, however many competent pictures she drew of her life for her mother in her letters home. Sally,
commenting to Jackson's biographer on her mother's breakdown, assessed
the question of her mother's mental control succinctly, if bitterly:

> She got the four kids and the big house and the smart husband and
> she went crazy anyway. And I think she felt really bad. She felt bad
> that the books weren't enough therapy, that writing a book every
> year or two didn't keep her sane. Because she put her guts into it. But
> it wasn't enough. (Opp. 248)

Sally is Jackson's daughter, and was only seventeen when her mother died.
Her bitterness is understandable. But what can never be determined is the
degree to which Jackson's writing had helped keep her fears at bay. Toward
the end of her life, Jackson worried about what she would be able to write
about were she to be cured of her anxieties. Oppenheimer quotes from her
last journal, kept while she was in therapy:

> If I am cured and well and oh glorious alive then my books should be
> different. Who wants to write about anxiety from a place of safety?
> Although I suppose I would never be entirely safe since I cannot

completely reconstruct my mind. But what conflict is there to write about then? I keep thinking vaguely of novels about husbands and wives . . . but I do not really think this is my kind of thing. Perhaps a funny book. A happy book. There's room for it and I could do it. (Opp. 258)

Jackson had begun *Come Along With Me* when she died of cardiac arrest in August of 1965. She seemed to be recovering from her breakdown, but too little of the novel was written (only twenty-nine pages) to be certain about where she was planning to take it. Still, it begins like one more vintage Jackson, with Angela Motorman a choice blend of the supernatural and homey, her voice saturated with Jackson's wit. I like to think that the border between the unknown and the comfortably known *was*, in fact, Jackson's "place of safety" and I take the fact that she had begun this novel with her usual droll blend of the two as a sign that she had come to appreciate her unique vantage point on life before she died.

NOTES

1. Shirley Jackson, "Notes for a Young Writer," *Come Along With Me; Part of a novel, sixteen stories, and three lectures*, ed. Stanley Edgar Hyman (NY: Viking, 1968) 234–243.
2. Judy Oppenheimer, *Private Demons: The Life of Shirley* Jackson (NY: Putnam, 1988) 121. Oppenheimer's bibliography was invaluable for this chapter and will be cited parenthetically, abbreviated Opp.
3. Shirley Jackson, "Experience and Fiction," *Come Along With Me*, 195–204.
4. Shirley Jackson, *Raising Demons*, 1957, rpt. in *The Magic of Shirley Jackson*. ed. Stanley Edgar Hyman (NY: Farrar, Straus, and Giroux, 1965) 533–753.
5. Shirley Jackson, *Hangsaman* (NY: Farrar, Straus, and Young, 1951).
6. Shirley Jackson, *The Bird's Nest*, 1954, rpt. in *The Magic of Shirley Jackson*, 147–380.
7. Shirley Jackson, *The Haunting of Hill House* (1959; NY: Viking Penguin, 1987).
8. Shiley Jackson, *We Have Always Lived in the Castle* (1962; NY: Viking Penguin, 1984).
9. Stanley Edgar Hyman, "Shirley Jackson: 1919–1965," *Sat Eve Post* 18 Dec. 1965: 63. Jackson was actually born in 1916, according to Oppenheimer. Hyman was the one born in 1919, but upheld the fiction they were the same age into her death.
10. *The New York Times Book Review* 10 Oct. 1959: 4.
11. *The New York Times Book Review* 23 Sept. 1962: 5.
12. Lenemaja Friedman, *Shirley Jackson* (Boston: Twayne, 1975) 31.
13. *The New York Times Book Review* 26 June 1949: 15.

14.   Shirley Jackson, *Life Among The Savages*, 1953 rpt. in *The Magic of Shirley Jackson*, 385.
15.   Walker cites *Life Among the Savages* as an example of a woman's double text—the wise warm mother is part of the "official" text, but there is also a subtler "unofficial" one. See *A Very Serious Thing* (Minneapolis: Univ. of Minn. Press, 1988) 31.
16.   Jackson, *Raising Demons,* 612.
17.   Jackson, "Experience and Fiction," *Come Along With Me*, 202.

5

Alison Lurie: "Writing was a Kind of Witch's Spell"

WRITING AS COMPENSATION

In 1982, Alison Lurie was invited to discuss her writing career in a special feature section of *The New York Times Book Review*.[1] The column was "intended to provide a forum for writers to consider the rewards and perils of their craft," explained an editor, who must have felt that including a column of personal reflections in a section devoted to reviewing books, even if these reflections *did* come from writers, needed some sort of explanation (13). Lurie wrote a delightful account of why she was encouraged to see herself as a writer when she was just a young child, and a more thoughtful, but equally delightful, account of why she renewed her pledge to writing after a thirteen-month defection in her late twenties. Lurie discusses a writer's sense of power as well as a writer's frequent identification with witchcraft, particularly when that writer is a woman. In fact, Lurie's account of her development as a writer is so pertinent to wit, witchcraft, and empowerment that the first section of this chapter will review her words carefully.

Lurie, who is an expert on children's literature as well as a writer of adult fiction, begins by acknowledging that creativity is always encouraged in the very young. The young child's "delightful paintings and naive verses" are displayed on kitchen walls (13). As the child grows older, she observes, more competitive and constructive projects are encouraged, like sports and baby-sitting, as well as more socially-viable ones, like personal appearance and manners. The child is being groomed for adult success. But, Lurie wickedly suggests, creativity can be encouraged for a longer period if the child appears to be a particularly unlikely candidate for adult success—and she claims that she was one of those children. *Her* creative work stayed up on the wall longer than most children's because she had no other talents.

Lest this be dismissed as traditional female self-deprecation, let me add that Lurie makes the same point in an interview with Dorothy Mermin which appeared the following year.[2] The repetition suggests that we take her assessment of her childhood failings as more than mere rhetorical deprecation. Lurie remarked to Mermin that when she was only six or seven, her position, encouraged by her parents, was that she was going to grow up to be a writer or an artist. Lurie then repeats the idea that she must have been encouraged to see herself as a writer while so young because she "obviously wasn't good at very many other things" (93). In the earlier *New York Times Book Review* article, Lurie provides specific details of her shortcomings:

> I was a skinny, plain, odd-looking little girl, deaf in one badly damaged ear from a birth injury, and with a resulting atrophy of the facial muscles that pulled my mouth sideways whenever I opened it to speak and turned my smile into a sort of sneer. . . . I couldn't seem to learn to ride a bike or sing in tune, and I was always the last person chosen for any team. (13)

It was evident to Lurie by the time she was eight that no one would ever want to marry her. She would never be able to have "any of those children whose names and sexes [she] had chosen at an earlier and more ignorant age" (13). She decided that she had better get to work on her writing skills.

Lurie's attitude as a young girl can be seen as a modern variation of the crisis or event Carolyn Heilbrun identified as instrumental in freeing earlier writers like George Eliot and Dorothy Sayers from the conventional male-scripted marriage plot. In Lurie's case, as well as in Nora Ephron's and Shirley Jackson's, a mere attitude, rather than any one event or crisis, was enough to shift the emphasis from the marriage plot to what Heilbrun identifies as the quest plot.[3]

Like the young Lurie, the teenage Ephron thought no one would ever want to marry her. She realized it the minute a high school friend reassured her that her breasts would grow as soon as she married. Her husband's kisses and caresses would cause them to develop:

> I became dizzy. For I knew instantly—as naïve as I had been only a moment before—that only part of what she was saying was true: the touching, rubbing, kissing part, not the growing part. And I knew that no one would ever want to marry me. I had no breasts. I would never have breasts.[4]

Ephron also recalls that she had been so aware of her lack of beauty as an adolescent that she spent hours working up conversation as a compensatory skill. Just once she went out with a young man who thought she was beautiful:

> He talked all night, while I—who spent years developing my conversational ability to compensate for my looks (my life has been spent in compensation)—said nothing.[5]

Shirley Jackson is another who seduced with words. She was a large and ungainly child. According to Dorothy Ayling, her closest childhood friend, Shirley Jackson

> . . . was sloppy about her appearance—hemlines never hung right, the newest clothes somehow ended up looking slightly askew the minute she put them on. Part of it was due to her figure. It was not that she was terribly fat; in fact, when Dorothy first knew her she was average in weight, "but she did have this fat stomach that just popped out."[6]

As she grew up, Jackson continued to develop her writing skills rather than her social ones. Fittingly, what sparked Stanley Edgar Hyman's interest in his future wife was a story she published in their college literary magazine. He had not yet met or seen her on the campus of Syracuse University, where they were both undergraduates. But he maintained later in life that as soon as he read that story he told a friend that he was going to marry her (Opp. 56).

What these anecdotes reveal is that all three young women found ways to think of themselves as something other than prospective brides. Granted, the route each used to reach this alternate self image was a negative one—language skills were meant to compensate for real or imagined physical lacks.[7] As Lurie put it, her stories were said to be " 'Perfectly lovely, dear.' Nobody every told me that *I* was perfectly lovely, though, as they did other little girls. Very well, then: perfection of the work."[8] Still, as Heilbrun points out, it is possible to give these compensating tactics a positive emphasis. The young girl who saw herself as plain was, in fact, fortunate in being unable to imagine bartering beauty to acquire a protective mate. Unable to imagine that she would ever have a husband, she felt she had to develop skills to succeed on her own. Heilbrun expressed this idea eloquently when assessing the shortcomings of Dorothy Sayers' male biographer, James Brabazon:

> He recognizes, but does not endorse, the possibility that it is precisely not having been sexually attractive in youth that enables women to develop the ego-strength to be creative and ultimately part of the instrumental rather than the expressive world in adulthood.[9]

Naomi Bliven was making a related point when she commented, rather wittily, that "behind any woman you ever heard of stands a man who let her down."[10]

In all three cases, Lurie's, Ephron's, and Jackson's, any fears of remaining single, of never being the center of a family, proved unfounded. Lurie was married for thirty-seven years and has three sons, Jackson married immediately after college and raised four children, and Ephron, with two sons from her second, is married to her third husband. But it is important to observe that even after Lurie, Jackson and Ephron were married, running homes, and involved with the time-consuming process of raising children, they all kept right on writing. What may have begun as compensation developed into a vital and valuable life work.

THE CONTROL OF WITCHCRAFT: EMPOWERING OR DEBILITATING?

The positive outcome of her childhood beliefs was unavailable to eight-year-old Alison Lurie in 1934. She believed she was going to be an ugly old maid "the card in the pack everyone tried to get rid of" (13). And it was but a tiny mental leap from old maid to witch, especially for someone like the young Alison Lurie, steeped in Victorian and Edwardian children's literature. She knew all about both figures:

> Old maids wore spectacles and old-fashioned clothes and lived in cottages with gardens. . . . Occasionally they shared their cottage with another Old Maid, but mostly they lived alone, often with a cat. Sometime the cat was their familiar, and they were really witches. You could tell which ones were witches, according to one of my children's books, because there was always something wrong with them: They had six fingers on one hand, or their feet were on backward, and so on. (13)

Imagining herself as a witch as well as a writer encouraged the young Lurie to enjoy the budding power of her pen. If we can trust the memory of the adult Lurie looking backward, the young Lurie anticipated the bravado behind the connection of women writers to witches celebrated by the French feminists fifty years later:

> With a pencil and paper I could revise the world. I could move mountains, I could fly over Westchester at night in a winged clothes basket; I could call up a brown-and-white spotted milk-giving dragon to eat the neighbor who had told me and my sister not to walk through her field and bother her cows. (13)

Lurie soon discovered that she could control non-fiction as well. All she need do was present the version of the truth she found most appealing. In letters to her parents from boarding school, Lurie realized she could describe her new English teacher with "a lovely wild curly brown beard" if he was in her favor or as "a small man with yellow teeth" if not:

> Or any of the two, three, 20 other versions of him, all of them the truth—if I said so, the whole truth. That was what you could do with just a piece of paper and a pencil: writing was a kind of witch's spell. (13)

Lurie continued to think of herself as a writer, and to write, throughout high school, college, and beyond, even though parts of her earlier image had to be readjusted. After graduating from Radcliffe in 1947, her writing proved not so irresistible, nor her person so unattractive, as she had once believed. Ironically, as she neared thirty, she had everything she had not dared to hope for as a young girl. She was married and raising two young sons. But she had not received an acceptance slip for her writing in seven years. She had two completed but unpublished novels. As her graduate-student husband suggested early in the seven-year spell of rejections, why not quit if rejections are so depressing? "After all, Alison, nobody is asking you to write a novel" was the way she reports that he put it.

After seven years of rejections and depressions, Lurie decided to take his insensitive advice and give up writing. For thirteen months she threw herself into family life with a vengeance. This happened in the mid-fifties, well before Betty Friedan published *The Feminine Mystique* in 1963, exploding the myth of the happy suburban housewife in America. In 1954, all women were expected to feel fulfilled staying at home and raising a family. Lurie felt no such fulfillment but no one noticed.

Then, in 1956, V.R. (Bunny) Lang died of cancer at age thirty-two. V.R. Lang was an eccentric poet, playwright, and one of the founders of the Poets' Theater in Cambridge, MA. More to the point, she had been a beloved friend of Alison Lurie. Lurie's reaction to this loss was to write down everything about her friend as a private way of remembering. She was not writing for others and certainly not for publication:

> When I worked, not worrying for once about whether my sentences would please some editor, I experienced a series of flashes of light. First, I noticed that I felt better than I had in months or years. Next I realized that I wasn't writing only about Bunny, but also about the Poets' Theater, about academia and the arts, about love and power. What I wrote wasn't the whole truth—I couldn't know that—

but it was part of the truth, my truth. I could still cast spells, reshape
events. (47)

Lurie knew that her friend had been considered difficult and neurotic. But
Lurie saw the point of Lang's brief life emerge on paper: *she* had done what
she wanted to, not what was expected of her. And what Lurie wanted to do
with her own life was to write. What difference would it make if her books
were never published? She went back to writing.

Writing the memoir of her friend was a breakthrough in two important
ways. First of all, obviously, Lurie was writing again. But secondly, friends
privately printed three hundred copies of the memoir. One of these copies
eventually reached an editor at MacMillan. This editor, favorably disposed
by the memoir, read and published Lurie's third novel, *Love and
Friendship*. And Lurie has been writing and publishing ever since. The
memoir itself was published as an introduction to a collection of Lang's
poems and plays Lurie brought out with Random House in 1975, almost
twenty years after it was written.

Lurie ends her article with an exhortation to all writers to keep on writing, to ignore the pressures to conform and succeed only along conserva-
tive and respectable paths. In her last paragraph she finally acknowledges
the debilitating side to the witchcraft connection. Clearly, the young Lurie
had enjoyed the sense of power behind her words, and recognized the way
they cast a spell over reality. But she had also identified with the isolation
of the witch, with the sense of being different—of being the one who was
always left out. Lurie suspects that she was not the only writer to make this
connection:

> Of course, this is not the end of the story. Nor is it just my story. Not
> all writers are born with their feet on backward, but most of them, in
> my experience, sometimes feel themselves to be witches or warlocks,
> somehow wicked, somehow peculiar, somehow damaged. At least
> until recently, this has been especially true of woman, who, in order to
> go on writing, have had to struggle not only with the ordinary evil spir-
> its of economic necessity, editorial indifference and self-doubt, but
> also with the fear that they are not "normal"—however this word is
> currently defined. (48)

A writer may try to stress only the empowering and creative sides to writing, but the darker, sinister, isolating ones are lurking just beneath. It is
immaterial whether the urge to write developed as a compensatory tactic of
the outsider or if it was the urge to write which caused the young writer to
feel isolated in the first place. What is relevant is that writing, like witchcraft, is *both* empowering and isolating.

CONTROLLING THE FRAME

Lurie's Non-Fiction: Breaking Patterns of Scholarship

Since 1962, Lurie has not only published eight novels, but has also brought out three books for children (*The Heavenly Zoo* and *Clever Gretchen* in 1980, *Fabulous Beasts* in 1981), a collection of short stories (*Women and Ghosts*, 1994), one somewhat unclassifiable work on what clothing signifies (*The Language of Clothes*, 1981), and one equally unclassifiable clever piece of scholarship about the world of children's books (*Don't Tell the Grown-Ups*, 1990). She has also written numerous articles and reviews.

The two works by Lurie that best illustrate innovative techniques of scholarship are *The Language of Clothes* and *Don't Tell the Grown Ups: Why Kids Love the Books They Do*.[11] The latter is not exactly your traditional scholarly book on the history of children's literature. Rather, it is a clever, free-wheeling book about the subversive make-up of the people who are receptive to fairy-tales: it assesses those who read them as well as those who write them. For the last twenty years, Lurie notes, college students have been enraptured by Tolkein's Hobbits and Milne's Winnie-the-Pooh. Lurie suggests several reasons for the appeal of elves, fairies, hobbits and other little people to such "grown-up" children: their imaginations may have been starved as young children, for one thing, while the world of little people presents less of a threat than does our modern world, for another (49–50). Lurie also points out the subversive element of so many children's favorites: *Tom Sawyer* was Twain's reaction against "goody-goody boys' books," and both *Alice in Wonderland* and *Through the Looking Glass* are filled with topical social and political satire (4–5). Even something as superficially innocuous as *Mary Poppins* presents an unsympathetic picture of incompetent parents. Lurie cleverly observes that the children's loyalty goes to Mary Poppins. They remain quite detached from their parents' unhappiness:

> "Children, Children!" Mrs. Banks was wringing her hands in despair. "Be quiet or I shall Go Mad!"
> There was silence for a moment as they stared at her with interest. Would she really? They wondered. And what would she be like if she did?[12]

Much modern fiction for adults follows patterns from fairy tales—a fact Lurie sees as an "underground connection" between the two (29). Lurie is suggesting that adults may be more subversive than they realize, as well as more susceptible to wish-fulfilling themes. Lurie points out the popularity of both the Snow White and Sleeping Beauty themes, particularly in the works of male novelists, who like to put their heroine in some sort of trance: "Often the princess is frigid, or sexually unawakened like Lady Chatterley; sometimes she is intellectually or politically unawakened, . . . like the Princess Casamassima in Henry James' novel of the same name" (30). Female writers have favored the Cinderella theme. *Jane Eyre* might be the most obvious example, but all of Brontë's fiction, as well as all of Austen's novels, support her observation (33).

Eleven of Lurie's sixteen chapters are innovative biographical chapters on well-known writers of children's literature, like Beatrix Potter, as well as writers less known in the genre, like Ford Maddox Ford. The opening paragraphs of both these chapters are captivatingly original, illustrating the way that Lurie has broken out of any established pattern of scholarship. Here is Lurie on Ford Maddox Ford:

> Once upon a time there was a large, pink-faced, yellow-haired man who liked to tell stories. All kinds of stories: adventure and spy thrillers, historical dramas, romances and fantasies, tales of war and personal reminiscence, social comedy and social criticism. Unfortunately he overdid it. Between the age of eighteen and sixty-five he published eighty-one books, including four juveniles and thirty-two novels. Of the latter, one, *The Good Soldier*, is a masterpiece; four or five others come near it, and the rest vary from interesting to awful. Overproduction, especially of inferior work, is hard on an author's imagination and also on his public reputation. If Ford Madox Ford had told fewer stories, he might be better known today. (90)

What is this exactly? It starts out as if "Auntie Alison" were going to tell her grown-up children (us) a story, but she ends up the literary guru, making a pithy pronouncement writers had better heed, especially second-raters. Is she being satirical, biographical or opinionated? I think she is being all three. The chapter is a delicate one, balancing Ford's strengths in fantasy and weaknesses in reality, offering biographical backgrounds for his fairy tales, and always well-grounded in both sympathy and history. Her opening paragraph on Beatrix Potter is equally riveting:

> Nearly ninety years ago, in London, a woman escaped from prison with the help of a rabbit. It was not a modern prison, with facilities for education and recreation and a chance of parole, but a tall, dark, stuffy Victorian house; and the prisoner, who had been confined there for most of her thirty-six years, was under sentence for life. The rabbit's name, of course, was Peter. (91)

The cuteness of the opening tone drops away, but Lurie continues with the theme of escape. Beatrix Potter's story is told in a simple, straightforward way that proves very moving. Lurie calls the chapter "Animal Liberation." The way Lurie presents Potter's life makes her one more example of a woman empowering herself through her wit, if we expand the definition of wit to encompass drawing skills.

The Language of Clothes is an even more extreme example of Lurie stepping off any expected path of scholarship. Lurie was, after all, a professor of folklore and children's literature at the time she wrote Don't Tell The Grown Ups. However innovative the end result, the subject was in one of her established areas of expertise. But what is The Language of Clothes? It is part a book of fashion, part a sociology text, part photographic documentary, with illustrations assembled by Doris Palca, and part literary criticism set free. Anne Tyler gave it a favorable review in The New Republic, saying it reminded her of the works of Erving Goffman, a sociologist "who, in such books as The Presentation of Self in Everyday Life interpreted the gestures and tiny formalities we'd hardly bothered to notice before, let alone analyse for hidden meaning."[13] Tyler rarely writes negative reviews, but here she gently suggests that some of Lurie's inferences seem forced: "Alison Lurie derives many of her most inventive theories from an almost breathtaking literal-mindedness" is the tactful way Tyler expressed her reservations. The example Tyler gives of such literal-mindedness is Lurie's interpretation of the shoulder pads worn by women during the Great Depression, which allegedly signaled women's "willingness and ability to bear the burdens of the world by literally squaring their shoulders" (32).

The Language of Clothes is occasionally a spoof of overconvoluted critical theories, where everything self-consciously signifies something else. Although (possibly because) Lurie is a member of the Cornell English Department, her fictional representations of academics are always satiric. She once speculated in an interview that there may be "something just a little silly about professors anyhow."[14] But exposing convoluted criticism was not the main motivation behind the book. Rather, writing this book shows that in 1981 Lurie was still under the spell of the lesson she had learned in 1956. As when she wrote the memoir of Bunny Lang, she was writing what she wanted to write, pleasing no one but herself. There could be no advantage for either Lurie the novelist or Lurie the expert in children's literature to writing this book on the signification of clothes. She had to have been interested in the topic. The end result is an odd and interesting book, with wonderful photographs.

Another interesting project was Clever Gretchen and Other Forgotten Folktales, a collection of neglected tales Lurie gathered and retold for children in 1980.[15] While others were inventing the contemporary feminist fairy tale to satisfy the "new" feminist consciousness, Lurie simply uncovered actual fairy tales which featured strong and clever young women.

These fairy tales, she explains to children in her introduction, had once been in circulation but were lost to tradition because they did not reinforce the principles that Victorian society (with male editors) wanted:

> Most of the editors who chose these stories [Snow White, Cinderella, Sleeping Beauty, Little Red Riding Hood] were men. The original tellers of folktales, on the other hand, were mainly women. And they were not frail Victorian ladies, but working women: farmers' wives, shopkeepers, craftsman, household servants, children's nurses, and midwives. They lived active, interesting lives, and the stories they told showed it. (Intro. xii)

In 1986, Jack Zipes brought out his edition of modern fairy tales with its wry title, *Don't Bet on the Prince*. Although he acknowledges Lurie's work in his bibliography, it is regrettable that he did not find room for these original tales alongside the newly-invented ones. His was a clever move, correcting an omission by invention, but hers was an even cleverer one, showing that the omission was a fabrication in the first place.

CONTROLLING THE FRAME

Lurie's Heroines: Breaking Life Patterns

The innovative forms of Lurie's non-fiction contrasts with the traditional form of her fiction. Most of her heroines are chafing at, if not struggling against, the traditional patterns for women's lives, but the forms of the novels which depict their struggles are traditional indeed. In fact, her novels fulfill that reviewer's worn caveat: they are all "good reads." Christopher Lehmann-Haupt saw *Foreign Affairs* as a masterpiece of classical form:

> But besides amusing us with its story, *Foreign Affairs* is wonderfully stimulating for its sheer performance as a novel. Perhaps by stressing this I'm admitting nostalgia for a classical approach to literature, but as I read *Foreign Affairs* I couldn't help visualizing a diagram with the rise of Vinnie's fortunes superimposed on the decline of Fred Turner's.[16]

Vinnie Miner, the "heroine" of *Foreign Affairs*, is a good illustration of the contrast between content and form. Before the creation of Vinnie Miner, the literary heroine most striking for her plainness was Jane Eye. According to Elizabeth Gaskell, Charlotte Brontë told her sisters they were morally wrong to make their heroines beautiful as a matter of course: "I will show you a heroine as plain and small as myself," Charlotte boasted, "who shall be as interesting as any of yours."[17] Then she sat down and created *Jane*

Eyre. But Lurie took Brontë's idea one step further: *her* heroine is both plain and middle-aged. Moreover, she contrasts Vinnie's story against a second plot where the hero, Fred Turner, is not only young but also gorgeous. Yet, when the novel ends, it is frumpy little fifty-four-year-old Vinnie who has been touched and changed by a loving affair, while the young and handsome Fred Turner has gained neither enlightenment nor happy memories from his.

Katherine Rogers wrote an insightful and pertinent article on Alison Lurie called "The Uses of Adultery."[18] Rogers justifies Lurie's use of adultery on the grounds that it was the only way to extricate her heroines from their smug acceptance of traditional roles. Something drastic was needed to make them realize that their pat middle-class lives were neither so solid nor so satisfying as society had led them to believe. As Rogers put it, "By involving them in extramarital affairs, Lurie forces them to part with their cherished illusions and to see themselves more realistically" (118). Lurie is using adultery strategically, as a way to urge her heroine towards a greater level of awareness, if not control, of what is happening in her life.

Love and Friendship, Lurie's first published novel, is the story of Emily Stockwell Turner from the day she realizes she no longer loves her husband until the day she realizes she is going to stay with him anyway.[19] In the days between, thanks to a passionate affair with a handsome, feckless member of the music department of Convers College, Lurie's fictionalized version of Cornell, Emily's sexuality is awakened. Lurie's plot can be read as a feminized version of the Snow White theme: the princess is awakened, but there will be no passive happily-ever-after ending. Will Thomas *seems* to love Emily, but will not promise her eternity. His refusal is in pointed contrast to her husband's claim that he'll *always* love her: " 'Always?' Emmy asks, in a tone of assumed flippancy. 'How can you promise that? What about when I'm old, and fat, and ugly?' 'What difference does that make?' " is his reply (306). So Emmy unpacks and crawls back into the mould. Emmy's reversal, after her year-long affair and initial desire to run off with her lover, shows that she has gained a better recognition of her own needs. Someday your prince *might* come, but you may well be better off enjoying him for a time and letting him go. For this sheltered, childish, wealthy, young matron, it is not a bad lesson to learn.

In *The Nowhere City*, the long-suffering Katherine Cattleman follows her husband from Cambridge to California, from Harvard to Nutting Research and Development Corporation.[20] She hates everything about California: the bright colors, the heat, the Disneyesque architecture, even the flowers, which she finds oversized and garish. Her sinus attacks increase. Meanwhile Paul, her husband, loves everything about California and immediately starts an affair with a pretty young "hippy." Although he

has been married only three years to a woman he claims to love, he has
already had several affairs. Katherine does not want to know about any of
them. She never appears very interested in sex anyway. But after she suffers
righteously for three quarters of the novel, one of the three psychiatrists she
works for at UCLA forces his attentions on her and she reverses her positions on sex and on California. By then Paul's affair has soured, and, after
he completes a successful interview for a job back East (at
Convers/Cornell), he can hardly wait to return and tell Katherine the good
news. He rushes in to the party where they are to meet but cannot locate his
wife. Katherine is there, in fact, but the "pretty girl in tight yellow pants,
with a smooth California tan and ash-blond hair piled up on her head like a
mound of whip cream" is so different from his outdated image of his wife
that he needs help locating her (332–3). He is too late. Katherine has
decided to stay in California. Not, it is important to add, to be with her lover.
That would be the traditional Snow White theme. But this party is a celebration of her lover's reunion with his wife. Katherine's lover has served
only as the means, not the fairy tale end: he has awakened her to some of
life's possibilities and she now chooses to stay in California to experience
more of them. This is the feminist Snow White theme with a vengeance.

  Real People presents yet another version of a feminist Snow White
theme. The heroine, Janet Belle Smith, already has a professional writing
career as well as a husband and family when the novel begins.[21] The novel
is set at an artists' retreat where the over-refined Janet has a brief affair with
a coarse, earthy sculptor. This jars her into some honest admissions about
her fastidious evasions in both her life and her novels. Admitting that "you
can't write well with only the nice parts of your character, and only about
nice things," Janet realizes that she had been expanding the "nice girl"
stereotype usually associated with wives and mothers to encompass her professional writing career (157). Since her behavior at the writers' retreat was
distinctly not that of a nice girl, she is forced to admit that she has been
diluting the truth in her life as well as her fiction. The book's conclusion
promises a dramatic change in Janet's writing style—the literary Snow
White awakens.

  The War Between the Tates is probably the sharpest example of Lurie's
urge to extricate the wife from her smugness but not her marriage.[22] As
Rogers notes, the ending is "ruthlessly realistic" (121). Brian Tate is the college professor, and Erica is his competent intelligent wife, mother of his
adolescent children. Parts of the plot can be anticipated: his affair with a
student and the young girl's pregnancy. But Erica's self-righteous insistence that her husband go live with this young mistress is an interesting
twist. In the end, the pregnant student runs off with a newer and younger
lover and the Tates are left to patch things up as best they can. Erica is left

with her husband minus her illusions. The ending of this novel reminds me of a conversation in a group therapy session in Ephron's *Heartburn*. Rachel has just told the group that her husband is in love with someone else:

> "Anyway, it's not over," said Eve. "He'll be back."
> "And then what?" I said. "It's like a beautiful thing that suddenly turns out to be broken into hundreds of pieces, and even when you glue it back together it's always going to have been horribly broken."
> "That's what a marriage is," said Sidney. "Pieces break off, and you glue them back on."[23]

At this point in *Heartburn*, Ephron changes the subject with a joke. But Lurie leaves Erica in her patched-up marriage. It is clear that Erica has learned humility but less clear how this will bring her happiness.

That a realistic assessment of yourself and your mate can lead to awareness and even control but not necessarily to happiness is also suggested in *Only Children*.[24] In this novel we are presented with contrasting types of women: Honey is the "Southern Belle," feminine, flirtatious, and silly, while Celia is the long-suffering wife, enduring the pain of watching her husband flirt with Honey. Against both these married women, Lurie contrasts Anne, the head of their children's school and owner of the farm where they all spend the weekend. Anne seems bright, competent, and sensible: in short, in control of herself and her fortunes. But her independence came with a price: she, too, it turns out, had once been in love with the man who is now Celia's husband. Her refusal to build her life around his caused them to break up. The memory of that distant time can still pain them both.

Breaking patterns, growing in self-awareness, edging up on control—possibly Lurie doesn't see this as necessarily leading to happiness. Her view of life is satiric, rather than celebratory. Anne is admirable but lonely. Nor is Erica the only Lurie heroine forced to "make do." Emily Turner was in that position before her. And although Vinnie Miner, the fifty-four year-old professor and heroine of *Foreign Affairs*, realizes she has finally loved and been loved in earnest, the realization comes after her lover's death. There are indications that she has become a kinder person on account of the experience, but not necessarily a happier one.

PERSPECTIVE AS CONTROL:
LURIE'S SATIRIC VIEW OF LIFE

While interviewing Lurie in 1983, Dorothy Mermin observed that many people see Jane Austen as a major influence in Lurie's writing. Lurie agreed to the influence, but trivialized the reason so many people make the association: "People make the connection because of the title of my first book [*Love and Friendship*], which was the same as the title of one of her juvenalia."[25] But Lurie probably has too flattering an opinion of the general public's knowledge of Austen's juvenalia. The more obvious connection is that Austen and Lurie both write domestic comedy: Austen concentrates on a small ingrown community remote from the distractions of eighteenth-century London, while Lurie sets many of her novels in a small, upstate, ingrown, academic community far from the distractions of New York City. Both then beam their satiric attention on the behavior of the sexes as they maneuver around each other in those isolated communities.

There are important differences between Austen and Lurie. Austen is generally kinder to her female characters. Granted, Austen can portray unredeemed silliness, as she does with Elizabeth Bennet's mother, or unredeemed lack of judgement, as she does with Elizabeth's younger sister Lydia. But in *Pride and Prejudice*, the main character, Elizabeth, as well as her older sister, Jane, are pictured as sensible, intelligent, admirable, and moral human beings who only have to overcome certain minor flaws before happiness (in the form of a loving male counterpart, who has only to overcome *his* minor flaws) can be rightfully theirs.

In a Lurie novel, the heroine's character is not so positively delineated, nor is her future so positively assured. Emily Stockwell Turner (*Love and Friendship*) is pictured as a wealthy, spoiled young matron who feels dissatisfied and lonely. She has always loved food and now she learns to love sex—for a while at least. There is nothing for us to admire, other than beauty and wealth, unless it is her awakened sensuality. Though we do not admire her behavior, we undoubtedly recognize it: she does what is most expedient. That it may also be the morally correct action is coincidental. Erica Tate (*The War Between the Tates*) cannot be accused of being frivolous, as can Emily, but there is not much to admire here either. In befriending her husband's impregnated girlfriend, she considers herself morally correct and sensible when she is merely self-righteous and masochistic. What these two heroines do learn is to modify their former flattering images, both of themselves and their husbands. They learn humility rather than happiness, and ultimately choose safety over risk. It is not clear what their futures will be like.

Lurie's world view is darker than Austen's. Satire, the use of ridicule or sarcasm to expose a character's folly, is the form her wit usually takes, especially in her early fiction. Lurie's satire is aimed at both sexes, mocking the behavior of all her characters and laughing at the accommodations they choose to make. This is why Walter Clemons was surprised to find himself touched by *Foreign Affairs*, since he felt Lurie had "not been famous for mercy." In fact, Clemons said what he liked about *The War Between the Tates* was its fury, and observed that the novel had prompted Gore Vidal to describe Lurie as "the Queen Herod of modern fiction."[26] Lurie's lack of sympathy towards her characters in the six novels between 1962 and 1986 has been toned down in her last two novels, *Foreign Affairs* (1984) and *The Truth about Lorin Jones* (1988)—but only to an extent. Vinnie Miner appears to become a more generous-spirited person for realizing she had fallen in love with her uneducated rustic, but it is questionable whether she would have reached this realization had he lived. And Polly Alter seems appealingly flexible when she changes her version of what happened to Lorin Jones, the artist whose biography she is writing (*The Truth about Lorin Jones*). But since it is definitely in Polly's own best interest to accept Lorin Jone's young lover's version of what happened, since he has now become Polly Alter's middle-aged lover, Lurie's tone is not very far removed from the bitingly cynical and satiric one of her earlier novels. The world Lurie writes about is a resilient and amusing one, but, with the exception of Vinnie Minor's belated efforts to live up to her lover's high opinion of her, it is not a particularly optimistic one. Lurie mocks all of her characters for their expedient accommodations, rather than create and reward heroes and heroines who are able to make morally correct choices, as does Austen.

CONTROLLING THE TRUTH

Lurie seemed to be aware of the relativity of truth at an extremely early age. She had bragged of her ability as an adolescent to impress her version of the truth by setting it down on paper. When she claimed writing to be a kind of witch's spell, she meant that writing something down convinced others, even if the writer knew it was only one version of the truth.

In a 1985 interview, Lurie observed that how people perceive the world is one of our central problems:

> Isn't that what all fiction is about in a way, the difference between views of the world, the conflict in people who see the world in completely different ways and see themselves differently?[27]

It is obvious that the relativity of truth still intrigued her in 1988, when she wrote *The Truth About Lorin Jones*.[28] Conflicting perceptions is certainly what that novel is about, so that the title is highly ironic. The "truth" about Lorin Jones, the dead artist, is precisely what her biographer, Polly Alter, will never be able to know.

Lurie is well aware that as soon as you have two people, you have two different versions of reality. In the brief interview by Sarah Ferrell, which accompanied Edmund White's review of *Lorin Jones*, Lurie again refers to her 1955 memoir of V.R. Lang to help make her point:

> I once wrote a memoir of a friend who died young. . . . But a memoir is different from a biography, because it is a view of someone from a single perspective. One of the difficulties of writing a biography is that you must interview many people. You discover that they all saw your subject differently. This happens to the heroine of my novel. . . . Also, the people who were closest to Lorin Jones want, very naturally, to appear as heroes rather than villains.[29]

Polly Alter is forced to see that her original intention of presenting Lorin Jones as a victim of patriarchal abuse can only be realized if she omits a lot of contradictory testimony. But Lurie allows her heroine no more than a few seconds of detached perception. Polly begins with one agenda and ends with another, since she falls in love with the man who had supposedly exploited and abandoned Lorin. But it is possible that even a few seconds of detached perception is more than many of us ever have, and that this, too, is Lurie's point: what we see as true is all too often what is in our best interest. Lurie's satiric view of the world runs deep.

SUBVERTING REDUCTIVE LABELS:

Feminism:

Lurie considers herself a feminist, but does not feel compelled to support every cause labeled feminist. Feminist co-eds were treated briefly but sarcastically in *The War Between the Tates* and lesbian feminists given a harsher and more extensive exposure in *The Truth About Lorin Jones*. What Lurie is concerned about is not lesbianism but rather the tendency of certain feminists, particularly lesbian feminists, to isolate themselves from the rest of society. She told Mickey Pearlman in a 1990 interview that she expected some hostile reviews for the treatment she gave Jeanne, the lesbian friend of Polly's who wanted to isolate Polly from all males, including her own son. People don't realize there can be different kinds of feminists, Lurie explained. Lurie is the kind who doesn't agree with separatism:

> I guess what I'm saying is that I'm upset by the *results* of separatism. I'm not sure that women are strong enough yet to profit by withdrawing from the male world. I think we're more apt to just be crowded into a corner. For example, in the academy, a women's stud-

ies department will set up a course in "Women Writers," and the result
will be that only *women* will take the course. The men who teach modern or early twentieth-century fiction will say, "Oh, now we don't have
to include Virginia Woolf or Edith Wharton" and they'll cut these
writers out of their courses, and male students will never hear of them.
We'll be back to where we were fifty years ago. Separatism can be
very divisive.[30]

Lurie knew that her position would cause a problem: "It's always risky to
point out the flaws in any group that's beleaguered," she told Pearlman (10).
But Lurie seems to have gone from a young woman who grew afraid to
keep writing and risking rejections to a well-published woman who does
not evade a touchy issue. Feminism is only one of them.

A WOMAN'S WRITING STYLE

A second issue is whether all women writers use a sentimental and intu-
itive style of writing. Lurie, interviewed by Dorothy Mermin, was trying to
describe her own style. Her words must be read carefully, for she is not
denying that she works in a female tradition. Mermin asked her if she had
been influenced by Elizabeth Bowen and Elizabeth Taylor. Lurie replied:

> I like them, but I wanted to move away from that sort of dreamy, sub-
> jective type of writing. It's not what I do best. . . . It's not the way my
> mind naturally works, although I've tried to imitate that way of think-
> ing in certain books because I know it's the way that a lot of people's
> minds works, women and men both; but I don't do it naturally. I don't
> think that way naturally.[31]

Dorothy Mermin fell into the deduction many would make: "So you don't
think of yourself as working in a female line, a female tradition?" It is
extremely lucky that she did, for it allowed Lurie to make her point more
clearly:

> Yes, I certainly do. I think it's a mistake to believe there's only one
> female line which is intensely personal, subjective, intuitive, emo-
> tional. That's not the only female line. There's also a line in Fanny
> Burney and Jane Austen that's just as true as the other. I think it's a
> mistake for women writers to feel that they've got to be subjective and
> dreamy and intuitive all the time.—There are some women whose
> minds honestly work that way. I've known them. And there are some
> men whose minds honestly work that way too. . . . On the other hand,
> there have been forces trying to push women into feeling that they're
> all like this and they should be like this. Even someone like Virginia

> Woolf was able to do both voices: she wasn't just subjective. If you
> read her essays, she's very much in the other tradition. (83–4)

Lurie rejects the reductive attitude that women write in one style only—an
attitude that undoubtedly stems from the idea that a woman's intellectual
capacity is different from (lesser than) a man's. Nancy Walker reviews the
"separate sphere" argument that crystalized in the nineteenth century:
"Logic, reason, and analytical thought became the province of man,
whereas to women were ascribed the qualities of intuition, feeling, and
morality."[32] That this is an artificially-imposed division is easily demonstrated by the fact that many women write in what has not been considered
the "typical" women's style—among them, as Lurie notes, herself, Burney,
Austen and Woolf.

PROFESSOR

When Alison Lurie received a Pulitzer Prize for *Foreign Affairs*, her
achievements were outlined in *The Washington Post*. Since Lurie is a
Professor of English Literature as well as a writer, the article included this
commentary on her teaching:

> Among Cornell students, Lurie's courses have been popular. She
> refuses to respond to anyone who addresses her as "Professor Lurie"
> and serves tea and cookies during her three-hour afternoon seminars.[33]

Lurie's classroom technique should not be dismissed as traditional maternal
nurturing behavior. Had Lurie's role been that of a full-time grandmother or
hostess, then using her first name and serving the tea and cookies might fit
a stereotype. But this is Alison Lurie the Professor, a professor who learned
as a young wife that you cannot control anything at all until you first break
out of expected patterns that control your behavior. While interviewing
Lurie, Dorothy Merwin observed that the women in her novels seemed

> to start off imagining themselves in terms defined socially by men and
> discover in the course of the book how inadequate those definitions
> are. (87)

And Lurie gave a telling and shrewd response: "I think that's true of all of
us" (87). It is no coincidence that all of Lurie's writings have either broken
patterns or questioned roles. Her wit has led her to examine both social and
scholarly restrictions—restrictions she has taken steps to overcome in her
life as well as her writing.

NOTES

1. Alison Lurie, "No One Asked Me to Write a Novel," *New York Times Book Review* 6 June, 1982: 13 & 46–48.
2. Dorothy Mermin, "Alison Lurie," *Women Writers Talking*, ed. Janet Todd (NY: Holmes & Meier, 1983) 81–95.
3. Carolyn Heilbrun, *Writing a Woman's Life*, (NY: Ballentine, 1988) 48.
4. Nora Ephron, "A Few Words Abour Breasts," *Crazy Salad Plus Nine* (NY: Pocket Books, 1984) 21.
5. Nora Ephron, "On Never Having Been a Prom Queen," *Crazy Salad Plus Nine*, 38.
6. Judy Oppenheimer, *Private Demons: The Life of Shirley Jackson* (NY: Putnam, 1988) 26.
7. For a related argument on how a sense of humor compensates for a lack of beauty, see Barreca, *They Used to Call Me Snow White . . . But I Drifted* (NY: Viking, 1991) 28–29.
8. Alison Lurie, "No One Asked Me To Write A Novel" 13.
9. Heilbrun 52.
10. Barreca, *They Used to Call me Snow White* 98.
11. Alison Lurie, *The Language of Clothes* (NY: Random House, 1981); *Don't Tell the Grown-Ups* (NY:Avon, 1990).
12. P.L. Travers, *Mary Poppins Comes Back* qtd in Lurie, *Don't Tell the Grown-Ups* 10.
13. Anne Tyler, "The Glass of Fashion," rev. of *The Language of Clothes* by Alison Lurie, *The New Republic* 23 Dec 1981: 32.
14. Mermin 84.
15. *Clever Gretched and Other Forgotten Folktales* retold by Alison Lurie, illustrated by Margot Tomes (NY: Cromwell, 1980).
16. Christopher Lehmann-Haupt, rev. of *Foreign Affairs* by Alison Lurie, *New York Times* 13 Sept 1984: C21.
17. Elizabeth Gaskell, *The Life of Charlotte Brontë* (1857; NY: Putnam, 1985) 308.
18. Alison Lurie, *Love and Friendship* (New York: Macmillan, 1962).
19. Alison Lurie, *The Nowhere City* (1965; NY: Avon, 1967).
20. Alison Lurie, *Real People* (NY: Avon. 1969).
21. Alison Lurie, *The War Between the Tates* (NY: Avon, 1974).
22. Nora Ephron, *Heartburn* 72.
23. Alison Lurie, *Only Children* (London: Heinemann, 1979).
24. Mermin 83.
25. Walter Clemons, "Lovers and Other Strangers," rev. of *Foreign Affairs* by Alison Lurie 24 Sept. 1984: 80.
26. Martha Satz, "A Kind of Detachment: An Interview With Alison Lurie," *South West Review* 71 (1986): 197.
27. Alison Lurie, *The Truth About Lorin Jones* (Boston: Little Brown, 1988).
28. Sarah Ferrell, "Research for a Love Affair," *The New York Times Book Review* 4 Sept. 1988: 3.

29. Mickey Pearlman, "Alison Lurie" in *Inter/View: Talks with America's Writing Women*, eds. Mickey Pearlman and Katherine Henderson (Lexington: Univ. of Kentucky Press, 1990) 10.
30. Mermin 83.
31. Walker 80.
32. James McGrath Morris, "Pulitzer Winner Alison Lurie: Still 'Driven to Writing,' " *The Washington Post* 25 April 1985: B12.

6

Grace Paley: The Ear is Smarter than the Eye

Grace Paley's wit is the most distinctive and arresting feature of her writing. It is found in her world view, her characters' voices, her choice of words, and even her accent, which she suggests by her language and syntax: "If you have a humorous view of the world, you have it and there's no way to fight it," Paley explains, "you can't write a story without something of that in it, there's just no way."[1] Asked whether she wrote her stories or talked them out loud, Paley said she did both: ". . . I do write out loud and I do feel very much that when I'm doing something wrong I hear it. I think the ear is smarter than the eye."[2] Every sentence Paley writes is filtered through, and quite purposefully flavored by, her own distinctive Yiddish/Russian New York ear. She feels that "you can't be truthful unless you're true to your tongue," and has said more than once that standardizing the tongues of immigrant speech would only deaden the English language.[3]

CONTROLLING LANGUAGE:
REVITALIZING CLICHÉS

Paley's "smart ear" can take the credit for the clever way her characters revitalize clichés. Consider this exchange between the mother and daughter in "A Woman, Young and Old." The sex-conscious, man-starved mother is wistfully reminded of her younger self when she looks at Lizzy, her attractive younger sister:

> "Look at Lizzy and you see the girl your father saw. Just like me.
> Wonderful carriage. Marvelous muscle tone. She could have any man
> she wanted."
> "She's already had some she wanted." (*DM* 27)[4]

The answer comes from her sassy fourteen-year-old daughter. By responding to the cliché as if it were the literal truth, and repeating its words in her ingenuous retort, the daughter has inadvertently freshened the cliché while deflating her mother's intended praise.

Or consider Faith's words when narrating "A Subject of Childhood." Faith is finally fed up with her boyfriend, Clifford, after he criticizes the way she is raising her two sons. Clifford gets angry when one of the boys bites him in the ankle. First he interrupted their solitary and peaceful amusements, insisting they punch and wrestle with him—his idea of play—and only then does he get hurt. He blames Faith—the boys are too tense, he claims. She has done a "rotten job" of raising them, "lousy," "stinking." Faith realizes she has reached the breaking point and revives an old cliché to voice her indignation over his daring to criticize the way she has managed to bring them up on her own: "For I have raised these kids, with one hand typing behind my back to earn a living" (*DM* 139). Faith only had to change "tied" to "typing" to refurbish the worn cliché.

Paley realized she had been refreshing clichés after the fact: "I never even thought of describing it until a couple of years ago when people asked me" she said in a 1981 interview, responding to Noelle Bott's observation that "You certainly use this freedom [to go ahead and write what and how you want] when you play with clichés and renew the language." Paley's hindsight description of what she had been doing captures both her technique and her distinctive playful/serious voice:

> You have to tell the truth. It's a hard business and to tell the truth
> you have the words of your own time, but sometimes, they don't work
> just quite right for you, partly because they become too old and too
> used up. The language has been used up a little bit, the sentences have
> been used up a little bit so that, sometimes, only to tell the truth, not to
> show off or to stand on your head, you really need to think of another
> way of saying things for your own time. Clichés are usually the result
> of a couple of generations refining a description and most of them are
> wonderful because they are so accurate. But, on the other hand, certain
> clichés and proverbs are so overused that, as accurate as they are, you
> don't really hear them because you have heard them so many times
> that they are like a string of old words that you can fling around with-

out their meaning anything. So the thing is to keep that, but to move it
off an inch or two inches, or two words, to move the whole business
aside a little bit so that you have almost that same old, old sentence but
you have shifted it, and in that way, attention is called to the truth
inside of it in a way that you wouldn't pay attention to otherwise.[5]

Paley's trick of keeping the cliché but moving it off by a word or two is
done both subtly and playfully. Faith, Paley's spokeswoman in many of her
stories, is again narrating in "Faith in a Tree." She is sitting in a tree in a
park when a man passing beneath looks up and recognizes her:

That is Alex O Steele, who was a man organizing tenant strikes on
Ocean Parkway when I was a Coney Island Girl Scout against my
mother's socialist will. (*EC* 81)

Inserting "socialist" immediately revitalizes the old phrase, while the added
irony of applying so ordinary a phrase ("against my mother's will") to so
unique a situation makes it even funnier. Most mothers and daughters clash
wills. But in America, only someone with Paley's radical political background would imagine they clash because the socialist-oriented mother
objects to her daughter joining the capitalist-oriented Girl Scouts.

At the beginning of the same story, Faith is describing a park, waxing
religious over the ethnic mixture of the people inside:

What a place in democratic time! . . . He can look down from His
Holy Headquarters and see us all: heads of girl, ponytails riding the
springtime luck, short black bobs, and an occasional eminence of
golden wedding rings. (*EC* 77)

Substituting "His Holy Headquarters" for the anticipated "on high" or
"heaven above" collapses any sense of sanctimonious piety. Faith can still
celebrate this ethnic Eden and escape being counted among the pompous.

Paley also renews clichés by expanding them, by pushing the stale image
imbedded in the cliché further than it had ever been intended to go.
Consider Faith's father's words in "Dreamer in a Dead Language:"

It's true. . . . Trotsky pointed out, the biggest surprise that comes
to a man is old age. . . . Years ago I didn't have the right appreciation
of him. Thrown out the front door of history, sneaks in the window to
sit in the livingroom, excuse me, I mean I do not feel old. DO NOT.
(*LD* 29, 1st ellipsis Paley's)

"Thrown out the front door of history" signals that what follows is a new
expanded version. Although it may not be stale enough to qualify as a bona-
fide cliché, it feels just familiar enough to make "sneaks in the window to
sit in the livingroom" hilarious.

Another good example of expanding a cliché to refresh the original image is from "Goodby and Goodluck." Aunt Rose is telling her life's story to her niece, going back over the accommodations she made with men: "Well, by now you must know yourself, honey, whatever you do, life don't stop. It only sits a minute and dreams a dream (*DM* 16). Pushing the image a bit too far, spelling out what life does when it doesn't stop, makes us pay attention to both the truth and the wit of the cliché.

CONTROLLING CONTEXT

Disparity as a Source of Wit:

When asked to speak about wit, asked if she felt that humor was a strategy of resistance to a dominant class or language, Paley responded that

> Humor is about disparity; a matter of the very tall and of the very small . . . If you see a very very tall man and a very very small woman walking along, you smile. But if you see a very very tall woman and a very very small man, you laugh. So both things are humorous, but one is more humorous than the other. That's just a very basic thing. I don't mean it's a big joke. But that's the most basic kind of thing that you can have smiled at. Disparity. And maybe for Jews or people in oppression, it's the disparity between power and suffering, but that's the way it works and I don't think in our case [Paley's and her father's], in my case, it was because of the oppression of language. I think that the English language welcomed me.[6]

Disparity is a key word for understanding Paley's wit. In fact, the disparity between the ordinary concerns of everyday life and life's fullest possible historical significance is the richest and most profound source of wit in her writing. Paley takes daily life and both juxtaposes it against and translates it into its larger historical picture. The wit lies in the disparity of the juxtaposition, while the (often tragic) significance comes from her ability to see the whole picture, to translate each little life into its most meaningful possible participation in the flow of history.

For example, in "Faith in the Afternoon," Faith's mother goes along with Mrs. Hegel-Shtein's project of knitting wool socks. The narrator suggests that this is a fabricated project designed to fill in the empty hours and concerns of the ageing knitters rather than meet the needs of the youthful recipients: ". . . because children today wear cotton socks all winter. The grandmothers who lose heat at their extremities at a terrible clip are naturally more sensitive to these facts. . . ." (*EC* 37). Mrs. Hegel-Shtein is mockingly referred to as the "president of the Grandmothers' Wool Socks

Association" and Faith's mother as the vice-president of this two-woman association (*EC* 37). The section describing these two old Jewish ladies working away needlessly in a retirement home in New York City ends: "They worked. They took vital facts from one another and looked as dedicated as a kibbutz (*EC* 38). The disparity between the fabricated chore in the comfortable room at the Children of Judea Retirement Home and the vital work on a kibbutz is what makes us smile. And yet these women are connected to the members of a kibbutz, both by their religion and their industriousness. Paley is both juxtaposing them against and translating them into one of the most significant events for the Jewish people in their time—the establishment of Israel as the Jewish nation.

The opening sentence of "Faith in a Tree" offers disparity as the starting point of the story:

> Just when I most needed important conversation, a sniff of the man-wide world, that is, at least one brainy companion who could translate my friendly language into his tongue of undying carnal love, I was forced to lounge in our neighborhood park, surrounded by children. (*EC* 77)

It is the narrator, Faith again, who is conscious of the disparity between runny noses and high passion, although it is possibly only Paley who is conscious of the further disparity between "important conversation" and "carnal love." The wit lies in the distance from the playground reality to the bedroom fantasy as well as in the magnificent language expressing that fantasy—language that suggests the impossibility of its realization by longing for a love *both* carnal and undying.

Disparity also operates as a strategy of wit on a simple language level. Paley's father, though an atheist, loved the Old Testament. There were always Bible stories in the home which Paley loved to read out loud when she was growing up.[7] Echoes of them, from both the Old and New Testament, find their way into her fiction at unexpected moments. Disparity explains what is funny about these biblical echoes: the clash between the ornate words and the common situation for which they are invoked. Yet the ornate phrase momentarily invests the common situation with an unexpected dignity.

"An Irrevocable Diameter" is told by Charles C. Charley, a man who sells and installs air conditioners: "People who have tried to live by cross ventilation alone have thanked me" (*DM* 105). It is not that what he is saying is not true, it is just that it is rarely expressed with such biblical, significant-sounding language. Charles is echoing Luke 4.4, "Man liveth not by bread alone," to describe the comfort of an air conditioner.

In "A Subject of Childhood," after Faith finally throws Clifford out, she wonders, as have so many women before and after her, why she had put up with such a man for so long. But since she is a Paley character, the language she wonders in is enriched by her creator's turn of phrase: "What is man that woman lies down to adore him?" asks Faith, echoing Psalm 8.5, "What is man, that Thou art mindful of him?" (*DM* 143).

When Virginia in "An Interest in Life" complains about a long rainy day confined to her apartment with her four young children, her complaint is witty because of her allusion to Cain and Abel: "after a rainy afternoon with brother constantly raising up his hand against brother" (*DM* 97). This is highly inappropriate language for a young non-religious, high-school educated mother. All Paley's characters talk from their own perspective but with Paley's own witty, intelligent, Yiddish/Russian-flavored tongue.

One of the most striking biblical echoes is not an echo of a phrase at all, but rather a fleeting allusion to the patriarchal myth of creation. In "Faith in a Tree," Faith is speaking of the one God who looks down over the racial mix in the park, and turns to describing herself: "But me, the creation of His soft second thought" (*EC* 78). This is vintage Paley: the subservience, the delicate mockery of soft femininity, the will of God—all the old male myths—captured in one brief appositional phrase.

CONTROLLING CONTEXT

Fighting the Arbitrary Control of a Plot

Paley told Joan Lidoff that she had probably invited misunderstanding ("screwed myself up" were her actual words) when she wrote "A Conversation With My Father," where her aging father asks her to write a simple story. She was only trying to explain what she disliked in the traditional time-bound plot, with a beginning, middle, and end, she explained to Lidoff, not denying the existence of *any* plot in her stories. But as soon as her critics read that imagined conversation they felt justified in criticizing her stories for lacking plot. They claim that nothing ever happens in them. But, Paley protested to Lidoff, a lot happens in her stories.[8] It is true that in "A Conversation With My Father" the narrator is herself, not Faith, and that she is imagining a conversation she could have had with her father, given her beliefs and his.[9] But what she imagines herself saying is that she had always despised "the absolute line between two points" in a *traditional* plot:

> Not for literary reasons, but because it takes all hope away. Everyone, real or invented, deserves the open destiny of life. (*EC* 162)

As Blanche Gelfant, a Paley admirer, accurately observed, "belief in the possibilities of change clashes with the literary convention of closure."[10] Yet many adventures can occur without closure.[11] It is only, as Paley explains to Lidoff, that her plot doesn't have to move "dead ahead in time." Her story "can curl around on itself, it can just fall down and slip through one of the spirals and go back again.[12] Gelfant shrewdly sees a connection between Paley's treatment of time, her jokes, and her optimism:

> Paley's joking seems a way of searching within life's inevitabilities for a loophole—some surprise opening in the concatenation of events that seem to serious and acquiescent observers inexorably linked. Refusing to follow the absolute straight line of causality, which she sees as the tyranny of plot, Paley traces loops and twists and unexpected turnings that circumvent doom. These curlicues seem comic, jokes that Paley plays on life; and whenever her twistings of plot pivot around death, as in "Samuel," "A little Girl," and "Friends," they allow the story a last laugh, for its final turn will openly defy death by invoking art.[13]

CONTROLLING CONTEXT:

The Wit to See When Beliefs Are Beyond Control

Paley is aware that her father's point of view, which she contrasts with her own open-ended optimism in "Conversation with my Father," is affected by his place in history: "He came from a world where there was no choice, where you couldn't really decide to change careers when you were forty-one years old."[14] Therefore, his belief in a traditional plot makes sense. He was a penniless immigrant who worked hard to move from point A to point B, and wanted his literature to reflect that movement. In short, he wanted a traditional plot. But his youngest daughter was born into a different world.

Paley explains that the time into which you are born is as crucial as the place in forming your attitudes and beliefs:

> ...people in my family who became grownups (which is my sister and my brother) during the Depression, they really have a much narrower view of what can happen, of what you can be and what you can't be and what you can do. I mean they have a very strong sense that you'd better do your homework and you'd better stay with it and you'd better move, you know. And that once you've got it, you stay there.[15]

Since Paley grew up fourteen years later, she connects her optimism and belief in new possibilities to the situation in America in the 1940s:

> . . . I think that growing up into the Second World War was a much more—it sounds crazy to say this—but it really was a more open time. Not for the Europeans, it was pretty bad for them. But for America,

for the people here, who were not fighting, it was a very exciting,
wide-open period. . . . The Depression ended; people began to make a
little money who hadn't made any. People began to go to work;. . . .
So I think some of my feelings really come from my particular time
and my particular place.[16]

One of Paley's stories that most explicitly juxtaposes the individual life
against that life's place in history is "Mom." This story appeared in the
December issue of *Esquire* in 1975. Since it has not been reprinted and
since the juxtaposition appears quite vividly at the outset, I have reproduced
most of the opening section, which comprises about one fifth of this very
short story. The translation of the woman from her apartment window into
history's window is nearly palpable:

Mom

The mother is at the open window. She calls the child home. She's a
fat lady. She leans forward, supporting herself on her elbows. Her
breasts are shoved up under her chin. Her arms are broad and heavy. I
am not the child. She isn't my mother. Still, in my head where remembering is organized for significance (not usefulness), she leans far out.
She looks up and down the block. . . . I play in the street, she stands in
the window. I wanted her to call me home to the dark mysterious apartment behind her back, where the father was already eating and the others sat at the kitchen table and waited for the child.

She was destined, with her meaty bossiness, her sighs, her suffering,
to be dumped into the villain room of social meaning and psychological
causation. When this happened to her she had just touched the first rung
of the great American immigrant ladder. Her husband was ahead of her,
her intentional bulk kept him from slipping. Their children were a couple of rungs above them. She believed she would follow them up into
the English language, education and respect.

Unfortunately, science and literature had turned against her. What
use was my accumulating affection when the brains of the opposition
included her son the doctor and her son the novelist? Because of them,
she never even had a chance at the crown of apple pie awarded her
American-born sisters and accepted by them when they agreed to give
up their powerful pioneer dispositions.

What is wrong with the world? the growing person might have asked.
The year was 1932 or perhaps 1942. Despite the worldwide fame of those
years, the chief investigator into human pain is looking into his own book
of awful prognoses. He looks up. Your mother, probably, he says.

As for me, I was not paying attention. I missed the mocking
campaign. (85)

Paley's language and presentation make the passage witty without subvert-
ing the potential for tragedy in the content. Placing the individual up
against history can show how well the person stacks up, but it can also

show how history has stacked the cards against the individual, as it does in this story. In this opening section, "Mom" is not a character but rather a generic mother of a particular time and place—she is any large-breasted family-oriented immigrant mother who landed in a New York tenement in the first half of this century. Later in the story, Paley will focus on her own mother (and her "aunt-mothers" and "sister-mother"), but here it is the historical situation that is more in focus. From her 1975 vantage point, Paley can see that these mothers never had a chance. The mothering role, the only one they knew, made them the target of blame and the butt of jokes. Mother love became smother love. Freud led the scientific "mocking campaign," but the practice of blaming Mom was hardly confined to Freudian psychology. Philip Wylie's influential sociological diatribe *Generation of Vipers* (1942) painted Mom as a castrating dominating tigress, and made the term "Momism," a term he had coined, a household complaint. The literary campaign lasted well into the sixties, with *Portnoy's Complaint* (Philip Roth, 1969) and *One Flew Over the Cuckoo's Nest* (Ken Kesey, 1962). Paley knows that all of us are caught up in our own particular time and place and feels the best we can do is to try to acknowledge our limitations, humorously if possible. We cannot all count on "not paying attention" to the potentially harmful ideas of our day.

WIT & POLITICS:

Paley's Family Background

Admirers of Grace Paley's fiction know she is also a political activist, one who protests, marches and is willing to be arrested for demonstrating on behalf of world peace and unilateral disarmament. With her usual modesty and everpresent sense of history, Paley traces both her writing career and her politics to her Russian Jewish immigrant family: "I was privileged to be the child of people who had been poor working people who had this love and respect for language and who carried on an old socialist tradition from Europe."[17] Her parents had immigrated to America in 1904, fleeing Czarist Russia. Paley was born in 1922, into a different world. In 1986, she was listing *her* politics as "Anarchist, if that's politics."[18] But she never had to consider her politics as a youthful idealistic revolt from parental values as did so many young Americans later in the century. Both her parents and her uncles had brought their socialist beliefs to the New World, and held onto them in their Bronx apartments. Paley told Gelfant that she was "brought up with a lot of their particular kind of idealism" and "just kind of inhaled their early lives."[19]

The fact that Paley embraced her parent's political beliefs should not mislead anyone into concluding that she was a docile adolescent who gave her parents an easy time. She told Ruth Perry that she remembered an incident in high school, or possibly junior high, when all the kids were protesting for a cause she could no longer recall ("we were wearing peace, something, armbands") and the principal told them that as long as they wore the bands they could not go to class. Slowly, the kids began to take them off. Not Paley:

> I knew that I would never, never, never take off that armband. It really was romantic you know. And I remember my cousin came down the aisle of the auditorium of the school and said, "Gracie, you better come up, you better come up because you know your mother's sick, you know you're making her sicker. You're going to kill her, you know that?"[20]

The irony of Paley's early political beliefs is that, while they had, in fact, developed from her parents' beliefs, they were so reprocessed through her youthful impatient idealism that she antagonized her parents with them. Her high school politics, Paley shrewdly observed, really came from the *romanticism* she felt about her parents, rather than from their actual lives: "I felt they were heroic, and I loved that stuff a lot. Of course by that time, they were very angry with me."[21]

When Paley was only thirteen, her mother developed cancer. She died seven years later, when Paley was twenty. So her cousin's words in the school auditorium were not empty rhetoric. Paley heightened her mother's anxieties by running around with boys in high school. Her mother worried that she would get pregnant: "She really knew she wouldn't live and she just couldn't bear the direction I was obviously going in" (towards "Badness. Trouble.").[22] As an adult, Paley wrote a brief but moving story of her mother dealing with her younger seventeen-year-old self:

> At the door of the kitchen she said, You never finish your lunch. You run around senselessly. What will become of you?
> Then she died.
> Naturally, for the rest of my life I longed to see her, not only in doorways, in a great number of places—in the dining room with my aunts, at the window looking up and down the block, in the country garden among the zinnias and marigolds, in the living room with my father. ("Mother," *LD* 112)

Meanwhile, the young Paley did not curb her experiments in living for the sake of her mother's peace of mind. She started at Hunter College when she was only sixteen, but disappointed both her parents by dropping out after a year:

I would go to school, but I could never get up to the classroom. I could sometimes get to the first floor, but I couldn't get into the classroom. I would meet someone, and talk to them, and that would be it. You know, a conversation any place stopped me from doing anything . . .[23]

Paley's parents valued education. They hoped she would become a doctor, lawyer, or teacher, and encouraged her in every way. Her elder brother was a doctor and her older sister a teacher. Her parents hoped that Grace, too, would "be as educated as any man."[24] Her father felt his own struggle to become a doctor had been worth it. He had arrived in America a poor immigrant and taught himself English by reading Dickens.[25] Looking back on her childhood, Paley explains it had been the social values outside her home that had encouraged her interest in boys, sex and early marriage.[26] She married Jessie Paley in 1942, at age twenty, the year her mother died. They remained married for over twenty years and raised two children, Nora and Dan.

But the young Paley only followed society's values when they coincided with her own inclinations and judgment. Her private rebelliousness and political savvy led her to a very early awareness of the political and social implications of language. Even as a child, she was angered by school speech classes where teachers tried to erase the children's ethnic accents. Long before academics realized the connections between linguistics and politics, Paley was incensed by her relatives' efforts to speak a slightly classier language, the "next-class-above-us" language: "I really rebelled against that then. I didn't like it. I just wanted to talk the way I was talking."[27] And she always has.

Paley's willingness to go to jail for her beliefs can be seen as connected to her parents' youth in Europe, but certainly not as a continuation of the middle-class life they followed in America. As youths in Eastern Europe, her father had been imprisoned in Siberia and her mother exiled to Germany. Not that they had to do much to warrant such punishment, Paley told Perry—just being socialists was enough. Fortunately, when the Czar sired a son in 1904, he released every prisoner under twenty-one. Both Paley's parents qualified. Once in America, they worked hard, brought over relatives, and eventually taught their two eldest children to play tennis and the piano, by which they proved to themselves they had joined the middle class. Paley thinks she must have been more exposed to stories of her parents' youth in Europe than were her elder two siblings, an exposure which encouraged her political idealism. Since her parents had still been in their own youth when her brother and sister were little, Paley speculates that they probably hadn't reminisced as much with them.[28]

Paley could take pride in her parents' lives, then, while still acknowledging there were parts she did not care to emulate. They had responded to *their* time and place in history, while she was responding to hers. Thus was she able to develop as a serious, compassionate and independent adult without having to make a clean break, or even any discernable break, from their beliefs. Today she not only actively participates in political demonstrations, and continues to write, but she also teaches creative writing at Sarah Lawrence. She has taught at Columbia and Syracuse University as well, and is always a popular visiting lecturer on other campuses, where she gives wonderful accented readings of her works-in-progress. Her mother need not have worried.

Paley connects her wit and sense of humor to both her father and her religion: "Jews have always had a sense of humor" she explained when protesting that wit was more than just a strategy of resistance to a dominant class or language:

> My father did not feel resistance to the language and he was the funniest man in the world, so I think it's just a Jewish sensibility. He felt nothing but joy in being in the United States, love of the United States, happiness that his children were going to be Americans. But he was as funny as hell.[29]

WIT AND POLITICS:

Convincing Your Public

Grace Paley has a limited but loyal following. Her public has always taken her seriously, both as a first-class wit *and* as a political thinker. Walter Clemons once wrote that he considered her "one of the best writers alive."[30] Nor have her politics been belittled or dismissed. Her name on a petition always lends it weight and credibility. Paley's career shows that a witty woman writer is no longer dismissed as a frivolous writer of light verse, although the fact that a woman can be given serious attention both as a witty writer and as a political presence is a distinctly new development.

Women writers have been taken seriously only reluctantly, and *witty* women writers hardly ever. In 1983, Alison Lurie reminisced that just being a woman had made it harder for her to be taken seriously professionally in the fifties and sixties:

> For instance, I think that it wouldn't have taken me so long to get a job at Cornell if I had been a man. I think if I had been a man who had just happened to be living in Ithaca, maybe married to some lady professor (if you can imagine that, in that climate), I wouldn't have had to publish four novels before I could get a job as a part-time lecturer.[31]

Shirley Jackson's writing career was well established when she entered the hospital to give birth to her third child in 1948. But she records this conversation between herself and the hospital desk clerk in her ostensibly light-hearted autobiography:

> "Name?" the desk clerk said to me politely, her pencil poised.
> "Name." I said vaguely. I remembered, and told her.
> "Age?" she asked. "Sex? Occupation?"
> "Writer," I said.
> "Housewife," she said.
> "Writer," I said.
> "I'll just put down housewife," she said.[32]

Dorothy Parker was born twenty-nine years before Grace Paley. Parker, like Paley, wrote short stories and poetry and had also been highly acclaimed for her wit. But though Parker was every bit as politically radical as Paley, and every bit as politically active, her friends and public always discounted her political activities as naïve and superficial. When Parker tried to support a waiter's strike at the Waldorf "the *Times* implied she was silly."[33] Undoubtedly one of the reasons for her friends' skepticism was the prevailing political cimate, with its hysterical fear of communism. Since Parker seemed sympathetic, if not actually a party member, some of her friends must have felt they were doing her a service to trivialize her alleged beliefs. Undoubtedly her reading public in the thirties would not have shared her radical political views. But the dismissal of Parker's leftist beliefs may also have had to do with the persona she projected: that of the extravagantly dressed city sophisticate, the daughter of a wealthy magnate of the garment industry, Henry Rothschild. Many of Parker's friends were themselves wealthy apolitical socialites. Her politics must have made them uneasy.

Since Parker recognized that her public used her wit as a reason to invalidate her politics, she would have been astonished that fifty years later one of Alison Lurie's interviewers could say she found it "strange that so many people feel humor and wit are incompatible with sympathy and seriousness."[34] Parker, writing in the middle of the century, found it a fact of life.

For Paley, the facts of life are different. Paley has been writing into the more liberal atmosphere of the sixties and beyond, while Parker was writing during World War II and the McCarthy era. Nor could Paley's family background undermine her credibility: she was born into a socialist immigrant family, while Parker was the daughter of wealth. Also, Paley was less established as a wit when she was establishing her politics. Indeed, many admirers of her fiction wish she would write more and protest less. While the reasons are speculative, the facts are encouraging: Paley has proven it is now possible to be respected both as a witty writer and as a political activist. And Parker's life stands as proof that this has not always been the case.

CONTROLLING YOUR AUDIENCE:

The Witty Exposure of Male Domination

"Mockery" is a term that has been used only sparingly to describe Paley's presentation of the relationship between the sexes. It is true that Patricia Waugh observes how "Paley often records the relations between men and women as a sort of serious but mockingly enacted contest"[35] and Jacqueline Taylor points out that "she refuses to take seriously any of the sacred cows of male dominance."[36] But most critics feel more comfortable discussing Paley's magnanimity toward men. Diane Cousineau discusses Paley's "generosity of vision" and the lack of hostility or bitterness in her female characters.[37] Ruth Perry opens her interview with Grace Paley by facing this issue head on:

> Ruth Perry: How come you're never angry in your stories? I always admire your generosity, the fact that you never add to the stock of anger and hate in the world. . . .
> Grace Paley: I think what happens is humor sometimes takes the place of anger, and it may even subvert it. You know, in a way, sometimes there should be more anger, and there's humor instead.[38]

This is an insightful answer, but leaves me wanting to reassure Paley that replacing the anger with humor may have been more effective. First of all, let us be clear that in Paley's handling of female-male relationships, humor *always* takes the place of anger or pain. And secondly, the anger or pain, had it not been replaced, would always have been the woman's. But the undeniable fact is that the offense still gets recorded. Whatever it is that would have caused anger, had it not been presented wittily, still gets described. Pompous egocentric male behavior is mocked, however obscurely or tenderly. And a witty presentation always garners more listeners than an embittered one. As Alison Lurie observes, "you don't want to convince only the converted." Thinking of the unconverted reader, Lurie adds that "you have a better chance if you write a book that is amusing and you sort of sneak around behind them."[39]

Consider Paley's clever aside about Mom's "American-born sisters" in the opening of "Mom" quoted earlier: "Because of them [science and literature], she never even had a chance at the crown of apple pie awarded her American-born sisters and accepted by them when they agreed to give up their powerful pioneer dispositions." That is, no woman, American or foreign born, will ever be adored by men until she learns to assume a subservient personality. But my way of explaining the thought is tendentious and stiff. Paley's way will, at the very least, insure an appreciative smile.

In "Wants" there is an equally clever instance of witty language replacing pain rather than anger. The narrator runs into her ex-husband from a twenty-seven-year marriage. He tells her that her problem in life has always been that she never wants anything. He, on the other hand, wants a sailboat. "But as for you," he says, "you'll always want nothing." The ex-wife then explains to her readers that:

> He had a habit throughout the twenty-seven years of making a narrow remark, which, like a plumber's snake, could work its way through the ear down the throat, halfway to my heart. He would then disappear, leaving me choking with equipment. What I mean is, I sat down on the library steps and he went away. (*EC* 5)

But that is not what she means. What she means is that he caused her pain. But hers is a devious and witty way of saying so, guaranteeing that she will not cause the reader pain as well. Nevertheless, the pain does get recorded, and registers in the reader's consciousness somewhere behind the appreciation for her clever metaphor.

Aunt Rose's life reminiscences in "Goodbye and Good Luck" is surely the most sustained example of a witty presentation displacing an angry one. Cousineau notes that Aunt Rose spoke "without self-pity or hostility."[40] Cousineau is accurate about the specific section she is discussing as well as for the entire story. But accuracy does not always give the whole picture. Aunt Rose is not hostile, true, but Vlashkin and all the men in her story are *worthy* of her hostility, Paley makes that quite clear. Their self-serving behavior does get recorded, quite cleverly, in spite of Rose's good will.

Aunt Rose is telling her life story to her niece, Lillie, on the day she and Vlashkin, now an old man, plan to marry. Vlashkin had been a large success in a very small arena—he was an actor in the Yiddish Theater in New York. As a young girl, Rose saw him as a god: "I cried to think who I was— nothing—and such a man could look at me with interest" (*DM* 12). However, her adoration did not blind her to the altered treatment she received from the other men, once she entered one illicit relationship:

> Meanwhile Krimberg went after me too. No doubt observing the success of Vlashkin, he thought, "Aha, open sesame . . ." Others in the company similar." (*DM* 14, ellipsis Paley's)

Although Rose breaks up with Vlashkin after meeting his wife, realizing the flesh-and-blood reality of what she had known only in the abstract, he crawls back into her life (and bed) several years later, with an updated Yiddish version of Marvel's "To His Coy Mistress" ("Had we but world enough and time"):

> "Rosie, Rosie," he said to me one day, "I see by the clock on your rosy rosy face you must be thirty."
>
> "The hands are slow, Vlashkin. On a week before Thursday I was thirty-four." (*DM* 17)

So they resume their affair. Rose had never been his only mistress, but she has always been able to excuse his other sexual liaisons:

> An actor's soul must be like a diamond. The more faces it got the more shining is his name. . . . a great artist like Volodya Vlashkin . . . in order to make a job on the stage, he's got to practice. I understand it now, to him life is like a rehearsal. (second ellipsis Paley's, 18)

The final irony is the reason Vlashkin is available to marry Rose in his old age. Although his wife had known of his affairs all along, only in old age does she use them as cause for divorce. For only when he retires does she realize that she cannot tolerate having him home all day. The way he describes the situation lets us know why:

> The truth is, Rose, she isn't accustomed to have a man around all day, reading out loud from the papers the interesting events of our time, waiting for breakfast, waiting for lunch. So all day she gets madder and madder. By nighttime a furious old lady gives me my supper. (*DM* 20)

Rose is neither bitter or hostile—at least not in front of her sister's daughter. Had she married young and lived in her own apartment she would have had "to live like a maid with a dustrag in the hand, sneezing" (*DM* 9). At least this is her rationale for why she has always preferred hotels. Nor, as a young girl, could she stand being stuck in a job if she couldn't sit by the window: "If you can't sit girlie, . . . go stand on the street corner" replied her boss (*DM* 9). So she ended up stuck in a Yiddish theater's ticket cage which was opened by Vlashkin who immediately stuck her in the role of one of his mistresses. But if Rose is not hostile, neither is she blindly romantic. She concludes her story for Lillie to relate to her mother, Rose's sister, on a cynical, if merry, note:

> Tell her after all I'll have a husband, which, as everybody knows, a woman should have at least one before the end of the story. (*DM* 21–22)

The ageing Rose is as wise as she is cynical. After all, she and Vlashkin had always enjoyed each other's company. And, maybe, once she is a legally married woman, she can mend the strained relations with her only sister, also ageing.

By suggesting that "mockery" is a highly suitable adjective to describe Paley's portrayal of men, I do not mean to suggest that Paley is not also generous-visioned. It is not that she set out to ridicule men, but rather that she began to spotlight the "lesser" concerns of women. Paley told Joan Lidoff that she feels "writing something to let someone really have it" is wrong. Writing, Paley believes, should be illuminating rather than distorting.[41] Paley remains true to this belief, for where relationships are concerned, she always writes to illuminate women's neglected lives rather than to attack men's.

Occasionally, she writes from the male point of view, as in "Contest," her first story. But as her fiction developed, she wrote more about women's lives:

> For a long time I thought women's lives . . . I didn't really think I was shit, but I really thought my life as a woman was shit. Who would be interested in this crap? I was very interested in it, but I didn't have enough social ego to put it down. I had to develop that to a point where I said "I don't give a damn." Women who have thought their lives were boring have found they're interesting to one another.[42]

Once Paley allowed herself to write about a woman's world, from a woman's point of view, much of her comic sense was aroused by male behavior. She found the inspiration for "The Used Boy Raisers" in real life. Paley had been visiting a friend who was serving breakfast to both her current husband and a former one, both of whom were complaining about the meal. This tickled Paley. "There were two husbands disappointed by eggs" is the way her story opens, a masterpiece of gentle mockery (*DM* 127). While the two men search for a drink, for something to criticize besides eggs (the children's poor reading skills are good for a few minutes), Faith sits embroidering "God Bless Our Home" at the breakfast table. "Go say goodbye to your father" she whispers to her sons. "Which one? they ask. "The real father" she replies ambiguously, and then, with Solomon-like justice, one runs to the old, the other is embraced by the new (*DM* 134). The men are not inordinately patronizing, bullying or pompous. But they are (or have been) her husbands and are therefore determinedly proprietary. They leave for work together. The ex-husband will not be returning that night:

> Goodbye now, Faith, said Livid. Call me if you want anything at all. Anything at all, my dear. Warmly with sweet propriety he kissed my cheek. (*DM* 134)

Then it is her present husband's turn:

> Ascendant, [he] kissed me with considerable business behind the ear. (*DM* 134)

The story closes with such delicate, almost innocent mockery that it is understandable why some critics choose to focus only on Paley's sympathetic handling of her male characters and ignore her mockery:

> I must admit that they were at last clean and neat, rather attractive, shiny men in their thirties, with the grand affairs of the day ahead of them. . . . Goodbye, I said, have a nice day. Goodbye, they said once more, and set off in pride on paths which are not my concern. (*DM* 134)

"Grand" affairs, not just "important" ones, and "attractive shiny men," not just "attractive men" rather tips her hand, so that when you reach the final sentence you are encouraged to read a touch of mockery in those paths that are not her concern, those paths on which they set out with such pride.

The response of Paley's women characters to male aggression can be less delicate than this. In "The Long Distance Runner" Faith is admiring her childhood apartment and appreciating how Mrs. Luddy has fixed it up, just as Faith's mother had done in her day. "Men," Faith notes, "don't have that outlet. That's how come they run around so much." "Till they drunk enough to lay down" Mrs. Luddy replies. Faith expands on the thought:

> Yes, I said, on a large scale you can see it in the world. First they make something, then they murder it. Then they write a book about how interesting it is. (*EC*, 188)

The connections between male aggression, achievement, war, and destruction have surely been noticed before Paley, but possibly never with such subtle and even tender wit. In "Enormous Changes at the Last Minute" Alexandra's frail and failing father objects from his hospital bed to her constant criticism of the United States, his adopted home:

> He remembered the first time he'd seen the American flag on wild Ellis Island. Under its protection and working like a horse, he'd read Dickens, gone to medical school, and shot like a surface-to-air missile right into the middle class. (*EC* 122)

Granted, the connection between achievement and war is only a simile, and it is even the unexpectedness of the comparison that makes us smile—but that is before its ominous appropriateness registers.

But while Paley is certainly able to mock male weaknesses, her emphasis always falls on uncovering female strengths. Her stories concentrate on the lives of women, on the way they love each other and their children, and on the way they summon the strength to survive their love of men. Her positive attitude is reflected in her assessment of women in history. Perry ends her wonderful interview by asking Paley why she thinks there haven't been great women writers in the past. Paley objects to this question. There *have* been great women writers, she protests, in spite of tremendous obstacles. Mostly women have been raising kids, that is true. So often they haven't been great at anything. But even so, we had Jane Austen, George Eliot, Mrs. Gaskell, Charlotte Perkins Gilman, George Sand, and Kate Chopin:

> The miracle is what women have done in this world. It's miraculous that they did the work they did on such a high level. Where did they do it? And wearing the clothes they were wearing? How could they even sit to do it? I mean they must have loosened something. But they were in the family parlor, they couldn't loosen everything. (Perry 56)

CONTROLLING GRACE AND LUCK

Paley speaks in terms of "grace" and "luck." She tries to explain to Hulley that the form of a story is granted by grace:

> I mean that it descends on you. You find it. You work and you work and you work. And you make connections, and you make connections, and you make connections. . . .
> Then you feel grace is a gift that comes from outside you? [asks Hulley]
> No, but it's like gifts that do come from outside. You have to do a lot of work.[43]

Paley explains to Lidoff that the way she broke into publishing was pure luck. She had a friend whose kids watched television with hers. This friend's ex-husband used to pick up his kids on Sundays, but usually had to wait for them to finish watching their program at Paley's house. So he'd sit around her livingroom and wait. He was a senior editor at Doubleday. "Well, the least you could do is read Grace's stories" his ex-wife, Grace's friend, said to him angrily one day. And he did. "Write seven more," he said, "and we'll publish them." That became *The Little Disturbances of Man*. Had it not been for him, claims Paley, she really might have stopped writing. Up until then every one of the stories had been rejected.[44]

Alison Lurie also speaks of the importance of luck. She ends her interview with David Jackson, who asks her what she would say to an aspiring young writer in the 80s, by saying:

> I think you've got to tell them you may have talent, you may have determination, but you've still got to have luck.[45]

Earlier in that interview, she acknowledges that there are many talented writers around, and that it is an accident that she is the one in print (24). Jackson politely protests. He opens the interview by asking her if she does not find it odd that so many of their friends have "come into their own." No, said Alison Lurie, emphatically, she does not:

> Let's put it this way: it takes a combination of effort and good luck, or inertia and bad luck, to succeed or fail noticeably. If you come from a comfortable background and you get a good education you end up being an editor, a lawyer, a doctor . . . circumstances carry you along. Then you have people who by unusual luck or unusual effort have climbed higher, or through another kind of luck or effort not made it. (17)

Both Paley's and Lurie's humility, as well as the indirect way they broke into print, put me in mind of an insightful essay by W.H. Auden on the relevance of fairy tales to life. We have to discount Auden's male orientation in his last sentence. Born in 1907, he is writing out of his own time and place in history, a time when the success seeker, the quester, was expected to be an aspiring young male:

> Success can never be achieved by an act of conscious will alone; it always requires the co-operation of grace or luck. But grace is not arbitrary; it is always there to assist anyone who is humble enough to ask for it. . . . Finally, and above all, one must not be anxious about ultimate success or failure but think only about what is necessary to do at the present moment. What seems a story stretched out in time takes place in fact at every instant; the proud and the envious are even now dancing in red-hot shoes or rolling downhill in barrels full of nails; the trustful and loving are already married to princesses.[46]

Lurie had little success until she forgot about publishing and concentrated on writing a private memoir of her friend V.R. Lang. That memoir, through no effort of hers, was passed on to an editor at MacMillan two years later— through the brother of a friend. In Auden's words, Lurie was only thinking of what was necessary to do at the present moment: memorialize her friend. And Paley? Paley was raising her children. She, too, was doing what was necessary to do at the present moment. She was creating a warm home environment, a home where her friends and her children's friends were welcome. As Paley said to Gelfant, you travel different roads at different times. It's not a question of preference, there's just no way out: "When your kids are small, or even when they're bigger, that's your main road" (26). Paley's road obviously embraced other mothers and children. Those mothers were her closest friends, women who considered her a loving and supportive friend. They were women who could perform loving and supportive acts in return, like waving Paley's clever stories under the noses of ex-husband senior editors.

NOTES

1. Noelle Batt and Marcienne Rocard, "An Interview with Grace Paley," *Caliban* 25 (1988): 131.
2. Batt and Rocard 122.
3. Batt and Rocard 130.
4. Quotations from Paley's stories will be cited parenthetically and abbreviated *Dm, EC*, and *LD*, referring to these editions: *The Little Disturbances of Man* (1956; NY: Viking Penguin, 1985); *Enormous Changes at the Last Minute* (NY: Farrar, Straus Giroux, 1960); *Later the Same Day* (Viking Penguin, 1986).
5. Batt and Rocard 124.
6. Batt and Rocard 131.
7. Joan Lidoff, "Clearing Her Throat: An Interview With Grace Paley," *Shenandoah* 32.3 (1981): 5.
8. Lidoff 18.
9. Batt and Rocard 136.
10. Blanche H. Gelfant, *Women Writing in America* (Hanover: Univ. Press of New England, 1984) 17.
11. Rachel Blau DuPlessis has written a book about the avoidance of closure in the works of twentieth-century women writers: *Writing Beyond the Ending* (Bloomington: Indiana Univ. Press, 1985).
12. Lidoff 18.
13. Gelfant 18.
14. Lidoff 19.
15. Lidoff 20.
16. Lidoff 20.
17. Kathleen Hulley, "Interview with Grace Paley," *Delta* 14 (1982): 40.
18. *Contemporary Authors Index: New Rev. Series* 13 (Detroit: Gale, 1986) 397.
19. Gelfant 22.
20. Ruth Perry, "Grace Paley" in *Women Writers Talking*, ed. Janet Todd (New York: Holmes & Meier, 1983) 46.
21. Perry 45–46.
22. Perry 41.
23. Gelfant 23.
24. Hulley 28.
25. Batt and Rocard 130–131.
26. Hulley 28.
27. Batt and Rocard 130.
28. Perry 44.
29. Batt and Rocard 131.

30. Walter Clemons, rev. of *Enormous Changes at the Last Minute*, by Grace
     Paley, *Newsweek* 11 March 1974: 78.
31. Dorothy Mermin, "Alison Lurie," *Women Writers Talking*, 95. Lurie is imag-
     ining her position reversed: she originally settled in Ithaca because her hus-
     band, Jonathan Bishop, was appointed to the English Department at Cornell.
32. Shirley Jackson, *Life Among the Savages* 1953, rpt. in *The Magic of Shirley
     Jackson*, ed. Stanley Edgar Hyman (NY: Farrar, Straus, Giroux, 1965) 426.
33. John Keats, *You Might As Well Live* (NY: Simon and Schuster, 1970) 221.
34. Martha Satz, "A Kind of Detachment: An Interview with Alison Lurie," *South
     West Review* 71 (1986): 194.
35. Patricia Waugh, *Feminie Fictions: Revisiting the Postmodern* (London & NY:
     Routledge, 1989) 165.
36. Jacqueline Taylor, *Grace Paley* (Austin: Univ. of Texas, 1990) 84.
37. Diane Cousineau, "The Desires of Women, The Presence of Men," *Delta* 14
     (1982): esp. 55–57, 63.
38. Perry 35.
39. Mermin, *Women Writer's Talking* 92.
40. Couisineau 55.
41. Lidoff 17.
42. Hulley 26.
43. Hulley 20.
44. Lidoff 8.
45. David Jackson, "An Interview with Alison Lurie," *Shenandoah* 31 (1980): 27.
46. W.H. Auden, "Grimm and Anderson" in *Forewords and Afterwords* (NY:
     Random House, 1973) 203–4.

7

Anne Tyler: Seeing Through a "Mist of Irony"

TYLER'S COMIC VISION:

1: In Her Life

Assessing her life as a writer, Anne Tyler explains that what she is constantly trying to communicate to her readers is her comic vision:

> People have always seemed funny and strange to me, and touching in unexpected ways. I can't shake off a sort of mist of irony that hangs over whatever I see. Probably that's what I'm trying to put across when I write; I may believe that I'm the one person who holds this view of things.[1]

Tyler cites the isolated Quaker community where she spent her childhood as the probable origin of her "mist of irony." Although born in Minneapolis in 1941, she was raised in a Quaker community in Raleigh, North Carolina. At age eleven, when her family left the commune, she had never used a phone and could strike a match on the soles of her bare feet.[2] Tyler admits she must have looked peculiar to her new schoolmates, but what proved more crucial for her subsequent writing career was the fact that they all looked peculiar to her. Moreover, her sense of the peculiar in others never

left her. It is not, the adult Tyler explains, that she purposefully chooses
"only bizarre or eccentric people to write about." Rather, it seems to her
"that even the most ordinary person, in real life, will turn out to have something unusual at his center."[3] Tyler's novels uncover and celebrate that
unusual center within each of her characters and she uses her wit to urge her
readers to share both her appreciation and compassion for them

Tyler's comic vision is captured in a story she tells about her father.
Although Tyler intends to focus on her father's approach to life, his attitude
is so related to her own comic vision that she inadvertently sheds light on
that as well. In the late 1970s, her parents went to the Gaza Strip to work for
the American Friends Service Committee. It had been a lifelong dream of
her father, and he had been preparing for it for years. But no sooner had they
arrived than her mother contracted a mysterious fever, obliging them to
return to America for treatment. Since they had sublet their home, they lived
with Tyler and her family for months, not knowing from week to week how
long they would have to stay. This period was hard on her mother, of
course, but, according to Tyler:

> . . . it should have been especially hard in another way for my father,
> who had simply to hang in suspended animation for four months while
> my mother was whisked in and out of hospitals. However, I believe he
> was as pleased with life as he always is. He whistled Mozart and put-
> tered around insulating our windows. He went on long walks collect-
> ing firewood. He strolled over to the meetinghouse and gave a talk on
> the plight of the Arab refugees.[4]

Finally her mother decided the fever was psychosomatic and should be
ignored. They returned to the Gaza Strip. The next summer Tyler and her
children went to visit. Her mother's fever was gone "and my father drove us
down the Strip, weaving a little Renault among the tents and camels, cheer-
fully whistling Mozart".[5]

Tyler tells this story to explain the way her father lives: "infinitely adapting, and looking around him with a smile to say 'Oh! So this is where I am!"
She admires this attitude, feeling it may be the only way to "slip gracefully
through a choppy life of writing novels, plastering the dining room ceiling,
and presiding at slumber parties."[6] Acceptance of and adaptability to the
unexpected and unavoidable is what Tyler is striving to achieve. She wants
to enjoy seeing through her mist of irony. To that end, Tyler strives to maintain an amused and tolerant smile for every situation, hoping to keep that
smile from slipping into a frown of exasperation or frustration. Tyler is
aware of the lurking passivity in such an attitude: "I could wind up as passive as a piece of wood on a wave," she acknowledges. "But I try to walk a
middle line."[7]

TYLER'S COMIC VISION:

2: In Her Characters:

Tyler's comic vision is one she allows certain favored characters to acquire. The amused but tolerant attitude such a vision encourages is exactly what Charlotte Emory achieves at the end of *Earthly Possessions*.[8] Charlotte has been feeling trapped in her life. Her father's death cancels her college plans and she continues to live in her childhood home after marrying. In fact, the only time she gets out of Maryland at all is when she is taken hostage by a small-time bank robber. With him she gets as far as Florida. It is amusing to read how Jake, the young robber, grows dependent on Charlotte. Hardly more than a teenager himself, he rescues his teenaged and pregnant girlfriend from a home for unwed mothers en route to Florida. Then the three of them travel together. In the end, when there is no more reason for Charlotte to stay, he begs her to stay on anyway. The words he uses are significant:

> . . . Charlotte, it ain't so bad if you're with us, you see. You act like you take it all in stride, like this is the way life really does tend to turn out. You mostly wear this little smile. (219)

The reference to Charlotte's smile, reminiscent of Tyler's father's smile, suggests that Charlotte is acquiring a comic vision of her own. When she returns to Maryland, to the site of her once-discontented self, Charlotte shows that her new attitude is one of amused wisdom in the way she reassures her worried husband that she is content with their life. He wonders if they should take a trip. She says no: "We have been traveling for years, traveled all our lives, we are traveling still. We couldn't stay in one place if we tried" (222). Doris Betts acknowledged in a 1983 article that the liberated coeds in her literature class found Charlotte's passivity in this resolution too close to masochism. They had read *Earthly Possessions* just after Fowles's *French Lieutenant's Woman*. And Betts observes, undoubtedly with an amused and tolerant smile of her own, that "the coeds want and fully expect to become Sarah Woodruff, and never Charlotte Emery."[9]

Jenny Tull's effort to reshape her approach to life (*Dinner at The Homesick Restaurant*) highlights another side of Tyler's comic vision.[10] Jenny had always wanted to be a doctor. But when her internship coincides with both her divorce and the birth of her daughter, she collapses under the strain. Jenny then studies the protective devices of those she admires:

> It seemed to her the people she admired (one of her partners, who was a wry, funny man named Dan Charles; and her brother Ezra; and her neighbor Leah Hume) had this in common: they gazed at the world

from a distance. There was something sheeted about them—some obliqueness that made them difficult to grasp. Dan, for instance, kept up such a steady, easy banter that you never could ask him about his wife, who was forever in and out of mental institutions. And Leah: she could laugh off the repeated failures of her crazy business ventures like so many pratfalls. How untouched she looked, and how untouchable, chuckling to herself and covering her mouth with a shapely, badly kept hand! Jenny studied her; you could almost say she took notes. She was learning how to make it through life on a slant. She was trying to lose her intensity. (216–17)

Learning to make it through life on a slant, to gaze at the world from a distance, to keep up a steady banter, to laugh off failures—this is an important aspect of the control of wit, as well as a crucial component of Tyler's comic vision: the realization that it is your own witty perception that controls your own version, or vision, of the world around you.

The novel suggests that Jenny learns the distancing controlling strategy of banter in the way she jokingly fends off a young priest who comes in concern over the withdrawn behavior of Slevin, her eldest stepson. (She has remarried, and Joe, her new husband, comes with six young children.) Jenny is full of reassurances and jokes to allay the priest's concern. She walks him to the door assuring him that Joe is an excellent father. Not like others she could mention—her former husband, for example. That man left her before their child was even born, "moved in with a model named Adar Bagned" (196). "But," Jenny hastens to add, lest the priest transfer his concern and compassion from her stepson to herself:

> isn't that a hilarious name? For the longest time I kept trying to turn it around, thinking it must make more sense if I read it off backward. (196)

Shortly after the priest's visit, Sleven steals Jenny's mother's vacuum cleaner because it was the same Hoover upright model that his own mother used. Pearl Tull, Jenny's mother, voices the expected response: "I wonder if he might be calling for help in some way. . . . Maybe he's asking for a psychologist or some such." "More likely," Jenny retorts, "he's asking for a neater house." Amused by her own words, she imagines him stealing a broom from one neighbor, Ajax from another, until she laughs out loud:

> "Oh Jenny," her mother said sadly. "Do you have to see everything as a joke?"
> "It's not my fault if funny things happen," Jenny said.
> "It most certainly is," said her mother, but instead of explaining herself, she all at once grew brisk and requested the return of her vacuum cleaner. . . . (209)

It is possible to dismiss Jenny's mother's curious accusation as the illogic of exasperation, but this would be a mistake. Tyler would undoubtedly endorse the idea that it *is* your own "fault" (or doing) if funny things happen, explaining that of course it is your own perception that makes something appear funny in the first place. This is, in fact, exactly what Tyler means by seeing through a mist of irony.

GRACE PALEY AND ANN TYLER:

The Effect of Belief on Plot:

In a study of Tyler, Joseph Voelker suggests that both Tyler's life and fiction reflect a "conviction of human goodness" and a "quiet resistance toward moral authority" that he identifies as essentially Quaker characteristics.[11] Although Grace Paley was raised in a totally different environment, the Bronx apartment of Russian-Jewish-atheist-socialist immigrants, her life and fiction have demonstrated a "conviction of human goodness" and an ongoing "resistance toward moral authority" similar to Anne Tyler's. However, since Paley has organized demonstrations and been arrested for protesting injustices, *her* resistance would never be described as quiet. According to Blanche Gelfant, Paley has always acted upon the "belief, essentially, in the possibilities for social justice—a faith that the will of good people like her parents might prevail. **You know the idea that you can't fight City Hall—well you can.**"[12] If Tyler's quiet beliefs can be traced to her Quaker background and the examples set by her parents' lives, then Paley's more outspoken ones can be traced to her socialist background and the idealism she inherited from her parents' early lives. Traveling two very different roads, Tyler and Paley arrived at nearly the same point.

For it is Tyler's and Paley's resistance of any repressive authority, as well as their belief in human goodness, that has encouraged both writers to avoid plots that entrap, to reject story lines that lock characters inside one narrow, sad, little fate. Paley rejects the traditional plot line itself, suspicious of the closure implicit in moving from point A to point B. Paley saw closure as the repressive authority of a narrow fate. Although Tyler has kept the traditional plot form, she avoids closure by adding more points along the narrative line. After point B comes C, D, maybe even E. Adding more plot developments creates the impression that the novel is merely capturing one discrete time segment within any given life, suggesting that the developments of that life do not end when the novel does. Tyler certainly does not consider her characters' lives fixed: "And if I were remotely religious," she once wrote,

I'd believe that a little gathering of my characters would be waiting for
me in heaven when I died. *"Then* what happened? I'd ask them. "How
have things worked out, since the last time I saw you?"[13]

Both Paley and Tyler are optimists who refuse to believe that a person is
allowed but one story, either in fiction or life. Tyler has said several times
that she writes because she wants more than one life.[14] She grants many of
her characters a second chance. "What is important," Voelker noted
shrewdly, "is that Tyler imagines sane people who know that life is a trap,
but that grace is a distinct possibility."[15] Elizabeth (*The Clock Winder*) runs
from her parents who see her as awkward and incompetent and marries into
a family who see her as skilled and necessary.[16] She begins her new life as
a widow's "handyman," and the more the widow and her grown children
admire her, the more competent she becomes. Macon stays with Muriel
(*The Accidental Tourist*) because he can be a warmer, softer person with her
than with his wife.[17] With his wife he is "locked inside the stand-offish self
he'd assumed when he and she had first met. He was frozen there" (53). But
with Muriel, the brassy low-class dog-trainer, he

> was an entirely different person. This person had never been suspected
> of narrowness, never been accused of chilliness; in fact, was mocked
> for his soft heart. And was anything but orderly. (212)

Duncan Peck (*Searching for Caleb*) escapes from the stifling Peck clan
taking along his cousin Justine, whom he loves and marries.[18] His problem
is that he cannot settle: once he makes a financial success of anything, from
goat farming to selling antique farm tools, he despairs and lays out a soli-
taire formation while sipping Old Crow. Financial success is precisely what
he fears—it feels too much like the stodgy respectable family expectations
he is escaping. When he exhausts all his job possibilities, when it looks as
though they will have to return to their family compound in proper Roland
Park after all, Justine comes up with a delightful way out, a fortuitous second chance: they will join their friend's traveling circus, Duncan as the
mechanic, she as the fortune teller. They can finally "settle" into wandering
and enjoy a life lacking respectability and financial solidity but filled with
warmth and adventure.

In *Saint Maybe*, Tyler creates "The Church of the Second Chance," a
small religious sect where Ian Bedloe spends most of the novel and over
twenty years of his life atoning for a rash moment of adolescent anger.[19]
Exasperated and angry with his sister-in-law, who leaves him to babysit on
the very evening he and his girl were to have her home to themselves, he
blurts out to Danny, his older brother, that Danny's recent marriage to Lucy
made him nothing but a fall guy: their baby wasn't premature, as Lucy had

claimed, and, what's more, she is *still* running around. (Lucy had been divorced with two young children when Danny met and, two weeks later, proposed marriage. She probably *had* been pregnant with a third when she met Danny. But, craving security rather than sex, she had most definitely not been cheating on her new husband.) Immediately after Ian's outburst, Danny drives straight into a wall and kills himself. A few months later, his distracted young widow dies from an overdose of sleeping pills. Ian feels he is to blame for both deaths and tries to atone for them. He quits college and, directed by the Church of the Second Chance, which teaches "concrete practical reparation" (122), raises the three orphaned children himself. He becomes a cabinet maker, a permanent member of the Church of the Second Chance, and settles into his childhood home with his ageing parents and his brother's widow's three children. This life continues for over twenty years. At forty-one, Ian seems settled and sad. He owns six books on how to become a good person. These books, plus the nutmeg smell of his clothes, were the reasons Rita (the "clutter counselor" hired to clear the junk from his home) gives for why she cannot help but love him. They marry, and, as the novel closes, have a son.

Although Tyler believes in granting second chances to her characters, she does not alter their personalities significantly. Tyler does not believe anyone can change, but does allow that people can behave differently with different people Thus she creates an external change of circumstance rather than an internal change of character. Macon is one way with Sarah and a kinder warmer way with Muriel, but it is important to realize that this alteration does not signal any wilful personality change on his part. Whenever Macon returns to Sarah, he helplessly returns to his former stuffy self. He can only choose to change his environment. In 1972, after her fourth novel, Tyler said in a rare interview that

> something that tends to come out in all my books is an utter lack of faith in change. I really don't think most people are capable of it, although they think they are.[20]

Although over twenty years have passed since that interview, her subsequent novels show she still believes that only external changes are possible. By surrounding themselves with new people, her characters are able to adopt new roles, roles that allow them to develop sides of themselves which have been lying dormant all along.

Sometimes, what first appears as helpless scraps of eccentric goodness can build up into a tangible way of life, if the character can just endure the bad spells. *Morgan's Passing* can be read this way.[21] Morgan's indefatigable eagerness to be a different person, one who is relevant, loved, and respected, leads him to answer Leon's emergency call for a doctor in the audience which, in turn, leads him to deliver Emily's baby in the car on the way to the hospital.

Morgan is aware that he has become an embarrassment to his teen-aged children. He likes to wear various outlandish costumes and pretend to be someone else. But in a moment of candor one morning, he blurts out to his wife:

> "Ah, God, I have got to do something about this *life* of mine," he said.
> "What about it?" she asked, sliding a blouse off a hanger.
> "It's come to nothing, It's come to nothing." (163)

Each of his five daughters loves him until they reach age eleven or twelve, when they begin to consider him an embarrassment. His thirteen-year-old, Liz, comes down for breakfast one morning:

> "For heaven's sake," she said to Bonny, "what's that he got on his head?"
> "Feel free to address me directly," Morgan told her. "I have the answer, as it happens. Don't be shy." (36)

But Liz does not appreciate his wit and continues to ignore him. His competent wife endures him good-naturedly, but never relies on him for anything. Morgan feels excluded from their giggling, noisy, and bustling lives.

Morgan is able to endure his useless life by living through his imaginative roles and by attaching himself to Emily and Leon, whose simple life he idealizes. But meanwhile he continues to be kind to his own family, not only to his wife and five daughters but also to his ageing mother and sister, who lived in his large and cluttered household. In fact, he is heroically patient with his stubborn mother, who refuses to tell him anything of her life with his father, who killed himself when Morgan was a teenager. One day on their yearly vacation, mother and son go for walk. She is surprised by an A-frame under construction, a structure she has never before seen. Morgan explains the cost advantages of the design. Then he tries to get her to remember earlier vacations with his father. As always, she refuses to remember anything, and firmly changes the subject by spotting a second A-frame. This one is completed and occupied:

> "Why!" she said, "Wasn't that speedy."
> "What was, Mother dear?"
> "They've finished construction of the A-frame," she said. "It seems like no time at all." And she jutted her chin at him with a triumphant bitter glare.
> "So it does, dear heart," he said. (165)

Morgan is saddened but not resentful over the way his grown daughters ignore him. Whenever he is seized with a spell of letter writing, he writes to them all, even those still living in Baltimore. He cares for his whole huge family, however extraneous they make him feel, while also loving Emily's tiny family unit. He loves Leon and their only child Gina, as well as Emily herself. He makes an endearing fool of himself at Gina's gym meet. Gina vaults the horse with no problem but lands badly, in a "twisted heap on the mat." The teacher coaxes the tearful child to try again. Morgan puts "an unlit cigarette in his mouth with a trembling hand" (258). Then, when Gina lands in perfect form, Morgan

> . . . jumped up and flung away his cigarette. He galloped in her foot-steps all the way to the horse, and veered around it to hug her. Tears were streaming down his cheeks. "Sweetheart, you were wonderful," he said. She said, "Oh, Morgan," and giggled. (She was unscathed; she had forgotten everything.) She slipped away from him to join her team-mates. Morgan returned to his seat, beaming and wiping his eyes. (259)

But Morgan also loves Emily in a more focused personal way, and when she finally returns that love and they create a new household it is hard not to feel that Morgan is finally getting the second chance he has long deserved. Doris Betts' general comment on all Tyler's optimistic endings is extremely apt for *Morgan's Passing*:

> . . . Tyler usually resists the temptation to attach with Velcro a hack-writers's happy ending to her final page. She tries to make her charac-ters earn solutions, step by step, . . . [22]

Ezra Tull (*Dinner At the Homesick Restaurant*) is a Tyler character who clearly deserves a second chance.[23] Although his jealous older brother steals his girl, although he finds himself a middle-aged bachelor living in his child-hood home tactfully caring for his blind mother, Ezra never seems bitter. He may seem passive and resigned, as when he discovers a lump in his groin and tries to ignore it, but never bitter. He doggedly continues to try to get his fam-ily to sit through an entire family dinner at his restaurant, although someone inevitably walks out in a huff. Failure does not phase him. He is a shy nurturer who knows how to keep at a respectful distance from others, even though he once worried that he did not know what that was. His mother had asked him if he had found out whether or not his sister had left her husband:

> "I notice she still wears a ring," he said hopefully.
> "So what," said his mother. She went back to her groceries.
> "She wouldn't wear a ring if she and Harley were separated, would she?"
> "She would if she wanted to fool us."

> "Well, I don't know, if she wants to fool us maybe we ought to *act* fooled. I don't know." (127)

Then his mother frets over what she sees as Jenny's standoffishness, causing Ezra to think of his own personality:

> "I'm worried I don't know how to get in touch with people," Ezra said.
> "Hmmm?"
> "I'm worried if I come too close, they'll say I'm overstepping. They'll say I'm pushy, or . . . emotional, you know. But if I back off, they might think I don't care. I really, honestly believe I missed some rule that everyone else takes for granted; I must have been absent from school that day. There's this narrow little dividing line that I somehow never located . . ." (127)

One of the strengths of Tyler's wit is her ability to give voice to her character's worries in a whimsical and amusing way, as she does here, without undercutting her character's concerns.

Although Tyler chooses not to give Ezra a second chance within the novel, grace at a later date is a distinct possibility. Ezra is only in his early forties when the novel ends, his mother has just died and, at long last, he has finally gathered the family, including their long absent father, for the funeral meal. Hurt feelings cause his father to disappear once, granted, and Mr. Tull *does* claim he will leave again before the dessert wine is poured. Still, the fact that Ezra's family dinner takes place under any terms is a distinctly positive turn of events in this novel. It encourages the reader to imagine that Ezra's private life will also take a more positive turn at some later point. For Ezra has all the characteristics of a Tyler hero:

> The real heroes to me in my books are first the ones who manage to endure and second the ones who somehow are able to grant other people the privacy of the space around them and yet still produce some warmth.[24]

Tyler's optimism, her belief in the possibility of grace, and her frequent granting of second chances all contribute to the sense of the comic in her novels. For comedies end happily. Updike shrewdly observed that "we have lost familiarity with the comedic spirit," citing this loss as one reason some critics have had trouble taking Tyler seriously.[25]

ANNE TYLER'S WIT

Henri Bergson and George Meredith, two classical comic theorists, have argued that wit is a corrective device. They see the witty writer as an objective outside observer who uses his often ruthless wit to expose human failings. In 1900, Bergson wrote that "the comic demands something like a momentary anesthesia of the heart. Its appeal is to the intelligence, pure and simple." In 1877, Meredith explained that comedy "laughs through the mind, for the mind directs it."[26] But Tyler's wit does not allow for any such division of heart and mind. Her wit, in fact, moves in quite the opposite direction, working to unite the heart and head rather than to sharpen any intellectual distance from folly. She never uses wit to ridicule her characters, but rather to celebrate their eccentricities, which is why Susan Gilbert called it a kindly rather than sardonic wit.[27] Tyler uses her wit to present her characters sympathetically, to allow them room to be themselves—however odd they appear to us with our narrower, less tolerant vision of life's possibilities.

In one sense, however, Tyler's wit *can* be seen as a corrective device— if we allow that it can be the reading audience's attitude that is in need of correction rather than the behavior of her characters, and realize that this is not at all what either Meredith or Bergson had in mind. Tyler's wit is always bent on reshaping and expanding her readers' sympathies into a more compassionate and generous view of others. She never misses an opportunity to urge this view, however whimsical her presentation. Elizabeth, the young heroine of *The Clock Winder*, once described an insight that allowed her to stop hiding from life, paralyzed as she had been by her fear that she might cause harm to others. Elizabeth has been watching the people who were watching a parade:

> There were people crammed on both sidewalks, mothers with babies and little children, fathers with children on their shoulders. And suddenly I was so *surprised* by them. Isn't it amazing how hard people work to raise their children? Human beings are born so helpless, and stay helpless so long. For every grownup you see, you know there must have been at least one person who had the patience to lug them around, and feed them, and walk them nights and keep them out of danger for years and years without a break. Teaching them how to fit into civilization and how to talk back and forth with other people, taking them to zoos and parades and educational events, telling them all those nursery rhymes and word-of-mouth fairy tales. Isn't that surprising? People you wouldn't trust your purse with five minutes, maybe, but still they put in years and years of time tending their children along and they don't even make a fuss about it. Even if it's a criminal they turn out, or some other kind of failure—still, he managed to get grown, didn't he? Isn't that something? (*The Clock Winder*, 247)

Elizabeth realizes she is no more likely to cause harm than anyone else: "I'm like all the people I'm sitting here gawking at, and I might just as well stumble on out and join them!" (247). And she does just that.

Morgan Gower (*Morgan's Passing*) is Tyler's most whimsical character. Both his behavior and his mental processes follow unexpected and delightful paths. When he declares his love to Emily he also declares how foolish and wrong that love is—he is too old for her, for one thing, and he has no wish to harm her current marriage, for another. So he explains how he has been fighting it by trying to take pleasure in his daily routines:

> "I persuade myself," he said, "that there is some virtue in the trivial, the commonplace. Ha! What a notion. I think of those things on TV, those man-in-the-street things where the ordinary triumphs. They stop some ordinary person and ask if he can sing a song, recite a poem . . . they stop a motorcycle gang, I've seen this! Black-leather motorcycle gang and ask, 'Can you sing all the words to "Some Enchanted Evening"?' And up these fellows start, dead serious, trying hard—I mean, fellows you would never expect had *heard* of 'Some Enchanted Evening.' They stand there with their arms around each other, switchblades poking out of their pockets, brass knuckles in their blue jeans, earnestly sweetly singing . . ." (234–5)

And Morgan is off and musing. His imagination has carried him quite away from Emily, who sits bemused, staring both at Morgan pacing his office and the clutter around him. He continues his wonderful digression:

> "They stop this fat old lady," he was saying. "A mess! A disaster. Gray and puffy like some failed pastry, and layers of clothes that seem to have melted together. 'Can you sing "June is Bustin' Out All Over"?' they ask, and she says, 'Certainly,' and starts right up, so obliging, with this shiny grin, and ends with her arms spread and this little stamp-stamp finish—"
>
> He bit down on his cigarette and stopped his pacing long enough to demonstrate—both hands outflung, one foot poised to stamp. "*Just . . . because . . . it's* JUNE!" he said, and he stamped his foot.
>
> "I love you too," she told him.
>
> "JUNE!" he sang.
>
> "Eh?" he said.
>
> She smiled up at him. (235)

This passage captures Morgan at his most endearing. Fortunately, his engaging and imaginative efforts to stifle his emotions fail. For Emily, who has come to appreciate his endearing eccentricities, now realizes she loves him as well.

One feature of Tyler's wit is the way she allows her characters' minds this free play and then follows them on their whimsical and entertaining digressions, digressions which are both funny and endearing. Another character fond of wandering off the point is Jenny Tull (*Dinner at the Homesick Restaurant*). The same young priest makes a second visit after Sleven, her step-son, takes an umbrella stand shaped like a rhinoceros foot from the church. Slevin has already stolen Jenny's mother's vacuum cleaner because of its resemblance to his mother's. This time the priest comes to Jenny's bustling pediatrics office, where "A naked toddler shot out a door like a stray piece of popcorn, pursued by a nurse with a hyperdermic needle" while he explains his visit (218).

> Jenny said, "I wonder if his mother had a rhinoceros foot."
> "Pardon?" said the priest. (218)

Jenny laughs when she realized what she has said but, chastised by the priest, tries for a more sober tone:

> "I only meant, you see . . . I believe he steals what reminds him of his mother. Hoovers and umbrella stands. Doesn't that make sense?"
> "Ah," said the priest.
> "What's next, I wonder," Jenny said. She mused for a moment. "Picture it! Grand pianos. Kitchen sinks. Why, we'll have his mother's whole household," she said, "her photo albums and her grade-school yearbooks, her college roommate asleep on our bed and her high school boyfriends in our living room." She pictured a row of dressed-up boys from the fifties, their hair slicked down wetly, their shirts ironed crisply, perched on her couch like mannequins, with heart-shaped boxes of chocolates on their knees. (218–219)

Tyler's brand of wit might be better described by turning Bergson's statement on its head: in her novels, the comic demands something like a momentary anaesthesia of the *mind*, rather than the heart. Muriel, the spunky young dog trainer in *Accidental Tourist*, once offered a whimsical but utopian vision of the world that could only be achieved by ignoring the rational. She had spent many days inside a hospital, caring for her prematurely-born infant son and mopping hospital floors to defray the costs. This thought came to her when she took a break and looked out the window from one of the hospital's upper floors:

> You ever wonder what a Martian might think if he happened to land near an emergency room? He'd see an ambulance whizzing in and everybody running out to meet it, tearing the doors open, grabbing up the stretcher, scurrying along with it, "Why," he'd say, "what a helpful planet, what kind and helpful creatures." He'd never guess we're not always that way; that we had to, oh, put aside our natural selves to do it. "What a helpful race of beings," a Martian would say. Don't you think so? (179)

Such irrational but hopeful musings explain why Muriel never becomes a closed, bitter, or resentful person. She has every reason: abandoned by her young husband, saddled with a sick infant, she has no discernible skills—

except for a dogged, relentless determination to remain cheerful, resourceful, and hopeful. And those, in Tyler's world, turn out to be quite enough.

Tyler's characters often appear as comic bumblers, as people who seem
to stumble fortuitously onto the path that is best for them. Few are focused
on any tangible goal, fewer still are concerned with money or careers. They
are hardware store managers, fortune-tellers, and lackadaisical photogra-
phers. What they do is often so incidental to who they are that it is hard to
recognize a Tyler character by his or her occupation. Morgan Gower
(*Morgan's Passing*) manages a hardware store almost incidentally, when
he is not trying on other roles or working out his obsession with Leon and
Emily. Justine Peck (*Searching for Caleb*) may tell fortunes, but her main
occupation is making life possible for herself and her husband. A strong
secondary occupation is helping her grandfather search for his lost brother.
Charlotte Emory (*Earthly Possessions*) imperceptibly passes from helping
out her father in his shabby photography studio to becoming the photogra-
pher herself. The main business of Charlotte's life is to learn how to translate her feeling of helpless passivity—in acquiring a husband, an
occupation, children, boarders, brothers-in-law, and all their inevitable
possessions—to learn how to translate that feeling of helpless passivity
into a kinder, more optimistic, assessment of herself and her life. Charlotte
eventually succeeds. Tyler uses all her persuasive skills to bribe, cajole,
tease, and otherwise disarm us into sympathy with these hapless heroes
and heroines.

But Tyler's heros and heroines are not so hapless as they appear.
Without knowing how to go about it, they all want to live good, useful, and
happy lives. They remain patient and doggedly optimistic in the face of confusion and failure. The lucky ones are drawn to people who can help.
Success for a Tyler character means surrounding yourself with people who
not only love you but help bring out your best nature—a nature that allows
others to be loving and useful in return. All Tyler's main characters struggle towards this position. Elizabeth in *The Clock Winder*, Macon in
Accidental Tourist, Morgan in *Morgan's Passing*, Justine in *Searching for
Caleb* and Ian in *Saint Maybe* struggle successfully. Tyler's wit is continually urging her reader to accept this struggle as the only meaningful one.

THE WIT TO KNOW WHEN TO LET GO:

Anne Tyler openly acknowledges the limitation of her control over characters:

> What's hard is that there are times when your characters simply won't
> obey you. . . . Where did those little paper people get so much power?

I'll have in mind an event for them—a departure, a wedding, a happy ending. I write steadily toward that event, but when I reach it, everything stops. I can't go on. Sentences come out stilted, dialogue doesn't sound real. Every new attempt ends in the wastebasket. I try again from another angle, and then another, until I'm forced to admit it: The characters just won't allow this. I'll have to let the plot go their way. And when I do, everything falls into place.[28]

Voekler ingenuously connects Tyler's respectful attitude toward her characters with her Quaker belief in tolerance:

Invariably, Tyler hands over spontaneous inspiration to one of her characters, . . . each of whom is permitted captainship of his or her destiny within the confines of a random and ungovernable external world. Tyler has cannily observed the abdication of authority at the heart of her emotional connection to her characters—the practice of tolerance become an artistic method. (3)

Tyler apparently believes in the autonomy of all created characters, including even the puppets created by her characters. In *Morgan's Passing*, Emily's puppets have a life of their own, which they assume even while she is making them:

She loved the moment when a puppet seemed to come to life—usually just after she'd sewed the eyes on. Once made, a puppet had his own distinct personality, she found. It couldn't be altered or submerged, and it couldn't be duplicated. If he was irreparably damaged—or stolen, which sometimes happened—she could only make a new one to fill his role; she couldn't make the same one over again. (89)

"That was ridiculous" her husband said when she explained this phenomena to him, voicing many a skeptical reader's reaction to everything I have just quoted. By anticipating and preempting such a response does Tyler defuse it.

Anne Tyler not only acknowledges the limitations of her control over her own creative ability, but she also suggests her faith in that limitation:

I sleep well at night, but I believe some sort of automatic pilot works then to solve problems in my plots: I go to bed trustful that they'll be taken care of by morning. And towards dawn I often wake up and notice, as if from a distance, that my mind is still churning out stories without any help from me at all.[29]

Tyler believes in the self-determination of all created characters, those imagined into life by other writers as well as those she created herself. She writes as if all these fictional characters deserved partial credit for the lives they lead. She concludes her Introduction to *The Best American Short Stories* for 1983 with these words:

I like to imagine that if you set this book on a table, it would almost
bounce; it would almost shout. It contains, after all, a 250-pound
Indian who keeps breaking out of jail, a mistress who mends her shoes
with electrical tape, nine women who live serenely in an ice cave in the
Antarctic, and a boy who hangs from high trees just to see what's out
there. All of these people have proven to be survivors, both in their
own worlds and in my memory. I am proud of them, and I am grateful
to the writers who created them.[30]

TYLER'S CONTROL OVER HER LIFE:

1: Her Public Image

Tyler's generosity as a writer is twofold: she is both prolific and supportive. Just as Tyler presents her fictional characters in the best light
possible, so she tries to stress the strengths of the writers whose fiction
she reviews. It has been said that she only chooses to review books she
expects to like.[31] But her generosity always takes place on paper. Tyler
dislikes giving lectures and most of the few "interviews" we have were
conducted through the US mail. Tyler says she doesn't talk easily, that
she is

the kind of person who wakes up at four in the morning and suddenly
thinks of what she should have said yesterday at lunch. For me, writing something down was the only road out.[32]

Mostly Tyler controls her public image by escape, both geographical and
verbal. Her "distrust of glamour"[33] is reinforced by her preference to stay
home. In 1977, Michaels noted that Tyler wore "bluejeans and size 10
dresses ordered out of catalogues," had "long brown hair that hasn't seen a
beauty parlor since 1958" and "wide blue-gray eyes without makeup."[34]
   Tyler also escapes her public by the distancing technique of wit. She
once wrote that she spent her childhood waiting for adulthood. Nor was she
disappointed:

I figure it was worth the wait. I like everything about it but the paper-
work—the income tax and protesting the Sears bill and renewing the
Triple-A membership. (Sternburg,15)

This is charming and offers details we can all relate to—which is precisely
the point. It doesn't actually tell us anything specifically personal about
Tyler at all. Tyler finds it odd that writers, in the most private of professions, should be hounded to go public:

Why do people imagine that writers, having chosen the most private
of professions, should be any good at performing in public, or should
have the slightest desire to tell their secrets to interviewers from
ladies' magazines? I feel I am only holding myself together by being
very firm about what I will do and I will not do. I will write my books
and raise the children. Anything else just fritters me away. I know
this makes me seem narrow, but in fact I am narrow. I like routines
and rituals and I hate leaving home; I have a sense of digging my
heels in. (Sternberg, 15)

TYLER'S CONTROL OVER HER LIFE:

2: Raising Children and Writing Fiction

Although Tyler sounds extremely organized about balancing her writing
with raising her children, the balance was obviously a strain. In 1977 Tyler
was 35, Mitra was nine and her older sister, Tzeh, an adolescent. Tyler
boasted to Marguerite Michaels in an interview for *The New York Times*: "I
have perfect control of time and I can organize it." Michaels reports Tyler
gave "Five minutes for a peanut butter sandwich lunch. Thirty minutes for
'the highlight of my day'—the mail."[35] But it was just a few years after this,
in 1980, that Tyler wrote of her admiration for her father's adaptability.
Tyler had undoubtedly discovered that no one can have perfect control of
time, or of anything else. Rather, what you can strive to exercise *some* control over is your *attitude* toward time, your *attitude* toward the unexpected
interruptions to your schedule. This adaptable attitude was precisely the
point of Tyler's story about her father's admirable reaction towards the
interruption of his Gaza Strip venture.

For the woman writer who chooses to have a family, children are a difficult hurdle. When Alison Lurie grew so discouraged over her rejections that
she quit writing, it was at the time when her sons were babies: "Did you
ever try to write in the living room with toddlers?" Lurie asks in an interview, "They take hold of the pieces of paper.—I always had playpen pals."
By "playpen pals" Lurie means that she found other mothers of young children who were willing to take turns watching the children, allowing each
mother alternating blocks of free time.[36] Even Tyler admits that when her
children were little "she wasn't half as productive as when they had grown."
Five years went by between the second and third novels. And even though
she inherited the family insomnia which allowed her to lie awake listening
to her characters between two and four in the morning, "when her children
were little she slept right through the night from fatigue?"[37]

Grace Paley took a different approach to motherhood and writing. She
claims she didn't even *try* for a balance, as did Tyler, but rather gave in to

the demands of the babies. But Paley admits this was hard too. Asked about the terrible conflict women poets like Plath or Rich describe, Paley answered, thinking of the fact that Plath had killed herself when her children were aged three and one:

> If Sylvia Plath could have gotten through the next year or two . . . Her period with those kids was probably the hardest, when they're very little, very demanding. Then, if you're trying to do something . . . but I can't speak exactly about that because one of the things I lacked at the time was ambition. It's not that I didn't want to be a writer; it's just that I didn't want to struggle.[38]

Tyler also tried to be philosophical during those years when she wrote very little and felt so useless:

> The only way I could explain my life to myself was to imagine that I was living on a very small commune. I had spent my childhood in a commune, . . . and I was used to the idea of the division of labor. What we had here, I told myself, was a perfectly sensible division of labor: one member was the liaison with the outside world, bringing in money; another was the caretaker, reading *Little Bear* books to the children and repairing electrical switches. This second member might have less physical freedom, but she had much more freedom to arrange her own work schedule. I must have sat down a dozen times a week and very carefully, consciously thought it all through.[39]

When her children were still babies, Tyler was working toward achieving an adaptable attitude, one that would eventually allow her "to accept a school snow-closing as an unexpected holiday, an excuse to play seventeen rounds of Parcheesi instead of typing up a short story.[40] Tyler was convincing herself to extend her mist of irony to include her own life in her comic vision. The fact that her now grown daughter, Tezh, painted the illustration for the jacket of *Ladder of Years*, her latest novel, suggests that her child-rearing philosophy was sound.

Tyler, like Paley, was striving to learn what she could not control. She learned to stop writing when her children came home from school. At one point she tried using a tape recorder to take notes while she was outside of her study, but this did not work: ". . . I was ignoring the partitions, is what it was; I was letting one half of my life intrude upon the other."[41] By learning when to let go, Tyler was also learning what to control. Although she has acknowledged the dangers of endlessly adapting, she is never guilty of the position she ascribes to young Ezra Tull (*Dinner at the Homesick Restaurant*) who, when asked why he would not stand up to a neighborhood bully, replied "I'm trying to get through life as a liquid" (169). The fact that

Tyler has written twelve novels, countless short stories, book reviews, and articles shows that she has learned to maintain an effective balance between adaptability and control.

NOTES

1. Anne Tyler, "Still Just Writing" in *The Writer on Her Work*, ed. Janet Sternburg (NY: Norton, 1980) 12.
2. Tyler, "Still Just Writing" 13.
3. Tyler, "Still Just Writing" 12.
4. Tyler, "Still Just Writing" 10.
5. Tyler, "Still Just Writing" 11.
6. Tyler, "Still Just Writing" 11.
7. Tyler, "Still Just Writing" 11.
8. Anne Tyler, *Earthly Possessions* (1977; NY: Berkley, 1984).
9. Doris Betts, "The Fiction of Anne Tyler," *Sourthern Quarterly* 21.4 (1983): 28.
10. Anne Tyler, *Dinner at the Homesick Restaurant* (1982; NY: Berkley, 1983).
11. Joseph C. Voelker, *Art and the Accidental in Anne Tyler* (Columbia: Univ. of Missouri Press, 1989) 3.
12. Blanche H. Gelfant, *Women Writing in America: Voices in Collage* (Hanover: Univ. Press of New England, 1984) 22. Gelfant boldfaces Paley's words.
13. Tyler, "Still Just Writing" 12–13.
14. Anne Tyler, "Because I Want More Than One Life," *The Washington Post* 15 August 1976: G1 &7. See also Laurie Brown, "Interviews with Seven Contemporary Writers," *Southern Quarterly* 21.4 (1983): 10.
15. Voelker 11.
16. Anne Tyler, *The Clock Winder* (1972; NY: Berkley, 1983).
17. Anne Tyler, *The Accidental Tourist* (1985; NY: Berkley, 1986).
18. Anne Tyler, *Searching for Caleb* (1975; NY: Popular Library, 1977).
19. Anne Tyler, *Saint Maybe* (NY: Knopf, 1991).
20. Clifford A. Ridley, "Anne Tyler: A Sense of Reticence Balanced by 'Oh Well, Why Not?' " *The National Observer* 22 July 1972: 23.
21. Anne Tyler, *Morgan's Passing* (1980; NY: Berkley, 1983).
22. Doris Betts, "Tyler's Marriage of Opposites," *The Fiction of Anne Tyler*, ed. C. Ralph Stephens (Jackson: Univ. Press of Mississippi, 1990) 4.
23. Anne Tyler, *Dinner at the Homesick Restaurant* (1982; NY: Berkley, 1983).
24. Marguerite Michaels, "Anne Tyler, Writer 8:05 to 3:30" *The New York Times Book Review* 8 May 1977: 43.
25. C. Ralph Stephens, introduction to *The Fiction of Anne Tyler* xi.
26. Henri Bergson, "Laughter," and George Meredith, "An Essay on Comedy" in *Comedy: Meaning and Form*, ed. Robert W. Corrigan (NY: Harper & Row, 1981) 239, 327.

27. Susan Gilbert, "Anne Tyler," *Southern Women Writers: The New Generation*, ed. Tonnette Bond Inge (Tuscaloosa: Univ. of Alabama Press, 1990) 227.
28. Tyler, "Because I Wanted More than One Life" G7.
29. Tyler, "Because I Want More Than One Life" G7.
30. Anne Tyler, introduction to *The Best American Short Stories 1983* (Boston: Houghton Mifflin, 1983) xx.
31. A remark made without attribution by Doris Betts, "Tyler's Marriage of Opposites" in Stephens 12.
32. Sternburg 14–15.
33. Voelker 3.
34. Michaels 43.
35. Michaels 13.
36. Mermin, "Alison Lurie," *Women Writers Talking* 81–85.
37. Michaels 42.
38. Gelfant 28.
39. Tyler, "Still Just Writing" 8.
40. Tyler, "Still Just Writing" 11.
41. Tyler, "Still Just Writing" 9.

8

Lisa Alther: Playing for the Laugh: Comic Control in Kinflicks

THE STAND-UP COMIC'S ROUTINE:

The opening segment of Lisa Alther's first novel reads exactly like the "shtick" of a very clever stand-up comedian. A shtick is the yiddish term for a comic routine, a series of exaggerated comments on any given subject composed for the sake of a laugh. If the audience laughs at one joke, the comedian will quickly offer five more. "My family has always been into death," opens *Kinflicks*, Alther's first and funniest novel.[1] This entire brief first chapter, "The Art of Dying Well," could easily be the material for a fifteen-minute shtick on death: how the mother woos it and the father plots against it. Mother decorates the walls of her home with rubbings from her forebears' tombstones and constantly revises her funeral ceremony, obituary, and epitaph. Father keeps "an ice pick next to his placemat at meals so that he could perform an emergency tracheotomy when one of us strangled on a piece of meat"(1). The comic voice belongs to Ginny Babcock, the twenty-seven-year-old daughter. Ginny means to be funny and she is. Ginny sticks to her comic routine on her parents' attitudes towards death for the entire five-page chapter, although she cleverly works in brief allusions to her husband and two earlier boyfriends, promising more about them later. Her tone is merry and her pacing fast. Each paragraph serves up another funny facet of her family's absorption with death.

Alther wisely doesn't try to sustain Ginny's shtick any further. It has served to establish Ginny's wisecracking, defensive personality immediately. But Alther is not simply playing for laughs. Rather, she is establishing the merry tone of her novel. The second chapter switches from a first to a third-person narration. Although it begins as if it could be yet another comic routine, this one on the fear of flying, much in the spirit of Erica Jong's novel by that name, the quips about Ginny's flying fears soon meld into the narrative of her present situation. She is flying home to Tennessee to be with her widowed and hospitalized mother. And thus the pattern of the novel is established: Ginny's first-person chapters, all hilarious in tone and meant to catch us up on her life to date, alternate with chapters narrated in the third-person, where time slows down to the present month and wit moves into a distinctly lower gear.

Ginny's chapters may well be the funnier (as Ferguson points out, Ginny's "voice is almost compulsively witty about existential matters"[2]), but the narrator of the alternate chapters is far from a dry or objective reporter. Consider the way Ginny's father's death is presented in chapter two, the first chapter narrated in the third-person. Ginny is visiting her parents and drives her father to the airport for a business trip to Boston. Waiting to board, he first shocks Ginny by taking an anticoagulant for a minor heart attack he had the previous month, and then by telling her that he and her mother might soon move to Boston permanently. Ginny, shocked a second time, asks him how he could forfeit thirty-five years of memories:

> "Easily. Very easily," he said with a laugh. He threw down the rest of his coffee, stood up and kissed Ginny on the forehead, and raced for his plane, like the candidate for cardiac arrest that he was. Though how a heart of stone could be subject to malfunctions escaped Ginny at the time.
> Two and a half months later he was dead, of a heart attack. (24)

The narrator can be as droll and clever as Ginny, moving with comic ease in and out of Ginny's consciousness but without Ginny's constant compulsion to crack jokes.

One reason Alther inserts these chapters between those narrated directly by Ginny is to allow her readers access to Mrs. Babcock's thoughts, since the narrator moves with ease in and out of the mother's consciousness as well as her daughter's. One critic has presumed the "omniscient narrator" of these chapters is "the Ginny of later years" but I do not find this a helpful observation since Ginny-as-narrator can also be "the Ginny of later years."[3] In fact I see very little difference in tone or insights between the chapters, other than the intensity of the humor in those narrated by Ginny.

Alther's second novel, *Original Sins* (1981) also has a witty opening, although Alther chose not to continue in that direction. The upbeat witty tone doesn't last much beyond the first paragraph:

> The Five had always known they were special. During the summers of the polio scare, when their mothers insisted their legs would shrivel if they didn't take afternoon naps, they complied only to humor the poor women. They themselves had good reason to believe they were invulnerable.[4]

But the very next paragraph adopts a more sober voice, describing the children's grandiose dreams for their future with a mocking but wistful tone for the dreams both the reader and the narrator know will not come true. As Ferguson observed, "Critics who found wit the main attraction of *Kinflicks* have seen *Original Sins* as only a serious version of the same story" (108). There are witty touches in *Original Sins*, however, often in the form of epigrammatic comparisons like the one summing up Mrs. Price's futile attempts to instill a sense of beauty and culture in her two daughters by hanging etched prisms in her living room window and playing Bach fugues on her piano: "It was like trying to wave back a hurricane with a feather duster" (79); or the one describing her husband's indecisive personality, "He was like a live-in Hamlet" (80). Similar touches are found in her next two novels, *Other Women* (1984) and *Bedrock* (1990). But in all three the ratio of humor to seriousness has been reversed. *Kinflicks* was written in a tone of high glee with underpinnings of seriousness, while in the subsequent three the serious tone dominates. However, moments of humor do relieve the seriousness of *Original Sins* and the prevailing pain of *Other Women*. The comic is given even more play in the Vermont town featured in *Bedrock*, but Clea, the main character, is never able to engage her readers so winningly or maintain a comic vision so gleefully as Ginny Babcock does in *Kinflicks*, Alther's most thoroughly comic novel. In *Five Minutes in Heaven*, Alther's most recent novel, Alther strikes more of a balance between humor and seriousness. Her main character, Jude (short for Judith) is clever and perceptive, but the tone of the book is droll rather than gleeful.

THE COMIC FABRIC OF *KINFLICKS*

How does Alther move from that clever but glib opening of *Kinflicks* into so well-developed, thoughtful, and coherent a comic novel? For one thing, she continues to intersperse jokes about her parents' death fears throughout the text, so that the scattered references function like a leitmotif in a Wagnerian opera. When Ginny discusses her college experience at Worthley (a fancy women's college that suspiciously resembles Wellesley—Alther's Alma Mater, as well as Ephron's), she describes attending a production of *Aida* with Miss Head, her philosophy professor, class dean, and mentor. Although she loved the performance, she is unable to resist so golden an opportunity to jest at her parents' expense: "Being sealed in a tomb by a high priest and suffocating was one hazard Mother hadn't thought to warn me about" she observes archly (202).

While Ginny has excessive instruction on how to skirt death and disaster, she seems to have absolutely no parental guidance on sexual matters at all: "My family may have been into death in a big way," she says early in the novel, "but they definitely weren't into sex" (32). Ironically, she loses her virginity on the sleeping platform of the bomb shelter her father has built to outwit death by enemy attack. A few years earlier, she was horrified by her first menstrual period, not having received any preparation for the event. Her mother agreed it was "horrible—but quite normal:"

> "That's life," she concluded. She concluded many of her conversations with the phrase, like a fundamentalist preacher's "Praise the Lord." When she said it, though, the implication was not that one should accept the various indignities of corporeal existence with grace, but rather that one should shift one's focus to the dignities of the dead. (32)

These wry insights stay faithful to the original distinction Ginny drew between her father's desire to outsmart death and her mother's peculiar way of wooing it. But when Ginny goes out with Clem on his motorcycle, her parents' fears and warnings rise up in unison. We could hardly expect Ginny to miss an opportunity to protest this chorus of doom, albeit with what might turn out to be her last breath. Clem is speeding, she riding behind, wearing a yellow chiffon gown which suddenly blows up and blinds him. She loses her balance and falls off the bike. Rolling down a hill, she is sure she is about to die and waits to feel the pain. But:

> I felt nothing. Except a faint twinge of annoyance, as I floated through the air with my skirts billowing like a parachute, that once again my parents had been right. (146)

These allusions are not only funny in themselves but cleverly weave a comic fabric which unifies much of Ginny's humor in the novel.

But the death theme takes on a surprising new dimension when, about three-quarters of the way into the story, we get Mrs. Babcock's version of

who is obsessed with death in the Babcock family. According to her
mother, it is Ginny herself:

> You used to go on and on about it. Why did people die? What hap-
> pened to their bodies? How could God let people die? Would God die?
> Did He have a wife and would she die? Did you have to die? When
> would your father and I die? What would happen to you if we died
> right then and left you all alone? Could you have the car for your own
> after we died? It went on and on. It used to get so ridiculous that your
> father and I would finally collapse in laughter. And then you would
> start crying and accusing us of not caring if you died. I worried about
> it for years. (367)

This is an interesting twist, suggesting Ginny's opening chapter may not be
a simple comedy routine at all, but rather the tip of an extended dramatic
monologue, meant ultimately to illustrate how this character has been pro-
jecting her own fears onto her parents. This interpretation is only possible,
however, if we believe Mrs. Babcock's story, and disavow Ginny's. But
what are we to do with the details Ginny provided about her mother's obsession with her own epitaph, obituary, and funeral service? She asks her
mother this very question. Mrs. Babcock responds:

> You're exaggerating, dear. True, I *did* at one point do an epitaph and a
> format for a memorial service. But that's not unusual. It's like making
> up a will. . . . But I've *never* written an obituary for myself. I wonder
> where you got that idea? (367)

Alther wisely never resolves the issue. Nor could Ginny resolve it to her
own satisfaction. She simply

> . . . stared at her mother suspiciously. Whose version of their shared
> past was accurate? And how could their versions be so different? (367)

And these are the last words on the subject. But they are enough to show
the reader that Ginny is not unreliable intentionally. The jokes at her parents' expense drop off after this point. Her mother's blood disease proves
fatal, a solemn reminder that there was a serious underside to Ginny's
jokes about her parents' death fears. The novel ends with Ginny setting off
from home once again, this time without either parent alive to act as a
buffer against death, if only by having provided a handy receptacle onto
which she could displace her own fears. After several comically-presented
and half-hearted suicide attempts, Ginny acknowledges that she is "condemned to survival," accepts this fate, picks up her knapsack, and heads
off once more on life's journey.

CONTROLLING THE COMIC PLOT

One critic has called *Kinflicks* a "comic bildungsroman," and a "revital-ization of the picaresque novel."[5] Another has noticed that "it's cyclic struc-ture—the departure and return home—is essentially that of the comic epic."[6] Lisa Alther has been compared to Doris Lessing (*The Summer Before the Dark*), Erica Jong (*Fear of Flying*) and even Max Shulman (*Barefoot Boy with Cheek*). A reviewer for *The New Republic* describes Ginny's adventures as "Chaplinesque pratfalls."[7] And John Leonard sees Ginny's speech as "the speech of breezy survivors, of Holden Caulfield, Augie March and, ultimately, Huckleberry Finn."[8]

While these comparisons are useful, no single comparison can suggest the full play of Alther's comic art in this novel. The comic is not confined to voice, be it Ginny's or the narrator's, but is also firmly embedded in the plot, as the comparison to Chaplin implies. For *Kinflicks* is the slapstick version of Ginny's life to age twenty-seven. It may be more accurate to call this a slapstick, rather than a comic, bildungsroman, since slapstick always involves silliness of action and behavior, growing sillier as it gets more out of control, and Ginny's adventures are always recounted in an exaggerated, silly way, with just enough truth at the core to make a point. It is the way many of us would like to describe the adventures in our own past, were we clever enough to channel our regret and exasperation with our younger selves into comic exaggeration.

The delicate balance between truth and exaggeration is well done when Ginny recounts the people who have influenced her. While everyone is influenced by others to *some* degree, Ginny claims she let herself be utterly absorbed. The exaggerated degree of her imitation is reminiscent of Zelig in Woody Allen's movie of the same name. Alther unwittingly invites this comparison by focusing on the way Ginny adopts the other person's way of dressing. The detailed description of each new outfit is a sure sign she has fallen, once again, under another's spell, a clever way to suggest the super-ficiality of the influence and, of course, a very visual, cinematic technique in itself. In Woody Allen's movie, Zelig yearned so much for acceptance by whomever he was with that he could even take on their physical qualities. Standing next to a fat man, he blew up in front of our eyes. Ginny's chameleon-like behavior does not lag far behind Zelig's, although she begins her "clothes-change-the-woman" career modestly enough under the influence of Joe Bob Sparks, her high school's football hero and her first boyfriend.

The first time Ginny goes out with Joe Bob she wears "cordovan loafers with leather tassels and a madras shirtwaist with a Peter Pan Collar," while Joe Bob wears "tan chinos and a plaid Gant shirt and penny loafers" (33).

They are each pleased that the other, out of uniform (his football, her flag swinger), "looked clean and pressed and identical to every other member" of their high school—except for hoods like Clem Cloyd, who later becomes Ginny's second boyfriend (33). She and Joe Bob go window shopping, "each subtly instructing the other on what outfits to buy next" (34). She only takes up with Clem as a diversionary tactic for the benefit of her father and Joe Bob's coach, both of whom object to their relationship. But Clem soon becomes her boyfriend in earnest, and it is with him that Ginnie loses her virginity on the sleeping platform in the bomb shelter. She was sorely disillusioned: "You mean that's *it*?" she asked with dismay (130).

As Clem's girl, Ginny wears a long-sleeved cardigan sweater buttoned up the back, a bra with pointy cups, a small gold cross on a chain round her neck, and a too-tight straight skirt (137). The cheap look. She even wears this outfit when setting off to college, topped with Clem's red-dragon windbreaker. But by Christmas Clem has married the girl whose dress Ginny has been imitating, and Ginny falls under the spell of Miss Head, her philosophy professor and class dean. She buys wool suits, nylon blouses, a cameo brooch, and a green loden coat for the Boston winter. Even Miss Head fails to recognize her after the vacation. When Ginny quits college at the end of the year to live with "Eddie" (Edna) as a lesbian feminist marxist, she wears wheat jeans, "power to the people" t-shirts, and one long braid, "Red-Chinese like" (279). Next she marries Ira Bliss, a staid Vermonter who is more middle class than her own parents. She buys polyester pant suits, jersey tops, and unbraids her hair to wear it pulled back with a scarf. By the time she heads home to visit her ailing mother, she has fallen under Hawk's influence, the frightened army deserter who shows up at Ira's house, hiding beneath a full beard and a smattering of Eastern philosophy. So Ginny appears at the hospital in Tennessee in a patchwork peasant dress, combat boots, frizzy Anglo-Afro hairdo, knapsack and poncho. Mrs. Babcock silently acknowledges the transformation with grim wit: "Who was she this time, Heidi?" she thinks to herself (78).

The truth behind these amusing descriptions is temporarily hidden by the exaggeration of their presentations. Ginny's conversions also appear that much more foolish by virtue of their being added together, which is precisely what Alther encourages us to do. The narrator adds them together herself early in the novel, as a kind of preview, foreshadowing all the changes yet to take place. Ginny's different roles are emphasized by the novel's title, *Kinflicks*, the name Ginny and her brothers give to the pictures their mother snaps of every significant occasion in their lives:

A preview of the kinflicks of Ginny's arrivals and departures from this airport would have shown her descending or ascending the steps of

> neglected DC-7's in a dizzying succession of disguises—a black cardigan buttoned up the back . . .; a smart tweed suit and horn-rim Ben Franklin glasses . . .; wheat jeans and a black turtleneck . . . (16)

This section continues to describe Ginny's different outfits and then offers a series of jokes about Ginny's lack of conviction: "In a restaurant after ordering, she always ended up hoping the kitchen would be out of her original selection so that she could switch to whatever her neighbor had" (17). People seemed to sense her vulnerability and always approached her for donations: ". . . she was an easy lay, spiritually speaking." The narrator caps off the jokes with one final summarizing quip: "Normally, she was prepared to believe in anything. At least for a while" (17). This long paragraph on the topic of Ginny's too-ready conversions, situated early in the novel, can be considered a "mini-shtick" establishing a second comic theme. For scattered throughout the text are many subsequent references to her different outfits, her "disguises," which build into a second leitmotif, a second unifying comic theme in the novel.

But the comic presentation of Ginny's conversions has a serious underside, as do the jokes about the Babcocks' death fears. People do learn through imitation, which is a necessary stage of development. Alther appeals to the Hegelian dialectic of thesis, antithesis, and synthesis to suggest the necessary adoption, rejection, and eventual unification of the opposing fragmented selves in any person's development. But Alther manages to suggest the validity of the Hegelian dialectic even while incorporating Hegel into Ginny's limited, and thereby comic, vision:

> Fortunately, I no longer cared what Clem thought. I had studied Hegel. I knew that Clem had merely played the antithesis to Joe Bob's thesis, and that Miss Head was the pure and elevated synthesis. That Miss Head herself might be the thesis for a yet higher synthesis, as Hegel would have insisted, was unthinkable. (211–212)

Ginny makes this observation midway through her story, before she rejects Miss Head for Eddie. But the humor of her limited perception does not undercut the potential seriousness of Hegel's theory. The fact that the theory is pushed rather far in the novel is simply another illustration of Alther's wit.

VISUAL SLAPSTICK WITHIN THE COMIC PLOT OF *KINFLICKS*

The most blatant instances of wit embedded in the plot is what I will call visual slapstick, or exaggeration of action—Alther's literary version of the

pie-in-the-face routine. Sochen has described the slapstick style of vaude-
ville and burlesque as "a physically rough-and-tumble style," where

> even the verbal humor was accompanied by a lot of pushing and shov-
> ing. Punching your partner, flaying your arms and legs regularly, and
> presenting yourself as a physical clutz were integral parts of the comic
> routine.[9]

This is an apt description of certain scenes in Alther's novel. These slapstick
scenes almost always have a sexual theme. Ira's efforts to bring Ginny to
orgasm by faithfully following a sex manual is one obvious example. He has
them stand on chairs and each raise one arm so he can handcuff them together
over the ceiling beam. When Ginny calls a halt due to an aching arm, Ira accidentally drops the key and, in trying to retreive it, knocks their chairs over.
Eventually, Ira manages to dial the phone with his big toe, and calls Ginny's
hippy friends (from her life just before this one) to come and rescue them.
These old friends enter with dilated pupils and, a nice touch, see Ira and Ginny
dangling naked "with no more than passing interest" (395). Another example
of visual slapstick is the scene when her roommate's vibrator causes a short
circuit, blowing out the lights and starting a fire in the walls. Nearly all the
scenes of Ginny's sexual fumbling with Joe Bob and Clem fall into this type
of graphic buffoonery—whether she is making out with Joe Bob in the trunk
of a car or with Clem on the sleeping platform of her father's bomb shelter.

LITERARY SLAPSTICK IN *KINFLICKS*

Related to this visual slapstick, or exaggeratedly silly action, is literary
slapstick, or exaggeratedly silly metaphors. Many of Alther's comparisons
and observations fall into this category, where either the imagery or the idea
expands to an unbelievably silly dimension. Once, when the teen-aged
Ginny met Joe Bob in the high school darkroom (their daytime trysting
place), in order to return his jacket and ring, she was settling in for a melo-
dramatic crying jag but

> The next thing I knew, I was holding his stiff cock in one hand as he
> lurched back and forth in front of me. I felt as though I were an animal
> trainer trying to lead a recalcitrant baby elephant by the trunk. (59)

During her first few months at college, Ginny settles into solitary self-pity:

> I wrote Clem lots of lonely letters. He wrote me lots of identical
> lonely letters. We could have saved enough money in postage to have
> financed an elopement by writing lonely letters to ourselves. (181)

Even the weather can be subjected to such exaggeration. Ginny endures a Memorial Day picnic with Ira's relatives, where she has absolutely nothing to discuss but the weather, since she has absolutely nothing in common with them "—other than living under identical cloud cover" (391). Finally, the storm they are all discussing rolls in and Ginny observes that:

> It was the first storm of the season, a treat in snow country after endless months of silently drifting white fluff. There was something so refreshingly candid about an electric storm. You knew where you stood. Nature was out to sizzle you alive. (391)

The ratio of exaggeration to truth may be ninety-nine to one, as it is in these three examples, but there has to be that small grain of truth for them to work. They work precisely because of that small truth which Alther captures, blows up, and offers to her readers with a merry, well-timed, and foolish flourish.

THE EFFECT OF RESTRAINT:

Since so much of the novel is steeped in the jocular tone of visual or literary slapstick, the few topics that are treated with a more delicate wit take on a greater significance by virtue of their restrained and tactful presentation. The scene where Ginny finally asks for her mother's advice is one of them. Unbeknownst to Ginny, her mother has been reviewing her own life and undergoing her own transformation while confined to her hospital bed. She cannot signal this by a change of outfit, but she does show some personality changes that startle Ginny. Mrs. Babcock's life had been devoted to serving her family, to keeping the peace, and accommodating everyone but herself. But in the hospital she begins to experience irritation, anger, and even the pleasure of minor insurrection. One day a fellow patient complains that he continues to be served a certain vegetable he has told the staff never to serve him:

> Mrs. Babcock—whom Ginny had never seen do anything more insurrectionary than prop open an occasional pay-toilet door—suggested under her breath, "Dump it on the floor and pretend you spilled it," (158)

Ginny ascribes her mother's uncharacteristic response to the peevishness of a hospital patient, not realizing that its roots are far deeper. Ginny is not aware that Mrs. Babcock has begun questioning why she has done what was expected of her all her life—as daughter, wife, mother, and now as hospital patient. So when Ginny finally asks her mother what to do about her troubled marriage to Ira, she is anticipating the traditional response. After all, Ginny has a young daughter as well as a husband. Her mother will certainly hand down the precept of doing one's duty that she has inherited from her own mother—Ginny does not know why she has even bothered to ask. But her mother surprises her:

> "I don't know what you should do, Ginny," she replied finally, with enormous difficulty. "You must do as you think best." (430–431)

Alther's delicate wit in describing Ginny's reaction to this response serves both to highlight its importance in the novel and to rescue the situation from banal feminist dogma:

> Ginny's eyes snapped open, as though she were Sleeping Beauty just kissed by the prince. She stared at her bruised mother. Mrs. Babcock opened her good eye and stared back. Was it possible that the generational spell had actually been broken? They smiled at each other, their delight mixed with distress. (431)

This is a crucial scene for Ginny. It means that at the end of the novel, when she sets out on a new path for an unknown destination, she goes with her mother's blessings.

One topic that Alther never ridicules is sex between women, although the novel has been described as "X-rated" and "ribald." But these adjectives describe the scenes between Ginny and Joe Bob, Clem, or Ira, or Ginny and an occasional blind date. Alther can never be accused of delicacy over matters (hetero) sexual. But when it comes to the actual act of sex between Ginny and a woman, Alther is close-mouthed and discreet. The first time Ginny spends the night in Eddie's (Edna's) room she "woke up delighted finally to know who put what where in physical love between women" (239). And that is all she has to say on the subject. Not that Alther exempts Eddie and Ginny's more public behavior from her expert mockery. Their feigned enthusiasm for soybeans, their righteous feminist/marxist dogma, and their lazy farming techniques all feed Alther's wit. But her refusal to discuss their physical coupling alongside all the heterosexual fumbling lends it a nice dignity in a book where very little has been exempt from ridicule.

THE ILLUSION OF CONTROL

What does Alther accomplish by creating so highly comic a version of a coming-of-age novel, by creating this slapstick bildungsroman? For one thing, Ginny's relentlessly comic presentation shifts much of the ridicule away from the main character onto her nearest neighbors. It does not matter if the values are those of right-wing citizens of Hullsport, Tennessee, of intellectual New England professors, or of members of a feminist/marxist commune—Alther finds them all a rich source for ridicule. The novel can be seen as a struggle between each one of these groups for Ginny's soul: each tries to fence her into a new belief system while she, by virtue of her comic aplomb, always manages to scramble out the other side.

To state this another way, the wit and perceptiveness of the presentation gives us the sense that Ginny is more in control of her life than she actually is. The novel ends on an ambiguously hopeful note, which is not quite the same as a positive one. The only firm fact we have is that Ginny will not kill herself. It seems fairly clear that she does not intend to go back to her marriage, but where she will end up is unknown to us and herself. And what exactly has she learned? That life (and death) goes on? That parents do not have the answers? That each of us is condemned to live (and die) alone? That another person's path cannot become our path?

But the end of the novel *feels* more reassuring than this, because we refuse to believe that so clever a character will not be able to figure out how she should best live her life. Wit has clearly given Lisa Alther control of her material, but this is not the same thing as saying wit has given Ginny Babcock control of her life. Paradoxically, the final fact of Ginny not having control can be seen in a positive light. Her bewilderment at the end saves this novel from too pat a finale and preserves the source of much of its humor and charm—Ginny's perplexity with the world around her.

LISA ALTHER'S LIFE

Lisa Alther was born on July 23, 1944 in Kingsport, Tennessee, a small city in the eastern part of the state that appears as Hullsport, Ginny's hometown in *Kinflicks*. And, like her comic heroine, she attended public schools there before going to a prestigious women's college in Massachusetts. Lisa Alther graduated from Wellesley in 1966, the model for Worthley, the college Ginny Babcock did *not* graduate from. Both author and character then moved to small towns in Vermont, although Lisa Alther made hers a permanent home, while life in a small Vermont town turned out to be just one more stage in Ginny Babcock's comic romp through adolescence. Both married and had daughters. Lisa Alther's daughter, Sarah Halsey, was born in 1968 when she was twenty-four. Ginny Babcock was about the same age when she gave birth to her daughter Wendy. Alther is now divorced and every detail at the end of *Kinflicks* suggests that Ginny Babcock was on her way to a divorce as well.[10]

But, as Ferguson wisely cautions, Alther's novels are never simplistically autobiographical:

> Her father did not die . . . as did Ginny Babcock's in *Kinflicks*; nor did her mother die of a lingering painful blood disease. . . . Her parents are alive and well in Tennessee, and she visits them frequently, as well as siblings still in the South . . .[11]

Her father, John Shelton, is a surgeon and her mother, Alice Margaret Greene Reed, taught English after college. Alther is one of five children. She returned to Kingsport for her large family wedding in August, 1966, after graduating from Wellesley. She married Richard Philip Alther, a painter.[12] Like Grace Paley and Dorothy Parker, Alther has kept her first husband's name, while Ephron, Jackson, Lurie, and Tyler never used any of their husbands' names professionally.

Alther told Ferguson that she writes fiction to answer questions about life that puzzle her. Most of her characters begin "as a conglomerate of four or five people."[13] This means Ginny is not Alther, then, in the same way that Faith is not Paley. Faith, the main character in many of Grace Paley's stories, began as Paley's friend Sybil, who was serving both her current and ex-husband eggs one day when Paley stopped over. ("There were two husbands disappointed by eggs" Paley's story "The Used-Boy Raisers" begins.) But no sooner did Paley create her than Faith ceased being just Sybil and took on the characteristics of at least four other friends. Paley was very familiar with the circumstances of their lives, she explained in an interview, but those circumstances were not hers.[14] Like Alther's, Paley's main characters grapple with issues that interest her creator.

WRITING FICTION AND RAISING A CHILD

Alther kept writing despite the rejection slips. She said she had tried to publish for over ten years before she had any success, piling up over 250 rejection slips in the process. Nevertheless, she kept at it even during her daughter's infancy. Her innovative approach to carving out the time to write during this difficult time may have added to the mood of frenetic merriment in *Kinflicks*. She told Ferguson that she wrote half of the novel in "a white heat of creativity," spending two weeks every two months in a boarding house in Montreal for over two years, leaving her daughter in the care of her cooperative husband. I find it telling that she needed to make few changes in this part.[15]

Like most writer/mothers, once her child attended school, Alther wrote during school hours. Shirley Jackson claimed that she wrote "The Lottery" in a single morning, and was finished before her kindergardener came home for lunch. Pregnant with her third, the idea for the story developed as she pushed her toddler back up the hill from her daily shopping routine: "Perhaps the effort of that last fifty yards up the hill put an edge to the story," she later teased, "It was a warm morning and the hill was steep." She sent it off the next day with only a few minor corrections.[16] Alther follows a less frenetic time frame, letting several months go by between drafts. Since she writes four or five drafts before sending anything off, she considers herself a slow writer.[17] She estimates that it takes her about five years to create each novel.[18]

Although all five of Alther's novels have been commercially successful, critical opinion is divided over which has the most merit. Each of her first three novels has been *someone's* favorite, although I had assumed everyone would prefer *Kinflicks*, her earliest and wittiest. Many do, to be sure. But Paul Gray reviewed *Original Sins* for *Time* magazine by raising the question so often asked the author of a highly successful first novel: What can she do for an encore? According to Gray, Alther answers the question with *Original Sins* quite nicely. She "does pretty much the same thing [as she did in *Kinflicks*] over again, except that she does more of it and better."[19] And Adrian Oktenberg ended her review of *Other Women* with this pronouncement:

> All comedy is tragic; all tragedy is finally comic. That Lisa Alther
> understands this, and fuses the two, is one of her great gifts as a writer.
> *Other Women* is a gift to its reader and her best book to date.[20]

Not all the reviews have been positive. With the exception of the reviews for *Kinflicks*, the balance may actually tip in the other direction. For Alther does take risks. She will talk about women loving other women. Lesbianism is a recurrent theme in her novels. However tempered by her wit, it is still a difficult topic to urge on the general public. A second hurdle for many is the way Alther mixes comedy and tragedy within one novel. Even some who agree with Oktenberg that all comedy is ultimately tragic and all tragedy comic do not care to see both in a single novel. And, finally, slapstick humor has to be the most difficult kind to achieve, since it can so easily get out of control. But if 250 rejections could not throw Alther off course, we need not concern ourselves over a few negative reviews. Alther will keep on writing. She told Ferguson she would continue to write fiction even without an audience, as she did for the first twelve years of her writing career.[21] But her loyal and growing following should ensure against that ever happening again.

NOTES

1. Lisa Alther, *Kinflicks* (1975; NY: NAL, 1977).
2. Mary Anne Ferguson, "Lisa Alther: The Irony of Return?" *The Southern Quarterly* 21.4 (1983): 104.
3. Bonnie H. Braendlin, "Alther, Atwood, Ballantyne, and Gray: Secular Salvation in the Contemporary Feminist Bildungsroman," *Frontiers* 4.1 (1979): 19.
4. Lisa Alther, *Original Sins* (NY: NAL, 1981) 3.
5. Bonnie Braendlin, "New Directions in the Contemporary Bildungsroman: Lisa Alther's *Kinflicks*," in *Gender and Literary Voice*, ed. Janet Todd (NY: Holmes & Meier, 1980) 168; and Braendlin, "Alther, Atwood, Ballentyne, and Gray," 19.
6. Ferguson 104.
7. Mark Shechner, "A Novel of the New South," *The New Republic* 13 June 1981: 34.
8. John Leonard, rev. of *Kinflicks* by Lisa Alther, *The New York Times Book Review* 14 March 1976: 4.
9. June Sochen, "Slapsticks, Screwballs and Bawds," *Women's Comic Visions*, ed. June Sochen (Detroit: Wayne State Press, 1991) 143.
10. Mary Ann Ferguson, "Lisa Alther," *Contemporary Fiction Writers of the South* ed. Joseph Flora and Robert Bain (Westport CT: Greenwood Press, 1993) 22.
11. Ferguson, *Cont. Fiction Writers 24.*
12. Ferguson, *Cont. Fiction Writers 22.*
13. Ferguson, *Cont. Fiction Writers 24.*
14. Joan Lidoff, "Clearing Her Throat: An Interview with Grace Paley," *Shenandoah* 22.3 (1981): 11.
15. Ferguson, *Cont. Fiction Writers 23.*
16. Judy Oppenheimer, *Private Demons* (NY: Putnam, 1988) 127.
17. Ferguson, *Cont. Fiction Writers 23.*
18. Carol Edwards. "Interview With Lisa Alther," *Turnstile* 4.1 (1993): 48.
19. Paul Gray, "Beating the Sophomore Jinx," *Time* 27 April, 1981: 71.
20. Adrian Oktenberg, "Odd Couple," *New Directions for Women* 14.1 Jan/Feb (1985): 20.
21. Ferguson, Cont. Fiction Writers 24.

9

Rita Mae Brown: "An Equal Opportunity Offender"

KNOCKING DOWN BARRIERS WITH HUMOR:

Rubyfruit Jungle, Brown's first novel, was an underground success by 1977. In that year Bantam bought it from Daughters Press, who had managed to sell 70,000 copies in four years by word-of-mouth advertising alone. The same month that Bantam bought the rights for $250,000, Judy Klemesrud interviewed Rita Mae Brown for the *New York Times*.[1] The caption for the photograph of Brown accompanying the interview read: "Rita Mae Brown: Knocking down barriers with humor," referring to Brown's comment that "Funny people are dangerous. They knock down barriers." The main barrier for Brown, as for Molly Bolt, the heroine of *Rubyfruit Jungle*, is that she is an unabashed and witty lesbian. Rita Mae Brown is an outspoken, funny, and often sassy writer who has always tried to maintain a not-so-delicate balance between knocking down barriers on the one hand and offending middle class sensibilities on the other. But any offence taken, to be fair to both writer and audience, is more likely due to literary high jinks and scatological language than to the presence of sympathetic lesbian characters. Brown dares to be silly and clearly enjoys using ribald language.

Since *Rubyfruit Jungle*, Rita Mae Brown has published eight more novels and three mysteries, cleverly narrated (and solved) by her cat, who

149

shares authorship credit on the covers: *Wish You Were Here* and *Rest in Pieces*, and *Pay Dirt* by Rita Mae Brown and Sneaky Pie Brown. In addition, Brown has brought out an unusual writers' manual, two volumes of poetry, a collection of feminist essays, and written screenplays. Her clever titles suggest her sassy voice: *The Hand that Cradles the Rock* is an early collection of rebellious revolutionary poetry and *The Plain Brown Rapper* is her apt title for the collection of hard-hitting feminist essays.

Starting From Scratch, A Different Kind of Writers' Manual is as crammed with the personal reminiscences of the established writer as it is with practical advice for the potential one. Brown explains her attitude towards wit early in the manual, when she recalls what her hopes had been for *Rubyfruit Jungle*:

> I wanted my novel to be so witty that even Republicans would be forced to enjoy it. I think my reach exceeded my grasp—it still does—but *Rubyfruit Jungle* was an energetic beginning.[2]

That it was. Brown claims that writing it taught her an important lesson, one that her subsequent writings show she has never forgotten. The lesson? That "seriousness is the refuge of the shallow," a clever adaptation of Samuel Johnson's observation that patriotism is the last refuge of a scoundrel (13).

Rita Mae Brown's recollections in the writers' manual move on to the years immediately following the initial publication of *Rubyfruit Jungle* in 1973, when she had finished writing her second novel, *In Her Day*, and had no money to begin a third. Recalling her desperation, her thoughts about wit grow serious:

> Try to remember back to that time. . . . Stories from a woman who was Southern, poor, and rebellious were not in big demand. I had an even worse strike against me: I was funny. Humor comes from self-confidence. There is an aggressive element to wit. It's one thing for a man to be funny on the page. Mark Twain was lionized for it (although for years people didn't realize he was writing for adults). It's another thing for a woman to be funny on the page. (*Starting From Scratch* 15)

Brown then added an important qualification:

> Erma Bombeck is screamingly funny but she's also on safe "feminine" territory. This is no criticism of her; I'm appreciative of her consummate skill. But I was not on "feminine" territory. (*Scratch* 15)

Bombeck's "feminine" territory is not so much her domestic subject matter as it is her self-deprecating approach. Brown prefers subjects like war, politics and sex and she would never be called self-deprecating. Not only does

Brown realize her territory was unsafe, but she admits her dreams were big, an admission too few women make:

> From the very beginning I was bucking for my chance to hit in the majors. I took on the individual versus society. I invaded sacred male territory: war. I took on the power imbalance between men and women without apologizing to either men or women. Why? I am an equal opportunity offender. (*Scratch* 15)

In 1976 Brown dedicated her powerful collection of feminist essays, *The Plain Brown Rapper*, to the co-organizers of "The Furies," a feminist collective she helped establish in 1970. Brown dedicated it to them even though she had been voted out of the collective by 1972. In her introduction she explains that she feels her expulsion was caused not only by her lack of sympathy with middle-class women's lives, but also by the problems women have facing strength in another woman. For by 1972 Brown was a budding young writer who was beginning to enjoy the powers of the pen:

> Since my gifts were more obvious at that time because of the circumstances of my life, I became dangerous. That I had gifts was sin enough. That I refused to apologize for them was unforgivable. That I blatantly enjoyed them was horrendous.[3]

For a woman writing in America in 1972, self-deprecation was still the safest route to acceptance, not only by the men in your audience, but, as Brown realizes, by the women as well.

Although she has never shied away from presenting the lesbian woman's story, Brown does not want to be remembered only as a lesbian writer. Such pigeon-holing angers her. In 1977 she told Judy Klemesrud that she planned to

> write a lot of books and hope people get over calling me "Rita Mae Brown, the lesbian author." I want them to remember me as "Rita Mae Brown, author." And I hope they say, "She was fun."[4]

She concluded an interview for *Publisher's Weekly* the following year with the same thought in sassier form, gamely threatening that the

> next time anybody calls me a lesbian writer I'm going to knock their teeth in. I'm a writer, and I'm a woman and I'm from the South and I'm alive, and that's that.[5]

Brown has always been open about her lesbianism, both in her writing and her life, a brave and occasionally belligerent position. Her refusal to hide her sexual preference made her an easy target for the administrators at the University of Florida who needed an excuse to expel her for joining black students in the struggle for civil rights in 1964. As Brown put it:

> The black individual was in danger but had a great deal to gain. The white individual was in danger and had a great deal to lose, namely the friendship of other whites. (*Scratch* 11)

Brown also had a scholarship to lose. She was accused of seducing other women, forced to see a psychiatrist daily, awarded a failing grade in a course where she entered the final with a 99% average, and, finally, separated from her funding.[6]

Her continued insistence on being heard as a lesbian caused her split with the National Organization for Women during its formative years in the late sixties and early seventies. According to Brown, in those years even the closet lesbians were purged from NOW.[7] There has subsequently been a major policy shift in this organization, since lesbians were highly visible at their twenty-fifth birthday celebration in January of 1992. Indeed, most of the standup comics brought in for a standing-room only Comedy Night and Dance were openly lesbian. But this change would probably have taken longer had it not been for Rita Mae Brown and others like her who risked offending in order to fight for lesbian interests when it was an even less popular fight than it is today.

RUBYFRUIT JUNGLE: THE POWER OF LAUGHTER

Rubyfruit Jungle is Brown's dynamic and merry rendition of coming of age in America in the sixties. Molly Bolt, like Rita Mae Brown, was born poor, white, and Southern. Although she gamely experiments with both sexes from an early age, she prefers her own. But, as Terry Curtis Fox observed in the *Village Voice*, "You don't have to be gay or female to identify with Molly Bolt—she is one of the outsiders many of us believe ourselves to be."[8]

Rubyfruit Jungle is highly autobiographical. Even some of the bizarre details of Molly's experience come from Brown's life. When Rita Mae Brown went to New York City, she actually did live briefly in an abandoned car. She was broke. It happened immediately after her University of Florida college scholarship had been revoked. In the novel, Molly Bolt, a coed at the same university, is called on the carpet for her lesbian behavior, for being in love with her roommate, and her scholarship revoked for "moral reasons," although the authorities admit her grades were excellent. Molly goes home only to be kicked out by her mother. So she hitchhikes to New

York City, with $24.61 in her pocket. Then Molly, like her creator, spends her first few nights in New York in an abandoned car.

Both Rita Mae Brown and Molly were adopted children whose natural parents were known in their communities, small towns in York County, Pennsylvania. Brown explains that her natural father

> a Venable (a Virginia family with a deep taproot in Charlottesville), was not married to my natural mother, a Young. Julia and Ralph Brown were fair people with beautiful gray eyes. Dad Brown had blond hair when young. There I was, with my dark hair, a living testimony to the persistence of Gallic genes. No one had to tell me. My natural father lived right there in York and my natural mother wasn't all that far away. In a fight at school the first word out of some kid's mouth was "bastard." (*Scratch* 8)

In *RubyFruit Jungle*, Molly's natural father was a Frenchman who hardly spoke a word of English. But, as her adoptive mother Carrie pointed out, "probably for what they were doing they didn't need no talking."[9]

Rita Mae Brown moved with her adoptive family to Fort Lauderdale in 1955, when she was eleven. Molly Bolt moves with hers to Florida between sixth and seventh grades. Both life and fiction offer the young girls a fresh start, providing them with communities where their illegitimate status is unknown. In Pennsylvania, both Rita and her fictional counterpart Molly used their fists to gain respect. In Florida, they could use their heads. As Rita Mae Brown puts it, "In Fort Lauderdale no one cared. I had an equal chance. I made the most of it.[10] So does Molly Bolt. Her school is divided between rich kids and red-necks. She does not fit in either group. Molly knows she is not rich but then again "she wasn't walking around with little plastic clothespins on her collar like all the red-neck girls either" (61).

In the novel, Molly maps out a strategy for survival. She makes good grades and learns to talk like the rich kids. She could *think* bad grammar, the way they talk at home, but she teaches herself not to speak it. This language barrier is not the same as the one that angered the young Grace Paley. As a child, Paley had objected to the standard English pronunciation the immigrant children were encouraged to imitate because she saw it as a way of erasing each immigrant group's cultural identity. Paley's English, and that of all immigrant groups, was flavored by the language of another proud culture. But Molly realizes that *her* speech patterns had been flavored by ignorance. Next, Molly decides to buy a few good outfits rather than her usual larger assortment of cheap clothes. But her ace in the hole is wit:

> I decided to become the funniest person in the whole school. If someone makes you laugh you have to like her. I even made my teachers laugh. It worked. (62)

This maneuver is similar to the strategy adopted by the young heroine of
Margaret Drabble's in *The Middle Ground*. Both characters recognize the
power of wit. Drabble's character, Kate Armstrong, is also eleven when she
enters a new school and invents a new persona. In her case, her family has
simply moved two miles away into a new and better neighborhood. Kate
was an outsider at her old school—she was handicapped by a fat, agora-
phobic mother, a skinny father who loved his job at the sewage plant, and a
fat, timid, older brother. She exacerbated the situation by fighting her class-
mates' aggressive teasing with her own fiercer aggression. She had no
friends. Then her family moved, and:

> . . . Kate realized, more or less overnight, that one of the ways to avoid
> being a butt or laughingstock yourself is to make people laugh—not as
> in the pious old cliché "*with* you rather than *at* you"; no they had to laugh
> *at* you, but they had to laugh because *you made them*, because you were
> funny . . . she realised that it was fine to be the centre of attention on
> one's own terms, and that there was nothing, literally, nothing, that
> couldn't be turned into a joke. In fact, the more horrible and discred-
> itable the subject matter, the better the joke.[11] (Italics Drabble's)

What both the young Kate Armstrong and Molly Bolt recognize is the power
of wit, the same power that Ephron's Rachel Samstat calls on in *Heartburn*
to fend off our pity, the same power Tyler's Jenny Tull acquires in *Dinner at
the Homesick Restaurant* when she needs to learn how to fend off sadness
and anxiety. Jenny is trying to make it through life on a slant. Molly Bolt,
unlike Jenny Tull, prefers to face life head on, but she prefers to face it surrounded by friends and admirers whom she has won over by her wit.

RUBYFRUIT JUNGLE: AN UPDATED *JANE EYRE*

Rubyfruit Jungle has been called an "inspiring bravado adventure story
of a female Huck Finn."[12] Huck Finn certainly anticipates Molly Bolt's
sassy and indomitable tone, but another helpful comparison is to *Jane Eyre*.
Both *Rubyfruit Jungle* and Charlotte Brontë's novel share the satisfying pattern of the young outsider determined to remain true to her principles and
seek her fortune on her own terms. They are both feminized versions of the
archetypal quest pattern of myth and fairy tale, one Molly Bolt herself recognizes when Calvin, the young man with whom she shared an abandoned
car, asks her to join him hitching to San Francisco:

> This is going to sound weird, Calvin, but something tells me I have to
> stay in this ugly city for awhile. I don't know how long, but I have to

be here. It's like I'll make my fortune here or something. Remember
those old children's stories where the young son goes out on the road
for adventure and to make his fortune after he's been cheated out of his
inheritance by his evil brothers? (*RJ*, 151)

Both *Rubyfruit Jungle* and *Jane Eyre* begin with the child's point of
view. Fox's praise of Brown's novel, written for a 1977 issue of the *Village
Voice*, could have been describing the opening of Brontës 1847 novel just
as accurately:

> . . . her evocation of childhood is astonishing; without ever losing the
> perspective of an adult looking back, she enters into a child's con-
> sciousness, thus playing fair with both the reader and the character. (41)

Both Molly Bolt and Jane Eyre are orphans raised by women who cruelly
emphasize the children's marginal positions in their families. Neither
mother-substitute is a blood relation. Jane's aunt is grudgingly carrying
out a deathbed promise to her deceased husband, who was Jane's
mother's brother. Molly's stepmother adopts the illegitimate baby after
she learns of her husband's sterility brought on by syphilis. Both children
are surrounded by fatuous, dimwitted cousins, though Molly loves her
cousin Leroy while Jane understandably despises her tormentor John
Reed and his insipid sisters.

Both children learn to fend for themselves at an early age, even reinter-
preting theology when necessary. Each novel opens with an example of the
heroine's rebellious misbehavior. Molly is punished for running an after-
school sideshow featuring her friend Brockhurst (Broccoli for short) and
his yet-to-be-circumcised penis: five cents a look, ten cents a touch. Jane is
locked up for finally striking back at her cousin John, who habitually
abuses her. When Carrie, Molly's stepmother, angrily tells her she is a bas-
tard, whose natural mother is "A common, dirty slut who'd lay with a dog
if it shook its ass right" Molly yells back "I don't care. It makes no difference where I came from. I'm here, ain't I" (7). Molly runs off to be alone
and repeats the idea to get used to it herself: "Who cares how you get here?
I don't care. I really don't care. I got myself born, that's what counts" (9).
In Brontë's novel, Jane's aunt calls in Mr. Brocklehurst, the hypocritical
master of a school for poor clergymen's daughters, where she plans to
enroll Jane. He and Jane have the following exchange:

> "Do you know where the wicked go after death?' " [Mr.
> Brocklehurst]
> "They go to hell," was my ready and orthodox answer.
> "And what is hell? Can you tell me that?"

"A pit full of fire."
"And should you like to fall into that pit and to be burning there for
ever?"
"No, sir."
"What must you do to avoid it?"
I deliberated a moment; my answer when it did come, was objec-
tionable: "I must keep in good health, and not die."[13]

Jane may be more *polite* than Molly, but she is no less determined to stand
up for her right to live, come what may.

Eventually, both Molly and Jane grow up, continue to stand up to the
outside world, care for themselves when no one else will, and stay true to
their own ethical standards. Jane not only gets her man on her own terms,
but discovers an inheritance and a different set of loving cousins. Brontë
leaves no aspect of happiness unaccounted for. Molly's success is not so
palpable as Jane's, but she is moving in that direction. Thrown out of
Florida State on a morals charge, she finishes Summa Cum Laude and Phi
Beta Kappa at NYU. Her final project for her degree in filmmaking is a simple film of her aging lonely stepmother, rocking in her chair and talking
back to life. When her requests to sign out camera equipment are ignored,
she steals the equipment for the week it takes her to go to Florida and make
her film.

As young adults, both Molly and Jane learn to forgive the two women
who had caused them so much suffering as children, but only Molly can feel
love for the woman who raised her. For Jane it is too late for love. As her
aunt lies on her death bed, Jane speaks to her one last time:

My disposition is not so bad as you think; I am passionate, but not
vindictive. Many a time, as a little child, I should have been glad to
love you if you would have let me; and I long earnestly to be recon-
ciled to you now: kiss me, aunt. (*Jane Eyre*, 242)

But Mrs. Reed turns her head away. Jane forgives her anyway. Carrie,
Molly's stepmother, refuses to admit she ever did anything for Molly to forgive in the first place. Carrie simply denies she ever said that she was glad
that Molly was not her real child. Still Carrie, unlike Mrs. Reed, has always
had her adopted daughter's love. When Mollie finishes filming Carrie, she
calls for a taxi to start her trip back to New York. As her taxi is pulling away
from Carrie's faded pink stucco home, Molly looks back at her mother leaning in the doorway and waves, thinking:

Carrie, Carrie, whose politics are to the right of Genghis Khan.
Who believes that if the good Lord wanted us to live together he'd
have made us all one color. Who believes a woman is only as good as

the man she's with. And I love her. Even when I hated her, I loved her. Maybe all kids love their mothers, and she's the only mother I've ever known. Or maybe underneath her crabshell of prejudice and fear there's a human being that's loving. I don't know but either way I love her. (*Rubyfruit Jungle*, 242)

Molly's film is so startlingly different from the others that no one says a word when the lights come on. But no decent jobs reward her cinematic success. However spunky, outspoken, talented, and brilliant, Molly is still only a woman. The year was 1969. Even though women were beginning to protest unfair treatment, and women's support groups were forming, Molly senses that her rage "wasn't their rage." She felt that "they'd have run me out for being a lesbian anyway" (246). Never mind. Molly forms a group of one and holds on to her dreams. The last words of the novel are Molly's determined musing:

Damn, I wished the world would let me be myself. But I knew better on all counts. I wish I could make my films. That wish I can work for. One way or another I'll make those movies and I don't feel like having to fight until I'm fifty. But if it does take that long then watch out world because I'm going to be the hottest fifty-year-old this side of the Mississippi. (*RJ*, 246)

The ending of *Rubyfruit Jungle* not only captures Molly's fighting spirit, her determination to celebrate her talents however long it takes, but also uncovers another of Rita Mae Brown's own dreams. When *Rubyfruit Jungle* was published, Brown was twenty-nine. When *Starting From Scratch* was published, she was forty-four. In one of the manual's final chapters, "the circumflex chapter, the catchall," she tells us what motivated her toward film and television:

I believe in the process itself. I want, someday, to be able to write a cycle of feature films or films for cable that are my Brandenburg Concertos. I have had, since I was quite young, an idea that connects six separate stories. Like the music, each story is different from every other story. . . . But if you "hear" the entire cycle, . . . then you will realize that a single guiding theme is at work. I may never realize this dream. But if you want to know why I do what I do in this business, it is so I can finally make enough money for other people that they will give me that slender shot at creating what I long to create. (*Scratch*, 201)

While the realities of patriarchal Hollywood may have caused her to tone down the 1988 version, the dream was still alive. By January of 1992, Ephron had directed *her* first movie, a version of Meg Wolitzer's *This is Your Life*, for which Nora Ephron and her sister Delia wrote the screen play. If a tri-

umvirate of witty women writers can create, adapt and direct their own material, can Rita Mae Brown's creation of an original film cycle be far behind?

RITA MAE BROWN'S WIT, OR, HOW TO OFFEND
THE MIDDLE CLASS

Brown's other witty and celebratory novels are *Six of One, Southern
Discomfort*, and *Bingo*. All three share the high-spirited silliness and optimism that characterizes *Rubyfruit Jungle*. But Brown's relentless good spir-
its and resilience have been a stumbling block for many critics, just as
Tyler's optimism caused her novels to be overlooked for many years. To
write both optimistically and humorously is to invite comparison to glib television scripts. One critic called *Six of One* "310 pages of Gilligan's Island":

> It is a major sadness to report that Brown has made her women not
> only boring but false . . . Her only verbal tool is the josh—speech that
> is not quite witty, sly, wry, sardonic, ironic or even, God help us,
> clever, but only self-consciously breezy . . . These aren't human
> beings talking; it's 310 pages of Gilligan's Island.[14]

The women Brown portrays may strike Richard Boeth as false, but I dare-
say the women from Brown's childhood would probably strike him as
equally unreal.

One critic in the *New Boston Review* appreciates Brown's general picture but quibbles over the pieces that make it up. According to Henze, the
characters seem too simplistic. Henze writes that Brown fills an otherwise
"surprisingly accepting, even celebratory portrait of down-home America"
with men and women who display "the simplicities of heroes of a
Western."[15] Optimism and resiliency seem to be no more acceptable in a
character than in a writer.

This negative criticism of *Six of One* is balanced by Cynthia Macdonald
writing for *The Washington Post Book World*, who observes that

> The vision of women we have usually gotten from women novelists
> is of pain and struggle or pain and passivity; it is seldom joyous and
> passionate, and almost never funny. And what humor there was has
> been of the suffering, self-deprecating New York Jewish stand-up
> comedian type. *Six of One* by Rita Mae Brown is joyous, passionate
> and funny. What a pleasure![16]

Rita May Brown's humor is closer to the tradition behind Chaucer's and
Rabelais' than Lenny Bruce's or Woody Allen's. In fact, her literary hero is
Aristophanes, a master of silliness and scatological humor. Brown was a

classics major at NYU and wrote her senior thesis on "Evolving Metaphor in *The Birds*." "It figures," comments Leonore Fleisher in her interview with Brown, and continues:

> If you have read *Rubyfruit Jungle* and/or her new novel *Six of One* you have been struck no doubt by certain similarities to Aristophanes. Political points made through the use of ribald humor, and an emphasis on the poor (or hoi poloi, as old A. would say) as the fountain of homely, practical wisdom. And a funny approach to sex.[17]

Nine years after *Six of One*, Brown was writing its sequel, *Bingo*, when she published her writer's manual. In the manual, she made the connection between silliness, Aristophanes, and herself clear. This was her hope for *Bingo*, then under creation:

> I am aspiring to be silly. If you ever read Aristophanes you know there are moments of such sublime silliness in his plays that you shout at the sheer pleasure of being so assaulted. That's what I want to do. I probably won't get there but it's a goal worth a life's work. (*Scratch* 18)

Both *Six of One* and *Bingo* are set in Runneymede, a town straddling the Mason-Dixon line, half in Pennsylvania and half in Maryland. Brown herself lived the first eleven years of her life almost on the Mason-Dixon line in a small town in Pennsylvania. Nor is geography the only autobiographical element in these novels. The two sisters, Julie Ellen ("Juts") and Louise ("Wheezie"), appear in both. They are young children when *Six of One* opens, but, since the book covers sixty-nine years, they are in their seventies when it ends. In *Bingo* they are still going strong. Everyone has to pretend they are celebrating Louise's eightieth birthday when they all know she'll never even see eighty-six again. These two foul-mouthed characters are patterned after Brown's mother and aunt, just as their mother, Cora, is patterned after Rita Mae's grandmother. According to Fleisher's interview, which took place shortly after the publication of *Six of One*:

> The Julia Ellen in her [Brown's] book is absolutely modeled on Julia Allen Brown, Rita Mae's mother. ("I just talked to the Big Juts yesterday; she's preparing for stardom.") In Jut's sister Louise she drew a less flattering than is true portrait of her mother's sister Mary; but even so, "the two of them are just giggling and having such a good time with this book." And, as for Cora, the grandmother who could neither read nor write, but who possessed all the wisdom and joy of living the world could bestow, yes, Rita Mae's grandmother was like that.

Fleisher did have some reservation about *Six of One*. She feels that women could not have been "as free, as educated, as liberated" as Brown depicts them. But Brown's responds:

> I grew up with these two almost mythical figures around me, my mother and my aunt, who didn't give a rat's a—what anybody thought. They'd say anything to anybody and they did as they damn well pleased. We were so poor, who cares what poor people do? Literature is predominantly written by middle-class people for middle-class people and their lives were real different. As a girl, I never saw a woman knuckle under to a man, or a man to a woman, for that matter. Although once I did see my mother go after my father with a frying pan. The people closest to me were all very dominating characters. The men weren't weak, but somehow the women . . . they were the ones you paid attention to.[18]

Brown has always identified with the lower class. As a child she despised the middle-class children she encountered in school, children taught to repress strong language and violent behavior:

> They were competitive, snotty and devious. They learned to hide their emotions early, to bow to authority without question, and to keep their allowances to themselves. I came from an opposing world view. I was taught to express myself (throw dishes if it came to that), to question authority . . . I was also taught to stick to my own kind . . . If your friend gets in a fight, even if he or she is wrong, you back your friend. You can argue with her later.[19]

One of the favorite insults offered by Juts, the character who was "absolutely modeled on" Rita Mae Brown's mother, was to say that someone "sucked green monkey dicks." She said it at seven and was just as foul-mouthed at seventy. Her lifelong use of such language bothered the critic Henze, who observed that time progresses in *Six of One*, "but the characters do not: the two old biddies at the center of the narrative trade off the same scatological insults at seventy as at six."[20] But Henze's observation is probably tied to a middle-class orientation, the orientation that teaches us to repress anger and control both our language and emotion from an early age. Beneath such suave good manners seethe the emotions that these two old biddies still know how to express at seventy and already knew how to express at seven.

LIVING BY HER WITS:

Rita Mae Brown started from about as disadvantaged a place as one can imagine. She was an illegitimate child born on November 28, 1944 in

Hanover, PA. She was adopted by poor working class people, Ralph and Julie Buckingham Brown. Ralph Brown was a butcher and it has been reported that Julia Brown had at one time been employed by Rita Mae Brown's natural mother[21]

Living nearly on the Mason-Dixon line, Brown observed that she "had both cultures inside the house as well as outside," since her mother was a southerner, from Maryland, while her father was from Pennsylvania. Ralph Brown was Amish, or, as his daughter explained to Leonore Fleisher, "actually a Dunkard—its the agrarian mentality, slightly more modern. They drive cars but they paint them black."[22] Although Rita Mae Brown is not one to shun material comforts, her father's beliefs did make an impression on her, just as the Quaker beliefs of Anne Tyler's parents affected her outlook on life. "Material benefits aren't bad," Brown observed in "The Last Straw," an essay against the middle class youth culture's attraction to downward mobility, "what's bad is that everyone doesn't have them."[23] In 1988 Brown contributed to an article for *Omni* magazine which asked various public figures to send in their vision of Utopia. Her answer begins:

> The Amish come close to my idea of Utopia, except for two problems: the status of women and the desire to shut out the rest of the world. But their sense of community and productivity, of sharing and caring for each other, are splendid models. I have always been impressed by their view that they shall not be controlled by machines.[24]

Brown's parents were loving and resourceful parents who were proud of their daughter. Despite their poverty, Rita Mae's father managed to give his daughter a huge Underwood typewriter when she was only eight. He traded some meat for it. When she was fifteen, he replaced it with a new Smith-Corona. To emphasize the enormity of this gift, Brown tells us that when she was filling out college scholarship forms, the combined incomes of her father, her mother and herself came to around $2,000. And this was in 1961. Then, on August 13 of the same year, her father died.[25]

Brown's parents valued education. They taught her to read at age three. She received her first library card at age five. From then on, one or the other of her parents took her to the town library every Saturday. When they moved to Florida, Brown's reading habits were established. She soon developed a second love: tennis. In Fort Lauderdale she spent her days neatly divided between the library and the tennis courts, where a little girl named Christine Evert followed her around.[26]

Despite her inauspicious beginning, and despite the death of her father in 1961, Rita Mae Brown did enter college in 1962. She had been accepted by Duke, The University of North Carolina and the University of Florida.

Subsequent events proved Florida to be a poor choice, but, initially, it allowed her to study within visiting distance of her newly widowed mother. The university expelled her two years later.

Then she went to New York. It was the summer of 1964 and she was nineteen: "No money. No nothing" except for her dogged determination and optimism:

> . . . the theater was there. New York University. Washington Square campus took me and I could get free theater tickets. If I couldn't get a free ticket I would go in after the first act and find an empty seat.[27]

Reconstructing the first act, she tells us gamely, came in handy when she later had to learn how to build plots.

But the first few days in New York were rough, however optimistic and resourceful she could sound in hindsight. She was literally starving, reduced to eating out of a garbage can which held the scraps from a pizza joint. Yet she even manages to find something positive to take away from this experience:

> I reached down in the can and picked out a pizza rind and started to eat it. Tasted delicious. The stand owner glimpsed at me and screamed. I thought he would beat me. Instead this burly Italian man dragged me inside and served both B.J. [her cat, Baby Jesus] and me as though we were royal. New York did have a heart after all.[28]

In "Take a Lesbian to Lunch," however, she looks back on those early New York days with distinctly less buoyancy: "If you are young, female and poor, New York City is worse than Dante's Inferno."[29]

Despite starting with no money in 1964, by 1968 Brown had received a BA from NYU as a classics major and a cinematography certificate from New York School of Visual Arts. By 1973 she also had a Ph.D. from the Institute for Policy Studies in Washington, D.C. ("I can honestly tell you that it hasn't done me a bit of good."[30]) Scholarships helped her live while she was a student and, after graduating, she found jobs that would allow her the mental energy to write. For a while she painted houses and sanded floors. Somehow, she even managed to find the time to write when she was studying—the same year she received her Ph.D. is the year she published *Rubyfruit Jungle*.

It was just fourteen years after she looked for food in a garbage can that she was interviewed by Fleisher for *The Washington Post*. Brown was living in Los Angeles in her own house and dividing her time between writing screenplays and traveling to promote her third novel, *Six of One*. She told Fleisher that her immediate ambition was to earn enough money to settle in Charlottesville, Virginia "which is where I want to be." The interview appeared in 1978. Just a little over a decade later the *Contemporary Authors Index* lists her home as Charlottesville, VA. Her writing has not only brought her the fortune to enable her to live where she wants, but has brought her a fair amount of fame as well. Several of her novels have appeared on *The New York Times* best seller list and two of her screenplays have received Emmy nominations.

But Brown has stayed rational and humble about the degree of control she or anyone can have:

> The odyssey of any life surprises the sailor/seeker. It's so easy, looking back from the security of middle age, to find dramatic turning points. It reads better that way. But the truth of my life as an artist is that I was and still am being built the same way a coral reef is built. Millions of tiny microscopic creatures fall through glistening waters to land upon the ocean floor. Eventually enough of them fall to create a fanciful, habitable coral reef. The shapes of these reefs are fantastic and they provide refuge and sustenance for other creatures. So it is with this writer's life. The minutes have fallen until my life has a definite architecture. To pretend that I planned those minutes is a shout of egotism beyond even my rather sturdy self regard. . . .I planned the reading. I wrote until my fingers ached. But I never planned the humans that walked into my life. I never planned the historical events that shook me: . . . Historical events are counterbalanced by the joys of personal life, yet even those are out of my control.[31]

Like Alison Lurie and Grace Paley, Rita Mae Brown has learned that all you can do is what you have to do at the moment. For her this was to write until her fingers ached. She could not control success, but she could hone her wit and be ready with reams of material for the day when someone finally agreed to publish it. Until then she sanded floors.

NOTES

1. Judy Klemesrud, "Underground Book Brings Fame to a Lesbian Author," *New York Times* 26 Sept. 1977: 38.
2. Rita Mae Brown, *Starting From Scratch: A Different Kind of Writers' Manual* (NY: Bantam, 1988) 13.
3. Rita Mae Brown, *The Plain Brown Rapper* (Baltimore: Diana Press, 1976) 18.
4. Judy Klemesrud 38.
5. Patricia Holt, "Rita Mae Brown," *Publishers Weekly* 2 Oct 1978: 16.
6. Rita Mae Brown, "Take a Lesbian to Lunch," in *The Plain Brown Rapper* 81.
7. Brown, "Take a Lesbian to Lunch" 88.
8. Terry Curtis Fox, "Up from Cultdom—and Down Again," *Village Voice* 12 Sept 1977: 41.

9. Brown, *Rubyfruit Jungle* (1973; NY: Bantam, 1977) 235.
10. Brown, *Starting from Scratch* 8.
11. Margaret Drabble, *The Middle Ground* (1980; NY: Ballantine, 1989) 18.
12. Marilyn Webb, rev. of *Rubyfruit Jungle* by Rita Mae Brown, *Ms.* June 1974: 37.
13. Charlotte Brontë, *Jane Eyre* (1847; Oxford: Oxford Univ. Press, 1975) 32.
14. Richard Boeth, *Newsweek* 2 Oct. 1978 as quoted in *Contemporary Authors*: New Rev. Series, vol 35 (1990) 71.
15. Shelly Temschin Henze, *New Boston Review* April/May 1979, as quoted in *Contemporary Authors* 71.
16. Cynthia Macdonald, "Death in the American Novel," *Washington Post Book World* 15 Oct 1987: 1.
17. "Leonore Fleisher Talks with Rita Mae Brown," *Washington Post Book World* 15 Oct 1978: 2.
18. Fleisher 2.
19. Brown, *Starting From Scratch* 5.
20. Henze, 71–72.
21. Martha Chew, "Rita Mae Brown: Feminist Theorist and Southern Novelist," *The Southern Quarterly* 21.1 (1983): 68.
22. Fleisher 1.
23. Brown, "The Last Straw," *The Plain Brown Rapper* 105.
24. Marion Long, "Utopia," *Omni* 10.7 (April 1988): 42.
25. Brown, *Starting from Scratch* 9.
26. Brown, *Scratch* 8.
27. Brown, *Scratch* 11.
28. Brown, introduction to *The Plain Brown Rapper* 10–11.
29. Brown, "Take a Lesbian to Lunch" 84.
30. Brown, *Starting from Scratch* 44.
31. Brown, *Starting from Scratch* 19.

_10_

Conclusion: What Wit Controlled

THE EMPOWERMENT OF WIT

What all the writers in this book enjoy, both the contemporary writers and their forerunners, is the empowerment of wit. Neither they nor their main characters will accept the role of victim without a witty protest. But the form of their wit varies, and their success is related to the social climate of their day.

> In 1993, Alther questioned the form her wit took in _Kinflicks_: I wasn't entirely happy with the comedy in _Kinflicks_ because I thought some of it was pretty savage, and I wanted to find a way to soften it. The question I kept struggling with was, Is humor always based on putting someone else down? Is there some way to write humor that isn't at somebody's expense?[1]

The writer who best illustrates that Alther's questions can be answered affirmatively is Anne Tyler. Her wit is always used to endear her characters to us, to charm us with their amusing thought processes. Tyler always views her characters sympathetically rather than satirically. Grace Paley also tries to steer her wit towards magnanimity. She told Joan Lidoff that she feels "writing something to let someone really have it" is wrong.[2] So she concentrates on wittily illuminating the neglected lives of women rather that attacking their men. Paley does present male foibles, but in a gentle, mocking tone rather than a bitingly satiric one. Nora Ephron takes a similar approach in *Heartburn* by concentrating on Rachel's witty and resourceful reaction to her husband's betrayal rather than presenting a clear picture of her betrayer.

But satiric presentations are also a viable option for the contemporary writer. Alison Lurie never shies away from exposing the faults of her characters, be they male or female. And Rita Mae Brown reveals her character's shortcomings gleefully. Both writers have been well received, although their satire is as sharp as Dawn Powell's, who wrote earlier in the century. Since the critical consensus is that Powell's stinging satire of middle-class family values hurt her reputation, it appears that contemporary witty women writers are given a wider berth.

A growing respect for witty women writers is also apparent in the differing receptions granted Dorothy Parker and Grace Paley. Dorothy Parker could only gain a reputation for her wit, while her political writing was ignored. Yet today, Paley is taken seriously both as a witty writer and as a political activist.

But some attitudes remain the same. Shirley Jackson's autobiographical memoirs received the same sort of belittling reception as Betty MacDonald's: both have been dismissed as the breezy writing of pacifying domestic humorists, a label deserved by neither. Fortunately, there is a side to the empowerment of wit untouched by the public's reception: the author's satisfaction that she has set down her position on paper with verve and skill.

THE EMPOWERMENT OF THE WITTY FAÇADE

When Anne Tyler describes what destroys Macon's marriage in *The Accidental Tourist*, she describes the boxing-in aspect of an assumed façade. Her narrator explains that "In some odd way, he was locked inside the stand-offish self he'd assumed" when he first met Sarah at a high school dance. It was like the old warning of his grandmother's, a homey warning familiar to many: "Don't cross your eyes, they might get stuck that way" (53). But Macon was a shy, insecure seventeen-year-old who had forced himself to attend that school dance because he secretly yearned to fall in love. Once at the dance, of course, he wouldn't presume to approach so radiant, popular, and clearly out-of-his-league sort of girl as Sarah. So he stood in a corner watching her, trying to look cool and detached. Finally, *she* approached *him*. Alone in his room later that same night, Macon decided it must have been his aloof façade that had won her attentions for the evening. He immediately made up his mind to continue to hide his feelings, to keep his dignity in order to win Sarah. His plan seemed to pay off, for Sarah continued to find him appealingly mysterious and they soon became a couple. But not long after they were married, she found that she needed a more open and affectionate mate than the one she had—or the one she *thought* she had. And even when Macon tried to change, Sarah kept relating to the old familiar cool-headed person she had married, "someone more even in temperament than she but perhaps not quite as feeling" (53). And so it transpired that the façade Macon had originally adopted to win Sarah became the very one that caused him to lose her.

But façades do not have to be destructive ones. A witty façade, even if it starts as only a self-conscious and defensive ploy, can become an empowering technique. Jesting and bantering may hold off fear, pity and pain to such a degree that the fear, pity, and pain eventually disappear. Nora Ephron, Rita Mae Brown, and Ann Tyler have all created characters who adopt such empowering witty façades in times of stress. Rachel Samstat, Ephron's alter ego in *Heartburn*, is probably the most salient example in this study of a character who creates a witty façade to fend of pain and pity. When *Heartburn* begins, Rachel is in the same position Ephron herself had once been in: she is the mother of a two-year-old and seven months pregnant with her second child when she learns that her husband is having a serious affair. How does Rachel react? She opens her story by summoning wit to her side: "The first day I did not think it was funny. I didn't think it was funny the third day either, but I managed to make a little joke about it." And Rachel/Ephron continues to manage to make enough little jokes about her situation to complete a best-selling book which eventually becomes a popular movie. Most reviewers point out the revenge factor of *Heartburn*, but few, if any, allude to the empowering side of Ephron's wit. It is not that she does not feel any pain, but rather that she refuses to wallow in it. As Rachel says, "If I tell the story, I can get on with it." Ephron's witty front is empowering because she refuses to write *Heartburn* in a way that makes her the pitiful victim. She may have *started* with more bravado than laughter, but at some point, certainly by the time the movie opened, the ratio was reversed.

In addition to Rachel Samstat, Molly Bolt (*Rubyfruit Jungle*) and Jenny Tull (*Dinner at the Homesick Restaurant*) are fictional characters who consciously create witty façades to bolster themselves during difficult periods in their lives. In *Rubyfruit Jungle*, Rita Mae Brown grants Molly Bolt the insight to realize that adopting a witty façade will both compensate for her poverty and win her popularity at her new school. Her family moves to Florida when she is still a child. But they are dirt poor and have rented an inexpensive house very close to a power plant. They have to endure its constant hum in exchange for the low rent. Molly soon realizes her new school was divided into red-necks, whom she does not want to associate with, and rich kids, whom she cannot afford to invite to her home ("What would we all do, dance to the power plant hum?"). So she decides to become the wittiest person in the school, reasoning that people will like someone who makes them laugh. And, she tells us, it worked. Even the teachers laughed.

In Anne Tyler's *Dinner At The Homesick Restaurant*, Jenny Tull's efforts to lighten up, to lose her intensity by learning how to banter and laugh off failure make her another character who learns the advantages of a witty façade. Jenny is learning to control herself, to stem her tendency to take things too earnestly, a tendency which has already led to one breakdown. So Jenny studies the people around her who seem to know how to banter and joke to keep their fears at bay. One is a colleague whose bantering successfully keeps anyone from asking about his troubles at home. Jenny learns the technique. Her success suggests that a witty facade works in both directions—you are convincing yourself at the same time that you are convincing those around you.

Nor is a witty façade the exclusive province of the characters. All of the writers included in this study understand the effectiveness of wit and know how to let it work for them. Their wit serves to create narrators and characters with such clever insights that they appear distanced from their problems. Shirley Jackson presents a witty front in her autobiographical novels, as does Betty MacDonald in her family memoirs. If either woman ever grows desperate over family responsibilities or the relentlessness of thankless daily chores, neither is going to give weight to her despair by acknowledging it in writing. Both Jackson and MacDonald can *allude* to the injustices built into the wife/mother role, but only if they are terribly witty when doing so. Grace Paley once said that she feels wit takes the place of anger in many of her short stories. But Paley's witty presentation is also a palatable way of presenting injustices, while her lighthearted puns suggest a basic optimism in the future. Anne Tyler describes her efforts to achieve the endlessly adapting smiling front she saw in her father. Her wit is continuously urging her readers to aspire to the same patient, compassionate, and wise attitude toward which she is striving. Alison Lurie discovered the power of her wit while she was still an adolescent. Although the adult Lurie's wit is usually caustic, it can also help create sympathetic characters. What would Vinnie Miner (*Foreign Affairs*) have been like without her clever observations and her imaginary pet—that dirty cumbersome white dog who embodies her self-pity? Rita Mae Brown both acknowledges the aggressive element to wit and admits that she aspires to be silly. Despite Alther's concern that the wit in *Kinflicks* was too sharp, Ginny Babcock would lose her bouyancy and verve without it. Dorothy Parker was the young Nora Ephron's role model, or, to be precise, the witty façade

Parker offered her public was Ephron's model. For these writers, the grandmother's warning in Tyler's novel, relating to Macon getting stuck in his aloof role, should be reversed. For the role of a wit is exactly what they *want* to be stuck in. Rather than "Don't cross your eyes, they might get stuck that way" the injunction for them could read "Make a joke, and hope the laughter lasts."

The wit found in the works of these women writers, then, becomes a strategy to win their readers over tactfully as well as an empowering technique. At times, as Paley notes, wit masks anger: where anger repels, wit disarms; where anger alienates, wit charms. And there is also a distinct bravery to all women writers who write with wit, since they risk being labeled witches, shrews, or overcontrolling bitches. It is to be hoped that the day will soon dawn when witty women writers can be heard only as laughing ladies with not even the faintest echo of the cackling witch.

NOTES

1. Carole Edwards, "Interview with Lisa Alther," *Turnstyle* 4.1 (1993): 45.
2. Joan Lidoff, "Clearing Her Throat: An Interview With Grace Paley," *Shenandoah* 32.3 (1981): 17.

Bibliography: Women and Wit

Current feminist scholars have begun to turn their attention to the wit of women writers. In 1983, Judy Little published *Comedy and The Woman Writer* (Lincoln: Univ. of Nebraska Press), a study of the fiction of Virginia Woolf and Muriel Spark which includes a ground-breaking first chapter suggesting why women's wit differs from men's. As well as her book on women's strategic use of humor, *They Used To Call Me Snow White—But I Drifted: Women's Strategic Use of Humor* (Viking, 1991), Regina Barreca has edited and introduced two provocative collections of essays on women's humor: *Last Laughs: Perspectives on Women and Comedy* (Gordon and Breach, 1988) and *New Perspectives on Women and Comedy* (Gordon and Breach, 1992). As well as tracing the neglected tradition of women's humor in America in *A Very Serious Thing: Women's Humor and American Culture* (Univ. of Minn. Press, 1988), Nancy Walker, together with Zita Dresner, has brought out a comprehensive anthology of women's humor in America, with an excellent and informative introduction: *Redressing The Balance: American Women's Literary Humor from Colonial Times to the 1980s* (Univ. of Mississippi, 1988). In 1991, June Sochen compiled a collection of essays on women's humor called *Women's Comic Visions* (Detroit: Wayne State Univ. Press). She includes articles on performers as well as on theory and witty women writers in America. Walker, Dresner, and Little all contributed articles to Sochen's collection.

The growing number of recent anthologies on women's humor also attests to a heightened interest in the subject. Only two existed in America before 1976: Kate Sanborn's *The Wit of Women* (NY: Funk & Wagnalls, 1885) and Martha Bensley Bruère and Mary Ritter Beards' *Laughing Their Way: Women's Humor in America* (NY: MacMillan, 1934). Since 1976, however, six new anthologies have appeared. Deanne Stillman and Ann Beatts published *Titters: The First Collection of Humor by Women* in 1976, (NY: Collier) although they were mistaken in thinking theirs was the first. Gloria Kaufman and Mary Kay Blakely, *Pulling Our Own Strings: Feminist Humor and Satire* (Bloomington: Indiana Univ. Press, 1980) concentrates on the 1970s; Gloria Kaufman, *In Stitches: A Patchwork of Feminist Humor and Satire* (Bloomington: Indiana Univ. Press, 1991) concentrates on the 1980s; and Rosalind Warren's *Women's Glib: A Collection of Women's Humor* (Freedom, CA: The Crossing Press, 1991), and *Women's Glibber: State-of-the-Art Women's Humor* (Freedom, CA: The Crossing Press, 1992) mixes verse, cartoons, and short essays. The most comprehensive is Walker and Dresner's, which includes descriptions of many of the other anthologies. In addition to these six anthologies, one journal devoted a special double issue to witty women: *Regionalism and the Female Imagination*, vol.7, nos. 2–3, fall and winter, 1977–78.

BIBLIOGRAPHY OF WITTY WRITERS:

The entries, listed chronologically, are novels or memoirs unless otherwise indicated.

Alther, Lisa:

Kinflicks. New York: Knopf, 1976.
Original Sins. New York: Knopf, 1981.
Other Women. New York: Knopf, 1984.
Bedrock. New York: Knopf, 1990.
Five Minutes in Heaven. New York: Dutton, 1995.

Brown, Rita Mae:

The Hand That Cradles the Rock. New York: NYU Press, 1971 (poems).
Songs to a Handsome Woman. Baltimore: Diana Press, 1973 (poems).
Rubyfruit Jungle. 1973. New York: Bantam, 1988.
The Plain Brown Rapper. Oakland, CA: Diana Press, 1976 (essays).
In Her Day. 1976. New York: Bantam, 1988.

Six of One. New York: Harper, 1978.
Southern Discomfort. New York: Harper, 1982.
Sudden Death. New York: Bantam, 1983.
High Hearts. New York: Bantam, 1986.
Starting From Scratch: A Different Kind of Writer's Manual. New York:
    Bantam, 1988.
Bingo. New York: Bantam, 1988.
Wish You Were Here. New York: Bantam, 1990.
Rest in Pieces. New York: Bantam, 1992.
Venus Envy. New York: Bantam, 1993.
Dolly. New York: Bantam, 1994.
Pay Dirt. New York: Bantam, 1995.

Ephron, Nora:

Wallflower At The Orgy. New York: Knopf, 1970 (essays).
Crazy Salad. New York: Knopf, 1975 (essays).
Scribble Scribble. New York: Knopf, 1979 (essays).
Heartburn. New York: Knopf, 1983.
When Harry Met Sally. New York: Knopf, 1990 (screenplay).

Jackson, Shirley:

The Road Through the Wall. New York: Farrar, Straus, & Co., 1948.
The Lottery. New York: Farrar, Straus, & Co., 1949 (short stories).
Life Among the Savages. New York: Farrar, Straus, & Co., 1953.
The Bird's Nest. New York: Farrar, Straus, & Co., 1954.
Raising Demons. New York: Farrar, Straus, & Co., 1957.
The Sundial. New York: Farrar, Straus, & Co., 1958.
The Haunting of Hill House. New York: Viking, 1959.
We Have Always Lived in the Castle. New York: Viking, 1963.
Come Along With Me: Part of a Novel, Sixteen Stories, and Three Lectures.
    New York: Viking, 1968.

Lurie, Alison:

Love and Friendship. New York: MacMillan, 1962.
The Nowhere City. 1965. New York: Avon, 1967.
Imaginary Friends. New York: Avon, 1967.
Real People. New York: Avon, 1969.
The War Between the Tates. New York: Avon, 1974.
Only Children. New York: Heinemann, 1979.

The Heavenly Zoo. New York: Farrar, Straus, & Giroux, 1979 (children's book).
Clever Gretchen and Other Forgotten Tales. New York: Cromwell, 1980 (children's book).
Fabulous Beasts. London: Cape, 1981 (children's book).
The Language of Clothes. New York: Random House, 1981 (non-fiction).
Foreign Affairs. New York: Random House, 1984.
The Truth About Lorin Jones. Boston: Little Brown, 1988.
Don't Tell the Grown-Ups. New York: Avon, 1990 (non-fiction).
Women and Ghosts. New York: Doubleday, 1994 (short stories).

MacDonald, Betty:

The Egg and I. New York: Lippencott, 1945.
The Plague and I. New York: Lippencott, 1948.
Anybody Can Do Anything. New York: Lippencott, 1950.
Onions in the Stew. New York: Lippencott, 1955.

Paley, Grace:

The Little Disturbances of Man. New York: Doubleday, 1959 (stories).
Enormous Changes at the Last Minute. NY: Farrar, Straus, & Giroux, 1974 (stories).
Later the Same Day. NY: Farrar, Straus, & Giroux, 1985 (stories).
Leaning Forward. Penobscot. Maine: Granite Press, 1985. (poems).
Long Walks and Intimate Talks. NY: Feminist Press, 1991 (stories & poems).

Parker, Dorothy:

Enough Rope. New York: Boni & Liveright, 1926 (verse).
Sunset Gun. New York: Boni & Liveright, 1928 (verse).
Laments for the Living. New York: Viking, 1930 (short stories & sketches).
Death and Taxes. New York: Viking, 1931 (verse).
After Such Pleasures. New York: Viking, 1933 (short fiction).
Here Lies. New York: Viking, 1939 (stories).
Constant Reader. New York: Viking, 1970 (articles from *The New Yorker*).

Powell, Dawn:

Jig Saw: A Comedy. New York: Farrar and Rinehart, 1934.
Turn: Magic Wheel. New York: Farrar and Rinehart, 1936.

The Happy Island. New York: Farrar and Rinehart, 1938.

Angels on Toast. 1940. New York: Vintage, 1989.

A Time to be Born. 1942. New York: Yarrow Press, 1991.

The Locusts Have No King. 1948. New York: Yarrow Press, 1990.

Sunday, Monday, and Always. Boston: Houghton Mifflin, 1952.

The Wicked Pavillion. 1954. New York: Vintage, 1990.

Cage for Lovers. Cambridge, MA: Riverside, 1957.

The Golden Spur. 1962. New York: Random House, 1990.

Dawn Powell at Her Best. Ed. Tim Page. South Royalton, VT: Steerforth Press, 1994.

The Diaries of Dawn Powell. Ed. Tim Page. South Royalton, VT: Steerforth Press, 1995.

My Home is Far Away. 1944. South Royalton, VT: Steerforth Press, 1995.

Tyler, Anne:

If Morning Ever Comes. New York: Knopf, 1964.

The Tin Can Tree. New York: Knopf, 1965.

A Slipping-Down Life. New York: Knopf, 1970.

The Clock Winder. New York: Knopf, 1972.

Celestial Navigation. New York: Knopf, 1974.

Searching for Caleb. New York: Knopf, 1976.

Earthly Possessions. New York: Knopf, 1977.

Morgan's Passing. New York: Knopf, 1980.

Dinner at the Homesick Restaurant. New York: Knopf, 1982.

The Accidental Tourist. New York: Knopf, 1985.

Breathing Lessons. New York: Knopf, 1988.

Saint Maybe. New York: Knopf, 1991.

Ladder of Years. New York: Knopf, 1995.

Index